From Tent To Cabin

From Tent To Cabin

How to Live in Comfort
While Building Your
Own Country Cabin

DISCARD

Laurence Gadd

The Bobbs-Merrill Company, Inc.
Indianapolis — New York

Library of Congress Cataloging in Publication Data

Gadd, Laurence.
  From tent to cabin.

  1. Country homes—Design and construction.
I. Title.
TH4850.G32   690′.873   80-2732
ISBN 0-672-52687-5

Manufactured in the United States of America

First Printing

From Tent To Cabin

INTRODUCTION

With this book and basic carpentry skills you should be able to construct a country cabin without outside professional help. If, due to time or other factors, you cannot do some or all of the tasks involved any competent carpenter or builder can fill in for you. You can do as much or as little as you wish. Many people will find the laying of a foundation to be heavy work which they would prefer to have done professionally. Others will want the frame completed for them, or even the complete cabin built by others referring to the book only to follow construction stages. However much you do, the plans and instructions for this cabin have been carefully selected from hundreds prepared by the United States Forest Service and Department of Agriculture and should result in an attractive, well-designed all-year country cabin.

The basic concept of this book is that you can live comfortably in a platform tent while working on or supervising the cabin construction. With today's interest in camping, many products such as stoves, heaters, and even refrigerators are available for tent living. There is no need to "rough it" while living on your land. Of course, by having electric power connected prior to construction, you will be able to use products which can be used later in the cabin. The electricity will also be useful for power tools which will make construction much easier (all the carpentry can be accomplished with hand tools).

The first thing you will build is the deck. This structure serves three purposes. First, it is the ideal way to practice your carpentry skills. Mistakes made on the deck are relatively easy and inexpensive to correct and, although the deck is a simple structure, almost all the carpentry skills needed for building the cabin will be used building the deck. Second, it can be your living space while building the cabin. By erecting a tent or fly directly on the completed deck, you can have a temporary, but quite comfortable, living space. Third, this deck will serve as an addition to your cabin which can double your cabin area in warmer weather and serve as an outdoor living room.

Many of the skills required for the deck are explained in full in the cabin construction section of this book. It is therefore necessary for you to read the entire book before you begin any of the construction.

After your deck is completed, you will want to erect some kind of tent or fly to protect you from the weather. If you are in an area which will have cold temperatures during the construction period, you will want a full tent with heating. The warmer climates require only a top fly and if needed, insect screening for the sides. Some people who are familiar with and enjoy camping will need only a simple 2–4 person regular tent. The best supply sources for inexpensive larger tents are the many Army/Navy surplus stores.

Whatever tent you do buy, its use is greatly enhanced by having the wooden deck on which to set it up. The best method with a standard smaller tent is to install eye bolts on the deck surface instead of the stakes normally used. For the poles, pipe flanges at the base should prevent any slippage. All holes can be filled later after you remove the tent.

The tent can be as large or small as you wish, but remember you will have little use later on for a giant surplus tent, whereas a smaller tent can be used for camping or is easily re-sold.

Your living arrangements can be as spartan or luxurious as you wish. You can sleep on anything from air mattresses to finished beds which could be used in the cabin.

Since most construction will be done in the summer months, heat is really unnecessary for the tent. If you are in northern climates, you may wish to use one of the new kerosene heaters now available. This can be kept for later use as a space heater or emergency heater in the cabin. Although these heaters are very efficient, fumes do escape. So be sure to follow instructions for ventilation.

Camp stoves are the best for cooking. Fuel can be white gas or propane. If you are going to use the cabin only occasionally, the large two burner portable stoves are more than adequate for both tent and cabin use. If you plan to install a full kitchen in the cabin, however, then a small inexpensive stove is enough for now.

You also may want to build a permanent outdoor barbecue. This should be positioned on a side of the deck that is away from the cabin; if built by a professional, it could be on the common side with the cabin designed to become an interior fireplace by having the opening on the cabin side. The design and construction of fireplaces with proper draft and safety is quite tricky and is best left to a pro. Below, however, is a basic design for an outdoor cook fireplace which you can do yourself.

The other aspects of tent life are much the same as indoor living. You should already have dug a well. Access to that water can be with hand pump or, if electricity is available, with a permanent pump. Hot water of course, will not be available in quantity until the cabin is completed and a hot water heater is installed.

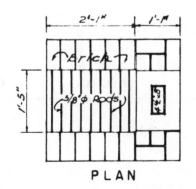

PLAN

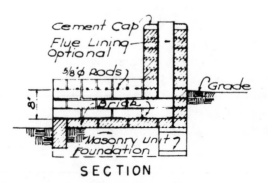

SECTION

An outdoor fireplace of modest design.

From Tent to Cabin

Part I
Deck Planning
and Construction

DECK PLANNING AND CONSTRUCTION

The location of the deck should be determined after you have decided on the exact location of your cabin. It is far easier to build the deck on a grade than it is the cabin. After you have located the cabin, and marked its true corners with pegs, you can decide on the exact deck location and size taking into account view, surrounding terrain and access.

The deck will be a low level deck with spaced floor boards and will be attached to the cabin for access and partial support. This deck can be simply supported on concrete piers or short posts closely spaced, thereby simplifying the horizontal structure. Drainage can be a problem on low decks; provision to insure good drainage should be made before the deck is constructed. Good drainage not only keeps the ground firm to adequately support the deck, but reduces dampness that could encourage decay in posts or sills.

The ideal soil for building is more than 5 feet deep, moderately permeable to water, free from flooding or high water tables, and level to gently sloping. Such soils will generally support both buildings and growing plants.

With the abundance of good soils in most parts of the United States, it is obviously better to select a site with minimum disadvantages than to try to correct serious soil problems.

Of course, some soils can be changed if for some reason a poor site must be used. Soil which is poorly suited for growing most plants or for supporting a building can be replaced with other soil material. Foundations or footings can be made to withstand the stresses of a particular site. Problems with wet-

From Tent to Cabin

ness can be overcome through drainage if someplace can be found to discharge the water. Slow soil permeability can be corrected for some uses by removing or altering the soil.

But these changes are costly and, in fact, often cost more than the original site. The upper 5 inch soil layer on one third of an acre weighs about 250 tons. To make a soil permeable to water and roots may require changing it from one that is one half clay to one that is one fourth clay. This can be done by bringing in many tons of sandy or silty materials. But to buy, haul and mix this new soil would be quite expensive and almost impossible to do on your own. Many people have tried adding organic materials instead. This process does improve the soil, but it is only a temporary improvement and does not substantially change the soil.

As you can see, a good hard scientific look at the soil before you buy or start building may save you a great deal of grief afterwards.

It is a major function of the USDA Soil Conservation Service to classify, map, and describe soil throughout the country. About 45 percent of all privately owned land in the United States has been surveyed. It is entirely possible that the land you are buying or planning to build on has a soil survey on record. If so, it will be at the office of the local soil conservation district or the county extension service.

Flood Plain: More than 10 percent of the land in the United States is subject to flooding. These areas can be found along small streams as well as near larger rivers. Flood plain soils are always adjacent to a stream, ditch, or drainage way and are nearly level. You can tell the size of the flood plain by standing on a stream bank and noting the width of the level area adjacent to the stream. If you dig in the soil you usually find a dark surface layer but no naturally developed sub-surface layers. Flood plain soil is often uniform in texture (sand, silt, and clay content) down to 4 feet or so. In some places there are layers of coarse and fine materials.

Clay Content: Soil with a high clay content often swells when wet and shrinks when dry, thus crack-

ing any foundations. This soil can expand up to 50 percent between dry and wet conditions. Unstable soil like this has its high clay content in the upper 3 to 4 feet. To check, press a small sample of the moist soil between thumb and index finger. If it is clay, a ribbon forms. Such soil is fine textured, sticky when wet, commonly dark and feels like putty. When dry, clay soil may have many cracks 2 to 4 inches wide and 10 to 20 inches deep. The surface may be sandy, silty, or clayey, underlaid by a dense plastic clay.

If you have questions about your site consult a professional. Don't take chances with your site selection as it is critical to the foundation of your cabin.

SITE PREPARATION

Grading and drainage.—Site preparation for construction of a wood deck is often less costly than that for a concrete terrace. When the site is steep, it is difficult to grade and to treat the backslopes in preparing a base for the concrete slab. In grading the site for a wood deck, one must normally consider only proper drainage, disturbing the natural terrain as little as possible. Grading should be enough to insure water runoff, usually just a minor leveling of the ground is required.

Weed and growth control.—There may also be a need for control of weed growth beneath the deck. Without some control or deterrent, such growth can lead to high moisture content of wood members and subsequent decay hazards where decks are near the grade. Common methods for such control consist of (a) the application of a weed killer to the plants or (b) the use of a barrier such as 4- or 6-mil polyethylene or 30-pound asphalt saturated felt. Such coverings should be placed just before the deck boards are laid. Stones, bricks, or other permanent means of anchoring the barriers in place should be used around the perimeter and in any interior surface variations which may be present. A few holes should be punched in the covering so that a good share of the rain will not run off and cause erosion.

FOOTINGS

Some type of footing is required to support the posts or poles which transfer the deck loads to the ground. In simplest form, the bottom of a treated pole and the friction of the earth around the pole provide this support. More commonly, however, some type of masonry, usually concrete, is used as a footing upon which the poles or posts rest. Several footing systems are normally used, some more preferred than others.

Footings for posts below grade.—Footings required for support of vertical members such as wood poles or posts must be designed to carry the load of the deck superstructure. In a simple form, the design includes the use of pressure-treated posts or poles embedded to a depth which provides sufficient bearing and rigidity. This may require a depth of 3 to 5 feet or more, depending on the exposed pole height and applied loads. In areas where frost is a problem, such as in the northern states, an embedment depth of 4 feet is commonly a minimum. But a lesser depth may be adequate in warmer climates. Soil should be well-tamped around the pole.

Concrete footings below the surface are normally used for treated posts or poles. Two such types may be used. The first consists of a pre-poured footing upon which the wood members rest. Embedment depth should be only enough to provide lateral resistance, usually 2 to 3 feet. The exception is in cold climates where frost may penetrate to a depth of 4 feet or more. Minimum size for concrete footings in normal soils should be 12 by 12 by 8 inches. Where spacing of the poles is over about 6 feet, 20 by 20 by 10 inches or larger sizes are preferred. However, soil capacities should be determined before design.

Another type of below-grade footing is the poured-in-place type. In such construction, the poles are pre-aligned, plumbed, and supported above the bottom of the excavated hole. Concrete is then poured below and around the butt end of the pole. A minimum thickness of 8 inches of concrete below the bottom of the pole is advisable. Soil may be added above the concrete when necessary for protection in cold weather. Such footings do not require tamped soil around the pole to provide lateral resistance. All poles or posts embedded in the soil should always be pressure treated for long life.

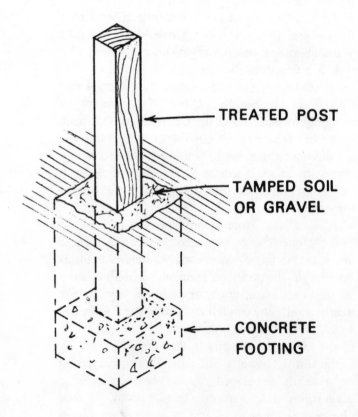

TREATED POST

TAMPED SOIL OR GRAVEL

CONCRETE FOOTING

Pre-poured footing.

BEAM-TO-POST CONNECTION

Beams are members to which the floor boards are directly fastened or which support a system of joists. Such beams must be fastened to the supporting posts. Beams may be single large or small members or consist of two smaller members fastened to each side of the posts. When a solid deck is to be constructed, the beams should be sloped at least 1 inch in 8 to 10 feet away from the house.

Single beams when 4 inches or wider usually bear on a post. When this system is used, the post must be trimmed evenly so that the beam bears on all posts. Use a line level or other method to establish the alignment.

A simple but poor method of fastening a 4- by 4-inch post to a 4- by 8-inch beam, for example, is by toe-nailing. This is poor practice and should be avoided. Splitting can occur which reduces the strength of the joint. It is also inadequate in resisting twisting of the beam.

A better system is by the use of a 1- by 4-inch lumber or plywood (Exterior grade) cleat located on two sides of the post. Cleats are nailed to the beam and post with 7^d or 8^d deformed shank nails.

A good method of post-to-beam connection is by the use of a metal angle at each side. A 3- by 3-inch angle or larger should be used so that fasteners can be turned in easily. Use lag screws to fasten them in place. A metal strap fastened to the beam and the post might also be used for single beams. A ⅛- by 3-inch or larger strap, pre-formed to insure a good fit, will provide an adequate connection.

Use 10^d deformed shank nails for the smaller members and ¼-inch lag screws for the larger members.

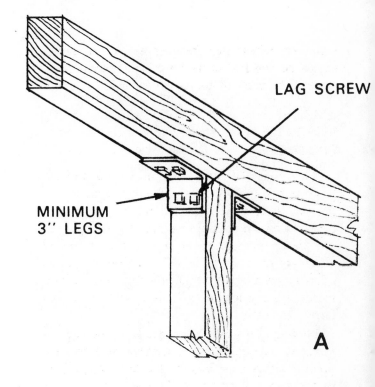

LAG SCREW

MINIMUM 3″ LEGS

A

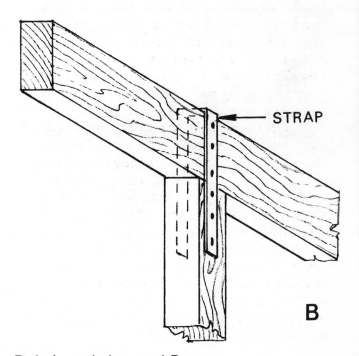

STRAP

B

Beam-to-post connection. Both A, angle iron, and B, strapping, are good methods.

JOIST-TO-BEAM CONNECTIONS

When beams are spaced 2 to 5 feet apart and 2-by 4-inch Douglas-fir or similar deck boards are used, there is no need to use joists to support the decking. The beams thus serve as both fastening and support members for the 2-inch deck boards. However, if the spans between beams are more than 3-½ to 5 feet apart, it is necessary to use joists between the beams or 2 by 3 or 2 by 4 on edge for decking. To provide rigidity to the structure, the joists must be fastened to the beam in one of several ways.

Joists bearing directly on the beams may be toe-nailed to the beam with one or two nails on each side. Use 10^d nails and avoid splitting. When uplift stresses are inclined to be great in high wind areas, supplementary metal strapping might be used in addition to the toe-nailing. Use 24- to 26-ga. galvanized strapping and nail with 1-inch galvanized roofing nails. When a header is used at the joist ends, nail the header into the end of each joist. Have the header overhang the beam by one-half inch to provide a good drip edge.

Joists located between beams and flush with their tops may be connected in two manners. One utilizes a 2- by 3-inch or 2- by 4-inch ledger which is spiked to the beam. Joists are cut between beams and toe-nailed to the beams at each end. The joint can be improved by the use of small metal clips.

Another method utilizes a metal joist hanger. The hanger is first nailed to the end of the joist with 1- to 1-¼-inch galvanized roofing nails and then to the beam. Several types of joist hangers are available.

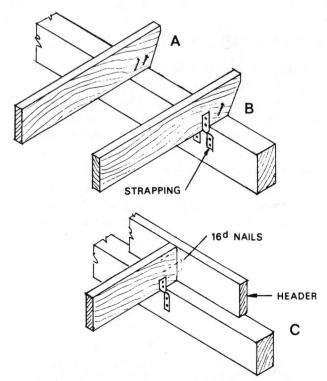

Joist-to-beam connection. A—toe nail; B—strapping; C—connection with header.

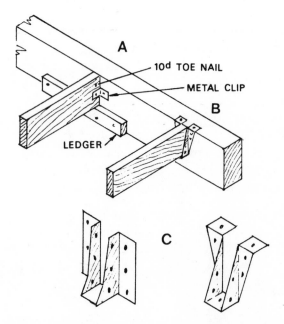

Joists between beams. A—ledger support; B—joist hanger support; C—joist hangers.

FASTENING DECK BOARDS

Deck boards are fastened to floor joists or to beams through their face with nails or screws. Screws are more costly to use than nails from the standpoint of material and labor but have greater resistance to loosening or withdrawal than the nail. A good compromise between the common smooth shank nail and the screw is the deformed shank nail. These nails retain their withdrawal resistance even under repeated wetting and drying cycles. Both nails and screws should be set flush or just below the surface of the deck board.

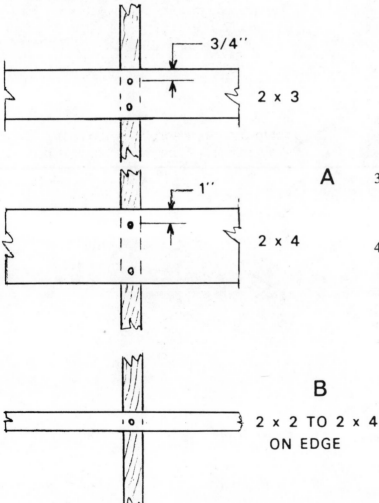

A

B

Some good rules in fastening deck boards to the joists or beams are as follows:

1. Number of fasteners per deck board—use two fasteners for nominal 2- by 3-inch and 2- by 4-inch decking laid flat. For 2 by 3's or 2 by 4's on edge, use one fastener per joist.

2. Size of fasteners—
   Nails (deformed shank, galvanized, aluminum, etc.):
   Nominal 2-inch thick deck boards—12ᵈ
   Nominal 2- by 3-inch deck boards on edge—5 inch
   Nominal 2- by 4-inch deck board (nailing not recommended)
   Screws (flat or oval head, rust proof):
   Nominal 2-inch thick deck boards—3 inch
   Nominal 2- by 3-inch deck boards on edge—4-½ inch
   Nominal 2- by 4-inch deck boards on edge—5 inch.

3. Spacing—space all deck boards (flat or vertical) one-eighth to one-fourth inch apart (use 8ᵈ or 10ᵈ nail for ⅛-inch spacing).

4. End joints (butt joints)—end joints of flat deck boards should be made over the center of the joist or beam. In flat grain boards, always place with the bark side up. When the upper face gets wet, it crowns slightly and water drains off more easily. End joints of any deck boards on edge should be made over a spaced double joist, a 4-inch or wider single beam, or a nominal 2-inch joist with nailing cleats on each side.

Fastening deck boards. A—flat deck boards; B—deck boards on edge.

When deck boards are used on edge, spacers between runs will aid in maintaining uniform spacing and can be made to effect lateral support between runs by using lateral nailing at the spacers. Spacers are recommended between supports when spans exceed 4 feet and should be placed so that no distance between supports or spacers exceeds 4 feet. An elastomeric construction adhesive or penta-grease on both faces of each spacer prevents water retention in the joints.

Always dip ends of deck boards in water-repellent preservative before installing.

Always pre-drill ends of 2- by 3-inch or 2- by 4-inch (flat) deck boards of the denser species, or when there is a tendency to split. Pre-drill when screws are used for fastening. Pre-drill all fastening points of 2- by 3-inch or 2- by 4-inch deck boards placed on edge.

To provide longer useful life for decks made of low to moderate decay-resistant species, use one or more of the following precautions:

(1) Use spaced double joists or beams and place end joints between.
(2) Lay a strip of building felt saturated with a wood preservative over the beam or joist before installing deck boards.
(3) Apply an elastomeric glue to the beam or joist edge before installing the deck boards.
(4) Treat end joints of deck boards made over a support with yearly applications of a water-repellent preservative. (A plunger-type oil can will work well.)

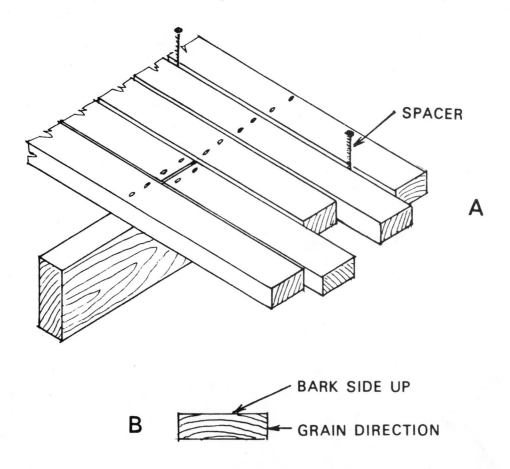

SPACER

A

BARK SIDE UP

B

GRAIN DIRECTION

Fastening flat deck boards. A—spacing between boards; B—grain orientation for flat grain boards.

Part II
The Cabin

1. Basic Cabin Plans

Figure 1. This is an exploded view of our cabin, showing all the major parts. The floor system, interior and exterior walls, and the roof are the major parts which when erected will make up the basic cabin.

Floor System

The floor system is constructed over a *crawl space* area. Supporting *beams* are fastened to treated posts embedded in the soil or to masonry *piers*. In the South, Central, and Coastal areas, provisions must be made for protection from termites. Construction of this type of support for the floor joists has a great advantage because grading is not required and thus it can be used on relatively steep or uneven slopes. Floor joists are fastened to these beams and the *subfloor* nailed to the joists. This results in a level, sturdy platform upon which the rest of the cabin is constructed.

Exterior Walls

Exterior walls, often assembled flat on the sub-floor and raised in "tilt-up" fashion, are fastened to the perimeter of the floor platform. Exterior coverings and window and door units are included after walls are plumbed and braced.

Interior Walls

Interior walls are usually the next components to be erected unless *trussed* rafters (roof trusses) are used. Trussed rafters are designed to span from one exterior sidewall to the other and do not require support from interior *partitions*. This allows partitions to be placed as required for room dividers. When ceiling joists and rafters are used, a *bearing partition* near the center of the width is necessary.

Roof Trusses or Roof Framing

Several systems can be used to provide a roof over the cabin. One consists of normal ceiling joists

Key words in italics appear in the glossary.

From Tent to Cabin

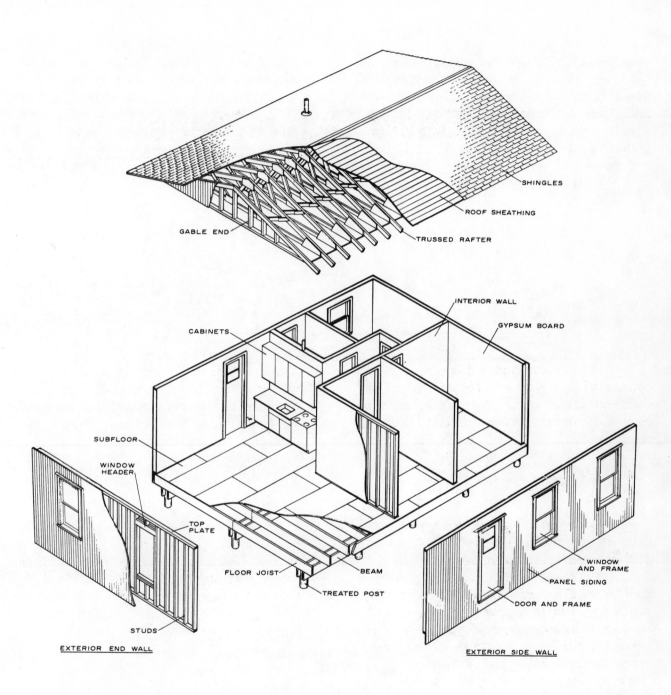

Figure 1—Exploded view of wood-frame house.

and rafters which require some type of load-bearing wall between the sidewalls (fig. 2A). Another is the trussed rafter system (figs. 1 and 2B) (commonly called *trusses*). This design requires no load-bearing walls between the sidewalls. A third design consists of thick wood roof decking (fig. 2C). A fourth is open beams and decking which span between the exterior walls and a center wall or ridge beam (fig. 2D). The truss and conventional joist-and-rafter construction may require some type of finish for the ceiling. The decking (fig. 2C) or the beam and decking (fig. 2D) combinations can serve both as interior finish and as a surface to apply the roofing material.

The type of roof system you use will be determined by room layout modifications you may make to the basic plan.

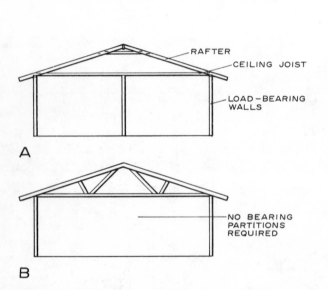

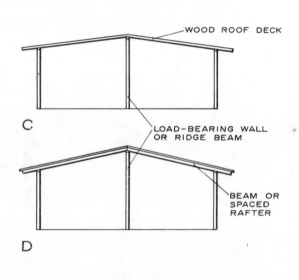

Figure 2—Types of roof construction. A, Rafter and ceiling joists—sloped roofs; B, trussed rafter—sloped roofs; C, wood roof decking—low-sloped roofs; D, beam with wood or fiberboard decking.

From Tent to Cabin

The following 27 pages are the actual construction plans for your cabin. Pages 28 through 49 make up the five separate sheets of the plans. Masters of each plan appear on pages 23 - 27 (in reduced form), showing how you are to piece the plans together.

Make photo copies or Xerox™ copies of pages *28* through *49* and tape together as indicated on masters. To keep your plans in good shape while working outdoors, spray them with artist fixative or cover them with clear contact paper; also, roll them up blueprint-style rather than folding. These plans can be used as they appear in the book but it is far easier to make copies and use blueprint-style.

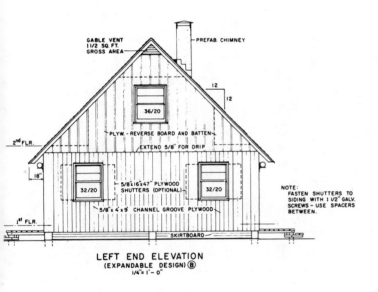

LEFT END ELEVATION
(EXPANDABLE DESIGN) Ⓑ
1/4" = 1'- 0"

FRONT ELEVATION
(EXPANDABLE DESIGN) Ⓑ
1/4" = 1'- 0"

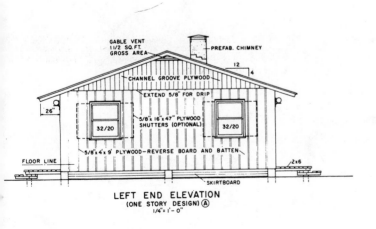

LEFT END ELEVATION
(ONE STORY DESIGN) Ⓐ
1/4" = 1'- 0"

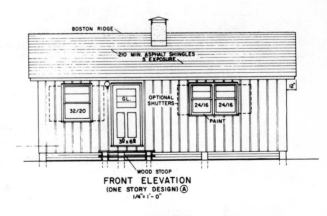

FRONT ELEVATION
(ONE STORY DESIGN) Ⓐ
1/4" = 1'- 0"

NOTE: (FINISHING)
SIDING - PIGMENTED STAIN - MEDIUM TO DARK COLOR
TRIM - PIGMENTED STAIN - LIGHT COLOR
WINDOWS - PAINT - WHITE OR LIGHT COLOR
NOTE: TRIM INCLUDES SHUTTERS, FACIA, FLY
RAFTERS, SOFFIT, MOLDINGS, ETC.

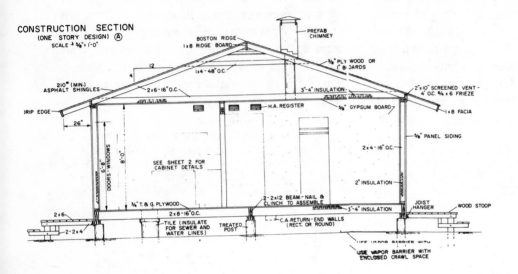

CONSTRUCTION SECTION
(ONE STORY DESIGN) Ⓐ
SCALE - 3/8" = 1'-0"

BOSTON RIDGE
1 x 8 RIDGE BOARD

PREFAB CHIMNEY

3/8" PLY WOOD OR 1" BOARDS

210# (MIN.) ASPHALT SHINGLES

12
4

1 x 4 - 48" O.C.

2 x 6 - 16" O.C.

3"-4" INSULATION

2" x 10" SCREENED VENT - 4' O.C. 5/4 x 6 FRIEZE

DRIP EDGE

H.A. REGISTER

3/8" GYPSUM BOARD

1 x 8 FACIA

26"

5/8" PANEL SIDING

DOORS - WINDOWS

6'-8"

8'-0"

2 x 4 - 16" O.C.

SEE SHEET 2 FOR CABINET DETAILS

2" INSULATION

3/4" T. & G. PLYWOOD

2 - 2 x 12 BEAM - NAIL & CLINCH TO ASSEMBLE

JOIST HANGER

WOOD STOOP

2 x 6

2 x 8 - 16" O.C.

3"-4" INSULATION

2 - 2 x 4

TILE (INSULATE FOR SEWER AND WATER LINES)

TREATED POST

C.A. RETURN - END WALLS (RECT. OR ROUND)

USE VAPOR BARRIER WITH ENCLOSED CRAWL SPACE

USE VAPOR BARRIER WITH ENCLOSED CRAWL SPACE

REAR ELEVATION
(ONE STORY DESIGN) Ⓐ
SCALE - 1/8" = 1'-0"

24/20   24/16

REAR ELEVATION
(EXPANDABLE DESIGN) Ⓑ
SCALE - 1/8" = 1'-0"

24/20   24/16

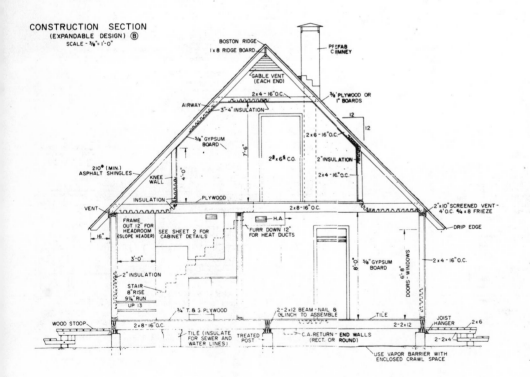

CONSTRUCTION SECTION
(EXPANDABLE DESIGN) Ⓑ
SCALE - 3/8" = 1'-0"

BOSTON RIDGE
1 x 8 RIDGE BOARD

PREFAB CHIMNEY

GABLE VENT (EACH END)

2 x 4 - 16" O.C.

3/8" PLYWOOD OR 1" BOARDS

AIRWAY

3"-4" INSULATION

12

3/8" GYPSUM BOARD

2 x 6 - 16" O.C.

12

210# (MIN.) ASPHALT SHINGLES

2 x 6 C.O.

2" INSULATION

KNEE WALL

2 x 4 - 16" O.C.

4'-0"

INSULATION

PLYWOOD

2 x 8 - 16" O.C.

2" x 10" SCREENED VENT - 4' O.C. 5/4 x 8 FRIEZE

VENT

7'-6"

FRAME OUT 12" FOR HEADROOM (SLOPE HEADER)

H.A.

DRIP EDGE

16"

SEE SHEET 2 FOR CABINET DETAILS

FURR DOWN 12" FOR HEAT DUCTS

3'-0"

3/8" GYPSUM BOARD

8'-0"

2 x 4 - 16" O.C.

2" INSULATION

DOORS - WINDOWS

6'-8"

STAIR 8" RISE 9 1/4" RUN

UP 13

3/4" T. & G. PLYWOOD

2 - 2 x 12 BEAM - NAIL & CLINCH TO ASSEMBLE

TILE

JOIST HANGER

2 x 6

WOOD STOOP

2 x 8 - 16" O.C.

TILE (INSULATE FOR SEWER AND WATER LINES)

TREATED POST

C.A. RETURN - END WALLS (RECT. OR ROUND)

2 - 2 x 12

2 - 2 x 4

USE VAPOR BARRIER WITH ENCLOSED CRAWL SPACE

RIGHT END ELEVATION
(ONE STORY DESIGN) Ⓐ
SCALE - 1/8" = 1'-0"

24/20   24/20

RIGHT END ELEVATION
(EXPANDABLE DESIGN) Ⓑ
SCALE - 1/8" = 1'-0"

34/20

24/20   24/20

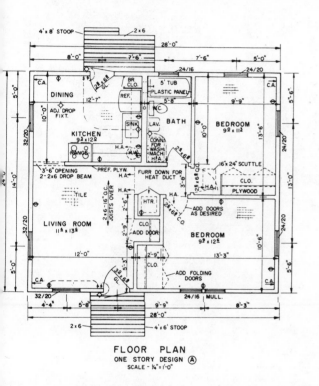

FLOOR PLAN
ONE STORY DESIGN Ⓐ
SCALE - ¼" = 1'-0"

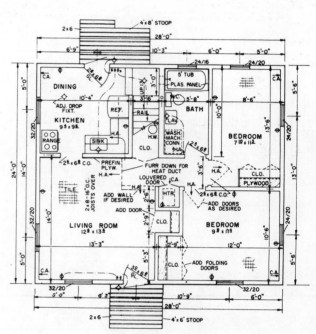

FIRST FLOOR PLAN
EXPANDABLE DESIGN Ⓑ
(SEE SHEET 5 FOR SECOND FLOOR PLAN)
SCALE - ¼" = 1'-0"

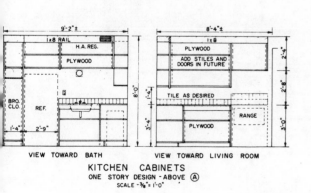

VIEW TOWARD BATH   VIEW TOWARD LIVING ROOM

KITCHEN CABINETS
ONE STORY DESIGN - ABOVE Ⓐ
SCALE - ⅜" = 1'-0"

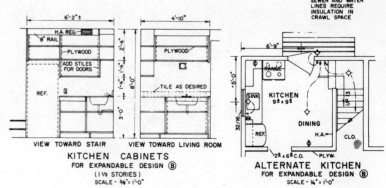

VIEW TOWARD STAIR   VIEW TOWARD LIVING ROOM

KITCHEN CABINETS
FOR EXPANDABLE DESIGN Ⓑ
(1½ STORIES)
SCALE - ⅜" = 1'-0"

NOTE:
SEWER AND WATER
LINES REQUIRE
INSULATION IN
CRAWL SPACE

ALTERNATE KITCHEN
FOR EXPANDABLE DESIGN Ⓑ
SCALE - ¼" = 1'-0"

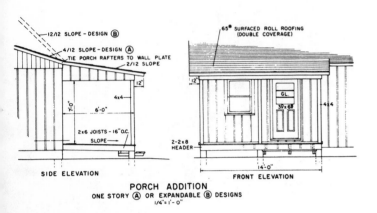

12/12 SLOPE - DESIGN (B)
4/12 SLOPE - DESIGN (A)
TIE PORCH RAFTERS TO WALL PLATE
2/12 SLOPE
12"
4x4
7'-0"
6'-0"
2x6 JOISTS - 16" O.C.
SLOPE →

SIDE ELEVATION

65# SURFACED ROLL ROOFING
(DOUBLE COVERAGE)
12"
GL.
3⁰x6⁸
4x4
2-2x8
HEADER
14'-0"

FRONT ELEVATION

PORCH ADDITION
ONE STORY (A) OR EXPANDABLE (B) DESIGNS
1/4" = 1'-0"

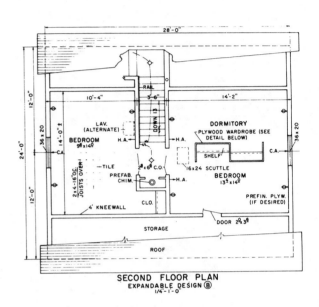

28'-0"
12'-2"
24'-0"
12'-0"
10'-4"
14'-2"
RAIL
3'-6"
DOWN 13
36 x 20
14'-0"±
LAV.
(ALTERNATE)
BEDROOM
9⁸x14⁰
H.A.
SHELF
DORMITORY
PLYWOOD WARDROBE (SEE DETAIL BELOW)
C.A.
36 x 20
TILE
2x4-16"O.C.
JOISTS OVER
PREFAB.
CHIM.
2"x6" C.O.
16x24 SCUTTLE
H.A.
BEDROOM
13⁵x14⁰
PREFIN. PLYW.
(IF DESIRED)
4' KNEEWALL
CLO.
DOOR 2⁸x3⁸
STORAGE
ROOF

SECOND FLOOR PLAN
EXPANDABLE DESIGN (B)
1/4"=1'-0"

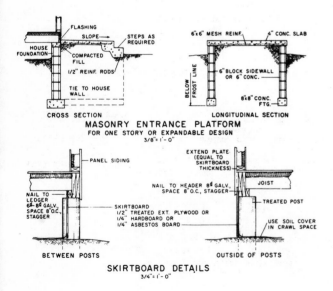

FLASHING
SLOPE
STEPS AS REQUIRED
HOUSE FOUNDATION
COMPACTED FILL
1/2" REINF. RODS
TIE TO HOUSE WALL

CROSS SECTION

6"x6" MESH REINF.
4" CONC. SLAB
BELOW FROST LINE
6" BLOCK SIDEWALL OR 6" CONC.
8"x8" CONC. FTG.

LONGITUDINAL SECTION

MASONRY ENTRANCE PLATFORM
FOR ONE STORY OR EXPANDABLE DESIGN
3/8"=1'-0"

PANEL SIDING
EXTEND PLATE
(EQUAL TO SKIRTBOARD THICKNESS)
NAIL TO HEADER 8d GALV,
SPACE 8" O.C., STAGGER
JOIST
NAIL TO LEDGER
6d- 8d GALV,
SPACE 8" O.C.,
STAGGER
SKIRTBOARD
1/2" TREATED EXT. PLYWOOD OR
1/4" HARDBOARD OR
1/4" ASBESTOS BOARD
TREATED POST
USE SOIL COVER IN CRAWL SPACE

BETWEEN POSTS   **OUTSIDE OF POSTS**

SKIRTBOARD DETAILS
3/4"=1'-0"

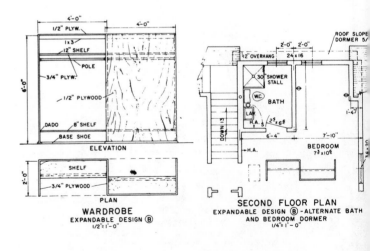

4'-0"
1/2" PLYW.
1x3
12" SHELF
POLE
3/4" PLYW.
1/2" PLYWOOD
DADO
8" SHELF
BASE SHOE
4'-0"
6'-0"

ELEVATION

SHELF
3/4" PLYWOOD
2'-0"

PLAN

WARDROBE
EXPANDABLE DESIGN (B)
1/2"=1'-0"

ROOF SLOPE DORMER 5/
2'-0" 2'-0"
4½" OVERHANG
24x16
30" SHOWER STALL
WC
BATH
LAV.
2"x6"
DOWN 13
H.A.
H.A.
6'-4"
7'-10"
BEDROOM
7⁵x10⁵
1'-4"

SECOND FLOOR PLAN
EXPANDABLE DESIGN (B)-ALTERNATE BATH
AND BEDROOM DORMER
1/4"=1'-0"

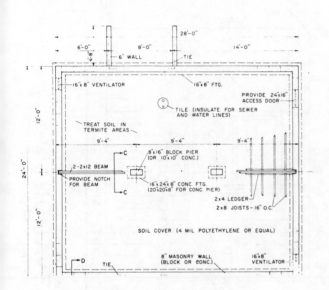

MASONRY FOUNDATION PLAN
1/4"=1'-0"

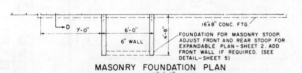

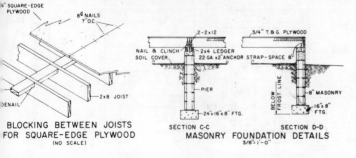

BLOCKING BETWEEN JOISTS
FOR SQUARE-EDGE PLYWOOD
(NO SCALE)

SECTION C-C   SECTION D-D
MASONRY FOUNDATION DETAILS
3/8"=1'-0"

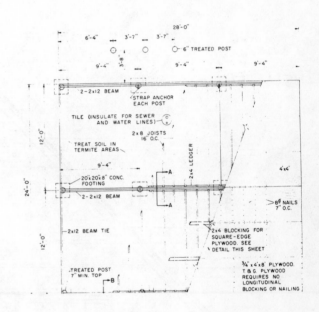

POST FOUNDATION PLAN
1/4"=1'-0"

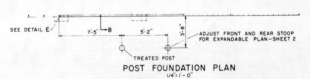

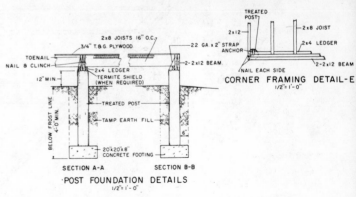

CORNER FRAMING DETAIL-E
1/2"=1'-0"

SECTION A-A   SECTION B-B
POST FOUNDATION DETAILS
1/2"=1'-0"

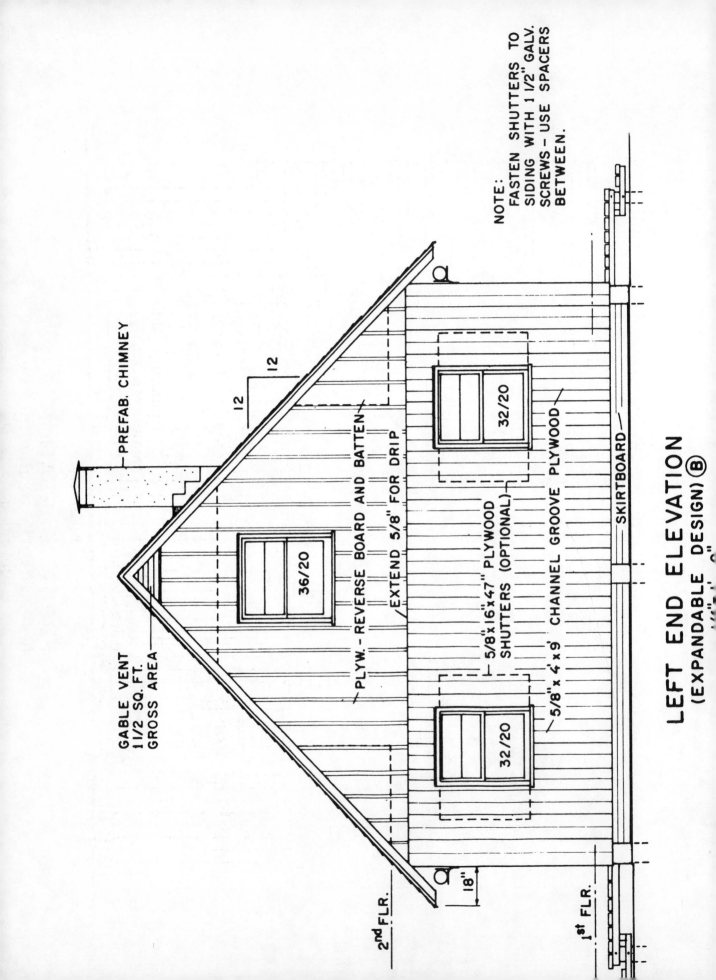

NOTE:
FASTEN SHUTTERS TO SIDING WITH 1 1/2" GALV. SCREWS – USE SPACERS BETWEEN.

PREFAB. CHIMNEY

GABLE VENT
1 1/2 SQ. FT.
GROSS AREA

12

12

PLYW.– REVERSE BOARD AND BATTEN

EXTEND 5/8" FOR DRIP

5/8"x16"x47" PLYWOOD SHUTTERS (OPTIONAL)

5/8" x 4' x 9' CHANNEL GROOVE PLYWOOD

SKIRTBOARD

36/20

32/20

32/20

18"

2nd FLR.

1st FLR.

LEFT END ELEVATION
(EXPANDABLE DESIGN) Ⓑ

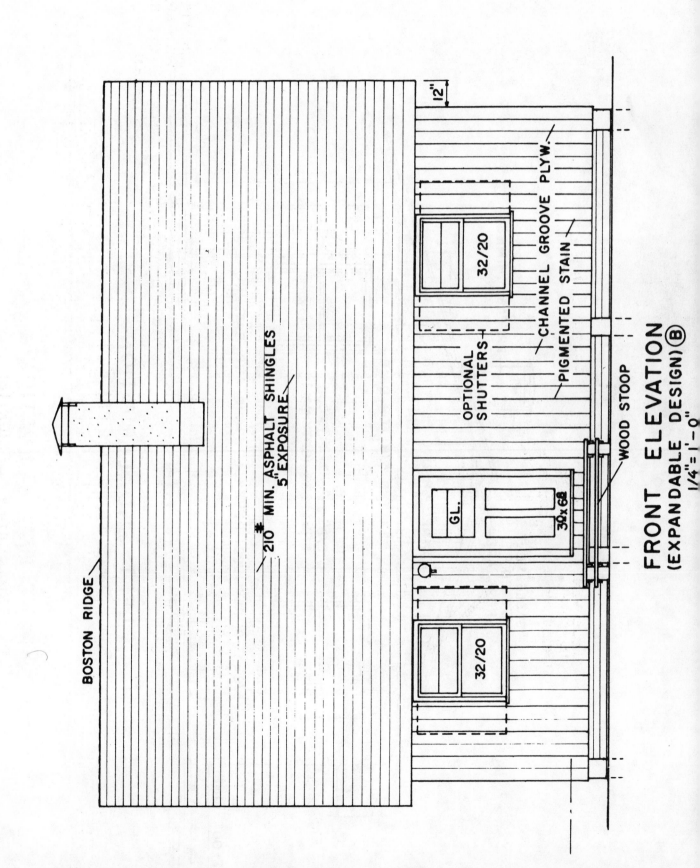

BOSTON RIDGE

210 # MIN. ASPHALT SHINGLES
5" EXPOSURE

12"

CHANNEL GROOVE PLYW.

PIGMENTED STAIN

OPTIONAL SHUTTERS

32/20

32/20

GL.

30 x 68

WOOD STOOP

FRONT ELEVATION
(EXPANDABLE DESIGN) Ⓑ
1/4" = 1'-0"

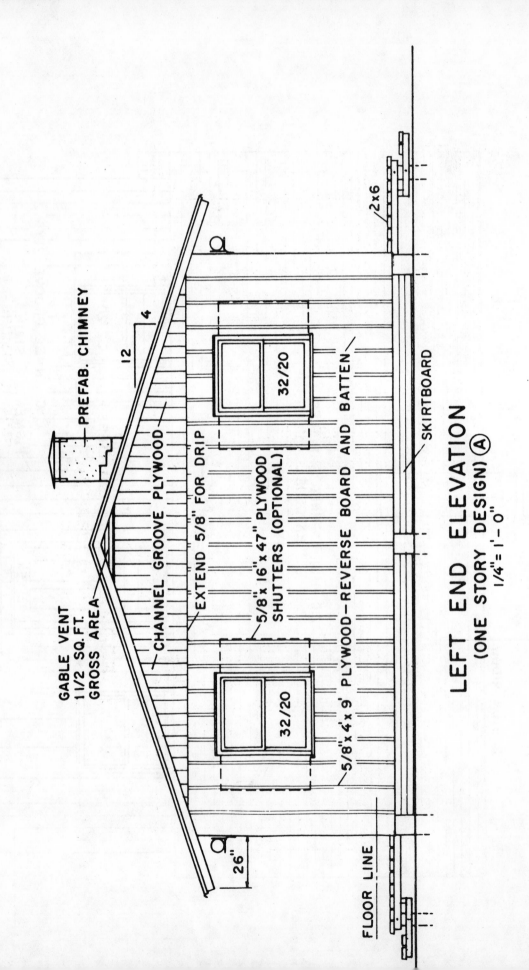

LEFT END ELEVATION
(ONE STORY DESIGN) Ⓐ
1/4" = 1'-0"

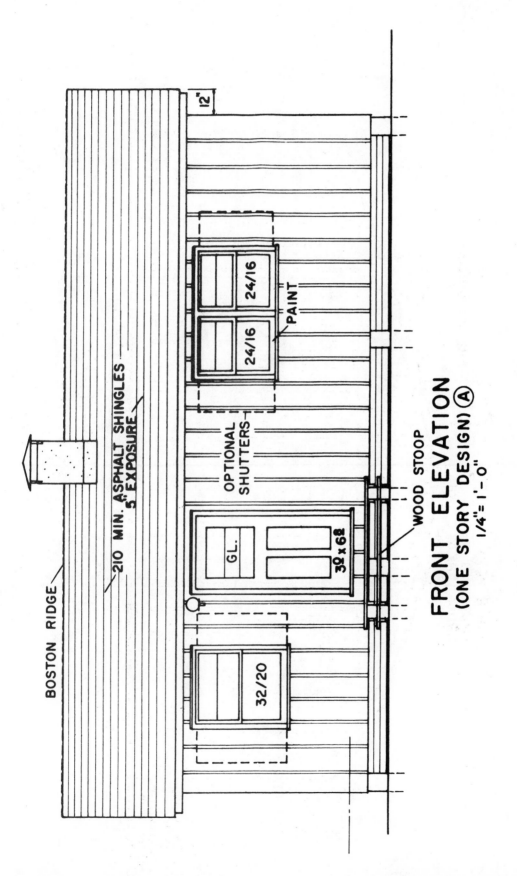

BOSTON RIDGE

210 MIN. ASPHALT SHINGLES
5' EXPOSURE

12"

24/16   24/16

PAINT

OPTIONAL
SHUTTERS

GL.

32 x 68

32/20

WOOD STOOP

FRONT ELEVATION
(ONE STORY DESIGN) Ⓐ
1/4"= 1'-0"

NOTE: (FINISHING)
SIDING–PIGMENTED STAIN – MEDIUM TO DARK COLOR
1] TRIM – PIGMENTED STAIN – LIGHT COLOR
WINDOWS – PAINT – WHITE OR LIGHT COLOR

1] NOTE: TRIM INCLUDES SHUTTERS, FACIA, FLY
RAFTERS, SOFFIT, MOLDINGS, ETC.

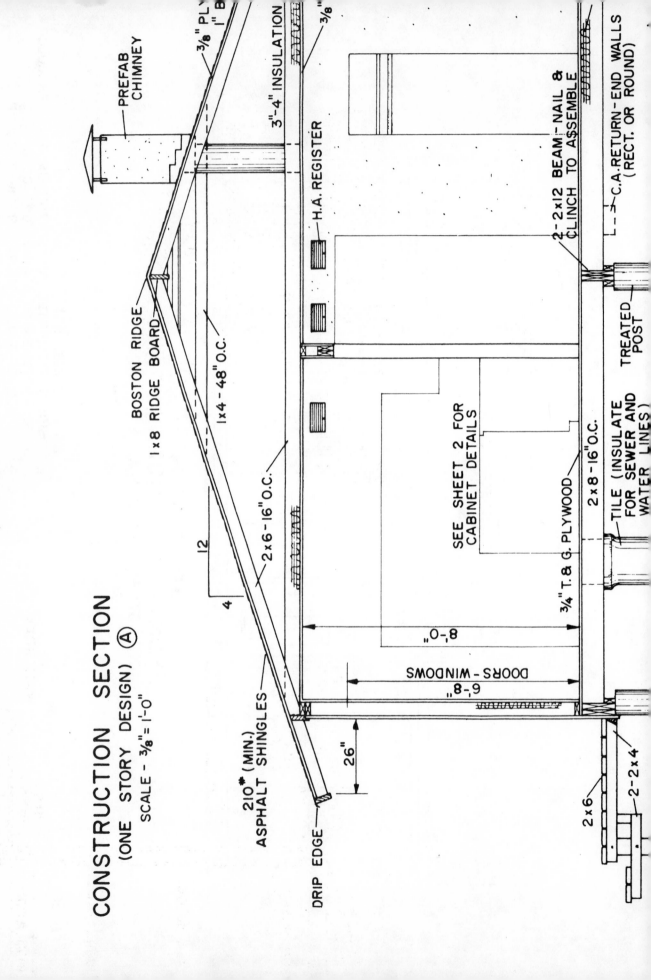

CONSTRUCTION SECTION A
(ONE STORY DESIGN)
SCALE - 3/8" = 1'-0"

PREFAB CHIMNEY

3/8" PLY

1" B

3/8" INSULATION

3"-4" INSULATION

3/8"

BOSTON RIDGE
1 x 8 RIDGE BOARD

1 x 4 - 48" O.C.

2 x 6 - 16" O.C.

12

4

H.A. REGISTER

2 - 2 x 12 BEAM- NAIL &
CLINCH TO ASSEMBLE

C.A. RETURN- END WALLS
(RECT. OR ROUND)

210# (MIN.)
ASPHALT SHINGLES

DRIP EDGE

26"

SEE SHEET 2 FOR
CABINET DETAILS

3/4" T. & G. PLYWOOD

2 x 8 - 16" O.C.

8'-0"

DOORS - WINDOWS

6'-8"

TILE (INSULATE
FOR SEWER AND
WATER LINES)

TREATED POST

2 x 6

2 - 2 x 4

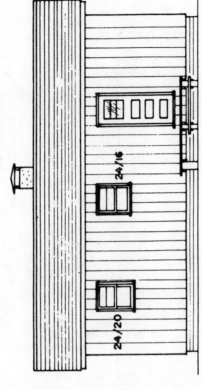

REAR ELEVATION
(ONE STORY DESIGN) Ⓐ
SCALE - 1/8" = 1'-0"

24/16

24/20

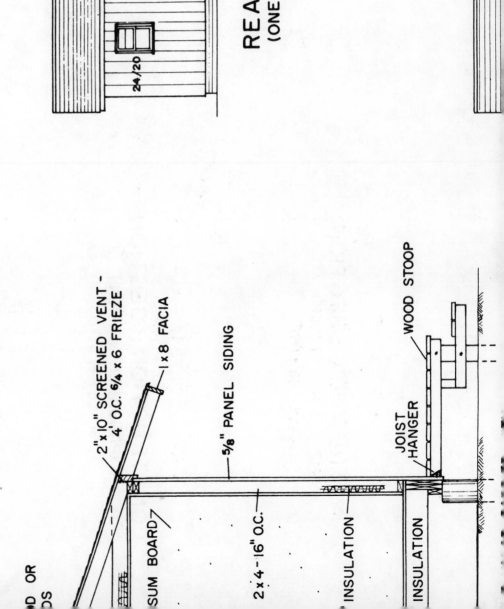

2"x 10" SCREENED VENT -
4' O.C. 5/4 x 6 FRIEZE

1 x 8 FACIA

5/8" PANEL SIDING

SUM BOARD

2'x 4 - 16" O.C.

INSULATION

INSULATION

WOOD STOOP

JOIST
HANGER

OR
DS

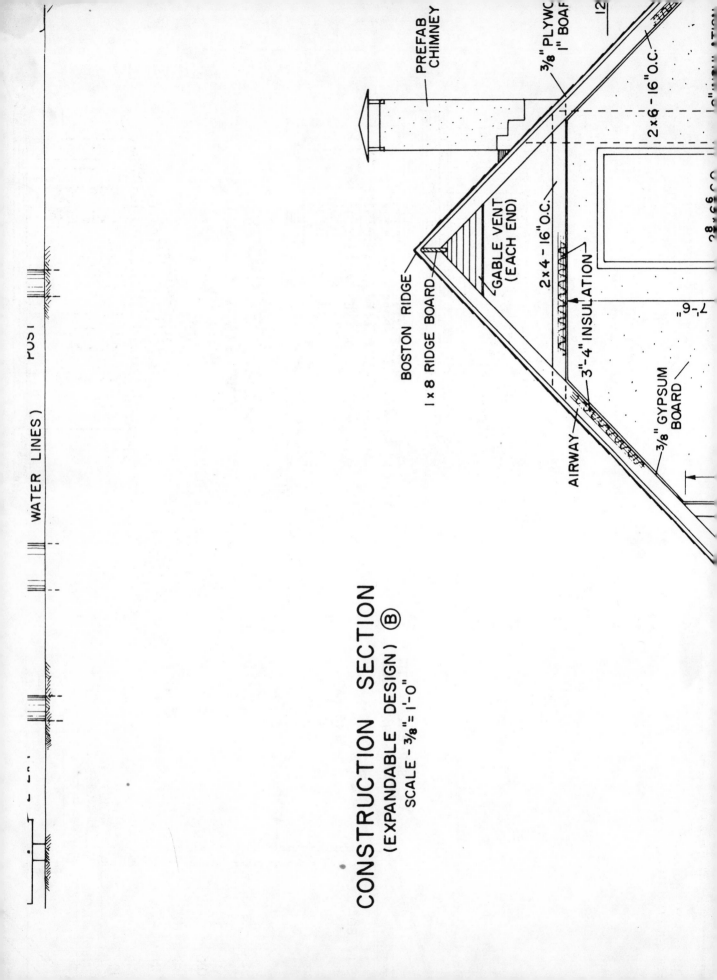

PREFAB CHIMNEY

3/8" PLYWOOD
1" BOARD

2 x 6 - 16" O.C.

BOSTON RIDGE

1 x 8 RIDGE BOARD

GABLE VENT
(EACH END)

2 x 4 - 16" O.C.

3"-4" INSULATION

AIRWAY

3/8" GYPSUM BOARD

7'-6"

2 x 6 - 16" O.C.

12

WATER LINES)

POST

CONSTRUCTION SECTION ⓑ
(EXPANDABLE DESIGN)
SCALE - 3/8" = 1'-0"

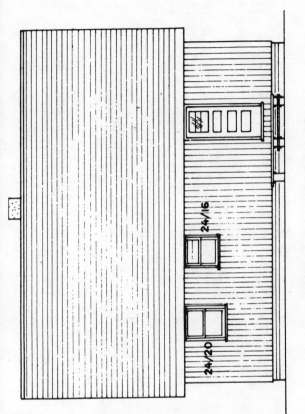

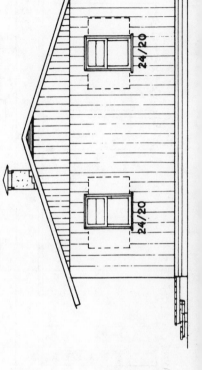

REAR ELEVATION
(EXPANDABLE DESIGN) Ⓑ
SCALE - ⅛" = 1'-0"

24/16

24/20

24/20

24/20

SE VAPOR BARRIER WITH
ENCLOSED CRAWL SPACE

OR

12

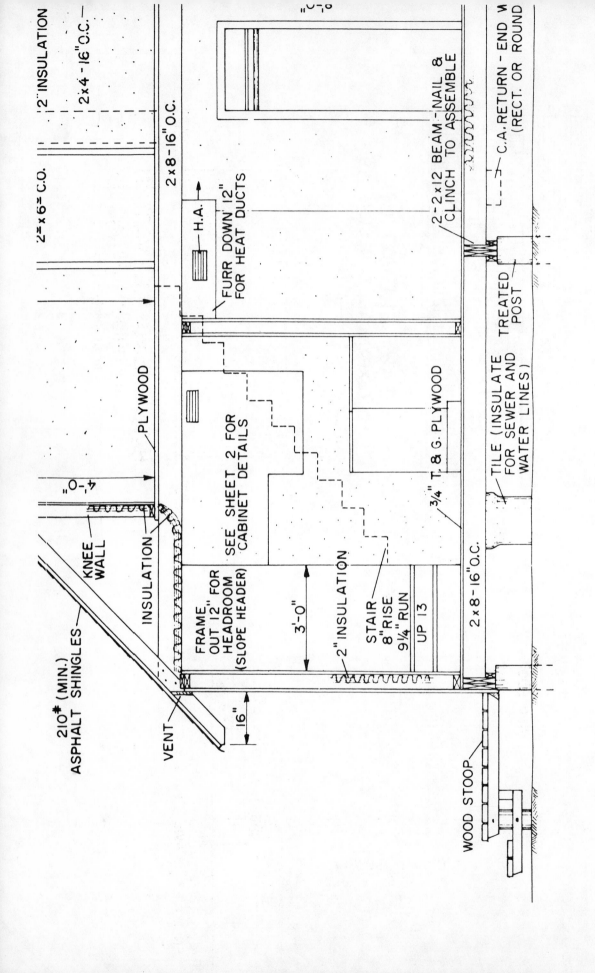

210# (MIN.)
ASPHALT SHINGLES

KNEE WALL

INSULATION

VENT

PLYWOOD

2"INSULATION

2×4-16"O.C.

2"×6"C.O.

2×8-16"O.C.

4'-0"

16"

FRAME OUT 12" FOR HEADROOM (SLOPE HEADER)

SEE SHEET 2 FOR CABINET DETAILS

H.A.

FURR DOWN 12" FOR HEAT DUCTS

3'-0"

2"INSULATION

STAIR 8"RISE 9¼"RUN

UP 13

¾" T.& G. PLYWOOD

2×8-16"O.C.

2-2×12 BEAM-NAIL & CLINCH TO ASSEMBLE

C.A.RETURN - END (RECT. OR ROUND

TILE (INSULATE FOR SEWER AND WATER LINES)

TREATED POST

WOOD STOOP

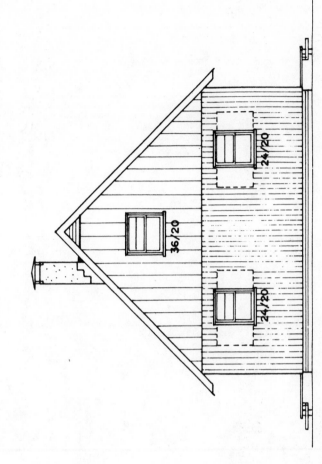

RIGHT END ELEVATION (A)
(ONE STORY DESIGN)
SCALE - 1/8" = 1'-0"

RIGHT END ELEVATION (B)
(EXPANDABLE DESIGN)
SCALE - 1/8" = 1'-0"

24/20

36/20

24/20

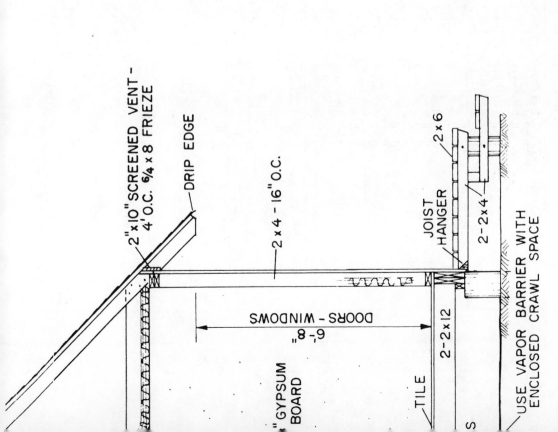

2"x10" SCREENED VENT - 4' O.C. 5/4 x 8 FRIEZE

DRIP EDGE

2 x 4 - 16" O.C.

2 x 6

JOIST HANGER

2-2 x 4

2-2 x 12

DOORS - WINDOWS
6'-8"

GYPSUM BOARD

TILE

USE VAPOR BARRIER WITH ENCLOSED CRAWL SPACE

S

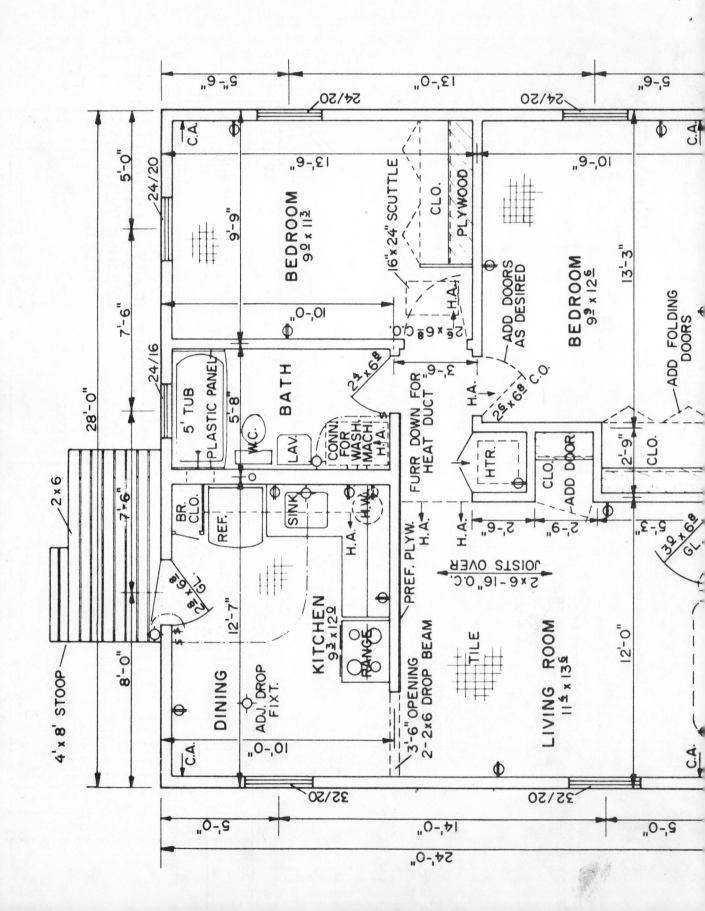

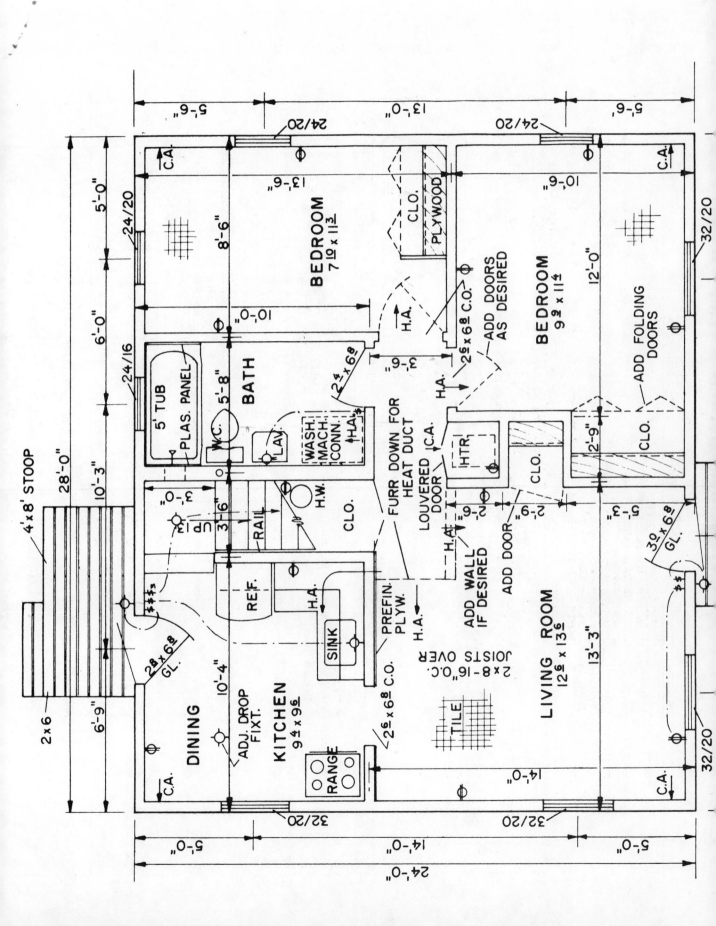

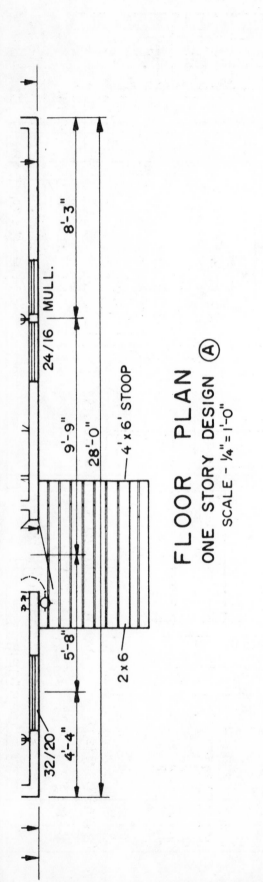

FLOOR PLAN
ONE STORY DESIGN (A)
SCALE - ¼" = 1'-0"

24/16 MULL.

8'-3"

9'-9"

28'-0"

4' x 6' STOOP

2 x 6

5'-8"

32/20

4'-4"

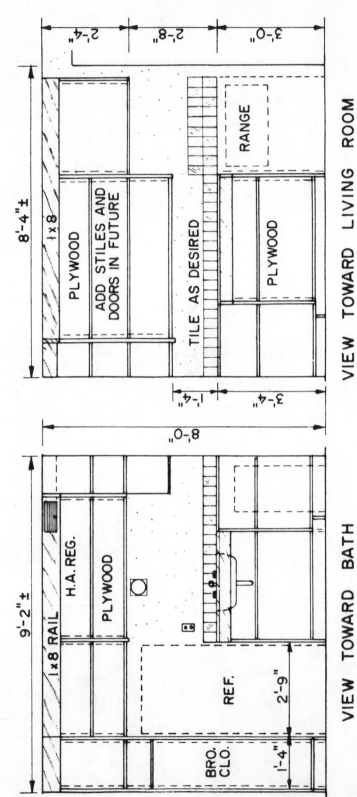

2'-4"

2'-8"

3'-0"

8'-4"±

1 x 8

PLYWOOD

ADD STILES AND
DOORS IN FUTURE

RANGE

TILE AS DESIRED

PLYWOOD

1'-4"

3'-4"

VIEW TOWARD LIVING ROOM

9'-2"±

1 x 8 RAIL

H.A. REG.

PLYWOOD

REF.

BRO.
CLO.

2'-9"

1'-4"

8'-0"

VIEW TOWARD BATH

KITCHEN CABINETS
ONE STORY DESIGN - ABOVE (A)

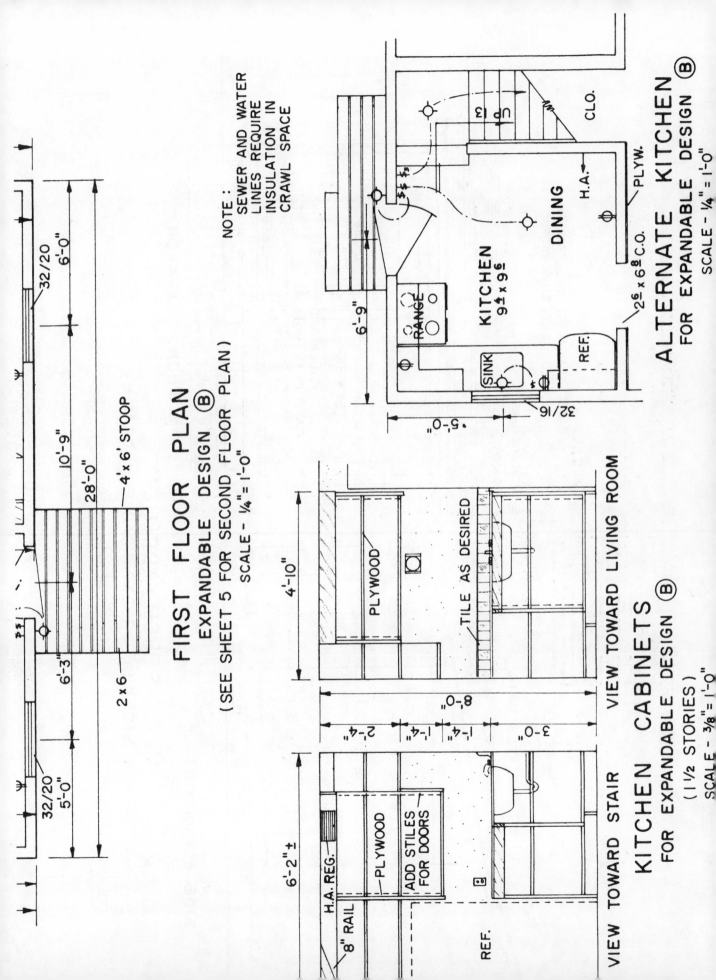

FIRST FLOOR PLAN
EXPANDABLE DESIGN Ⓑ
(SEE SHEET 5 FOR SECOND FLOOR PLAN)
SCALE - ¼" = 1'-0"

32/20

6'-0"

10'-9"

28'-0"

4'x 6' STOOP

2 x 6

32/20

5'-0"

6'-3"

NOTE :

SEWER AND WATER
LINES REQUIRE
INSULATION IN
CRAWL SPACE

ALTERNATE KITCHEN
FOR EXPANDABLE DESIGN Ⓑ
SCALE - ¼" = 1'-0"

CLO.

DINING

H.A.

PLYW.

KITCHEN
9⁴ x 9⁶

RANGE

SINK

REF.

2⁶ x 6⁸ C.O.

6'-9"

15'-0"

32/16

KITCHEN CABINETS
FOR EXPANDABLE DESIGN Ⓑ
(1 ½ STORIES)
SCALE - ⅜" = 1'-0"

VIEW TOWARD LIVING ROOM

VIEW TOWARD STAIR

PLYWOOD

TILE AS DESIRED

4'-10"

8'-0"

2'-4"

1'-4"

1'-4"

3'-0"

6'-2"±

H.A. REG.

PLYWOOD

ADD STILES
FOR DOORS

8" RAIL

REF.

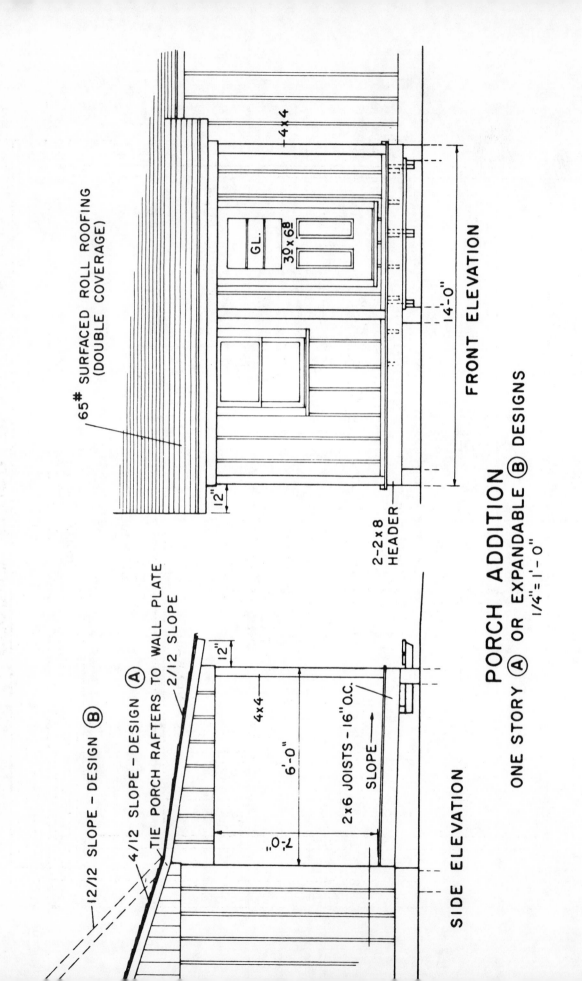

65# SURFACED ROLL ROOFING (DOUBLE COVERAGE)

4 x 4

GL.

30 x 68

14'-0"

12"

2-2 x 8 HEADER

FRONT ELEVATION

12/12 SLOPE - DESIGN Ⓑ

4/12 SLOPE - DESIGN Ⓐ

TIE PORCH RAFTERS TO WALL PLATE
2/12 SLOPE

12"

4 x 4

6'-0"

2 x 6 JOISTS - 16" O.C.

SLOPE

7'-0"

SIDE ELEVATION

PORCH ADDITION

ONE STORY Ⓐ OR EXPANDABLE Ⓑ DESIGNS

1/4" = 1'-0"

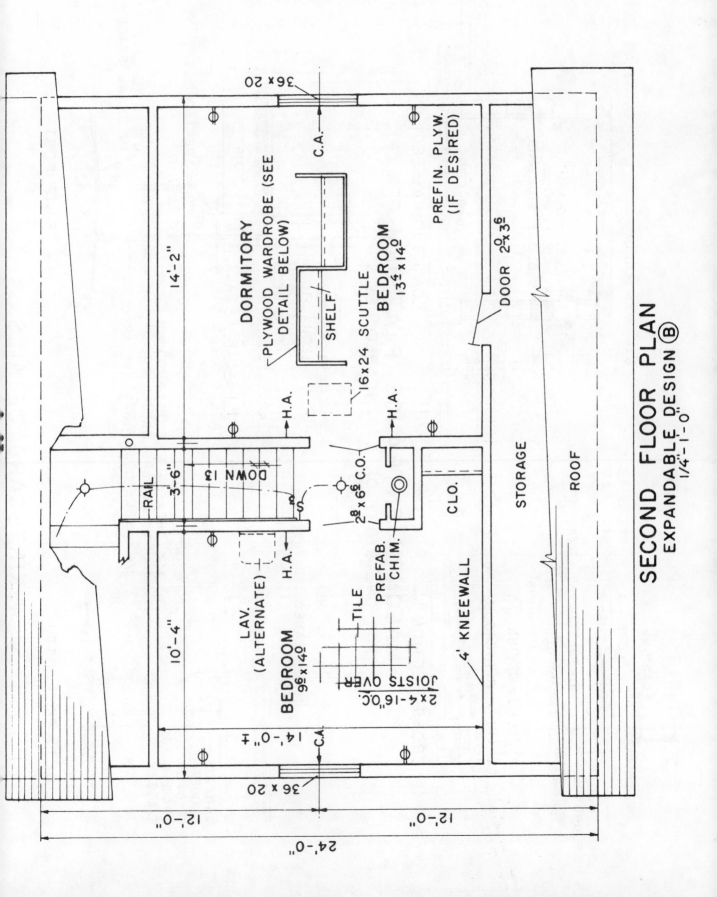

SECOND FLOOR PLAN
EXPANDABLE DESIGN Ⓑ
1/4"-1'-0"

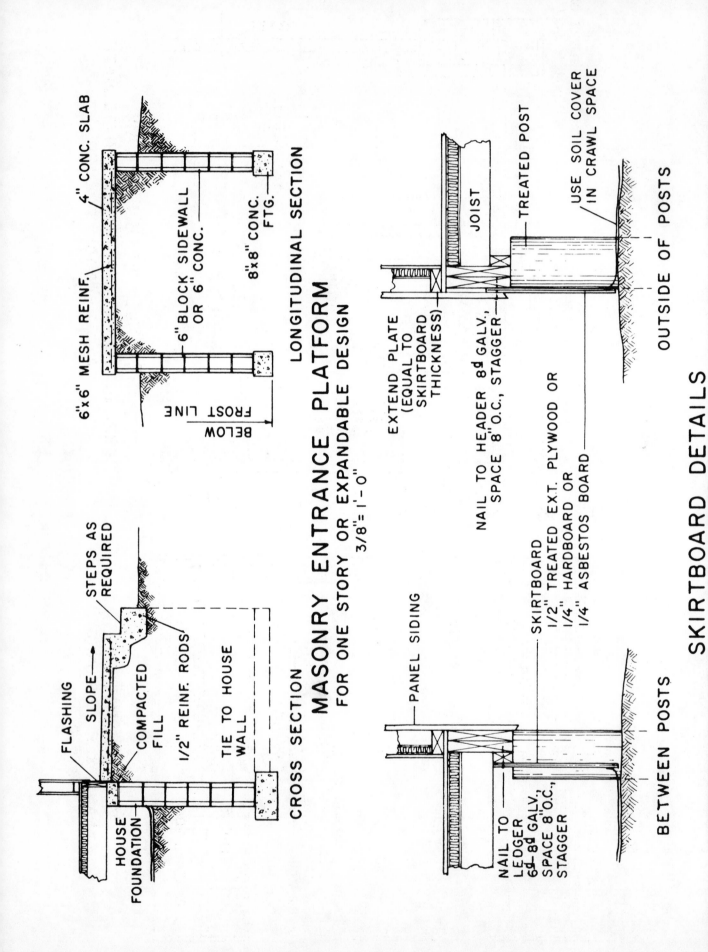

4" CONC. SLAB

6"x6" MESH REINF.

6" BLOCK SIDEWALL OR 6" CONC.

8"x8" CONC. FTG.

FROST LINE BELOW

LONGITUDINAL SECTION

FLASHING

SLOPE

STEPS AS REQUIRED

COMPACTED FILL

1/2" REINF. RODS

TIE TO HOUSE WALL

HOUSE FOUNDATION

CROSS SECTION

MASONRY ENTRANCE PLATFORM
FOR ONE STORY OR EXPANDABLE DESIGN
3/8" = 1'-0"

JOIST

TREATED POST

USE SOIL COVER IN CRAWL SPACE

OUTSIDE OF POSTS

EXTEND PLATE (EQUAL TO SKIRTBOARD THICKNESS)

NAIL TO HEADER 8^d GALV., SPACE 8"O.C., STAGGER

PANEL SIDING

SKIRTBOARD
1/2" TREATED EXT. PLYWOOD OR
1/4" HARDBOARD OR
1/4" ASBESTOS BOARD

NAIL TO LEDGER 6^d-8^d GALV., SPACE 8"O.C., STAGGER

BETWEEN POSTS

SKIRTBOARD DETAILS

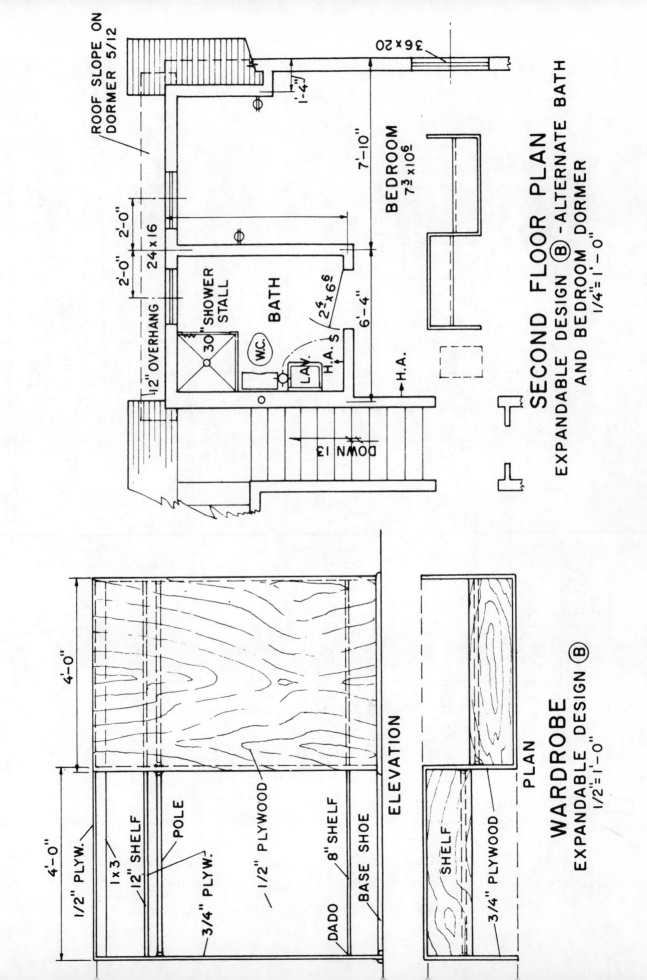

ROOF SLOPE ON DORMER 5/12

36×20

1'-4"

7'-10"

BEDROOM
$7\frac{3}{4} \times 10\frac{6}{8}$

2'-0" 2'-0"

24×16

2'-0"

12" OVERHANG

30" SHOWER STALL

BATH

$2\frac{4}{8} \times 6\frac{6}{8}$

6'-4"

W.C.

LAV.

H.A.S

H.A.

DOWN 13

SECOND FLOOR PLAN

EXPANDABLE DESIGN Ⓑ - ALTERNATE BATH
AND BEDROOM DORMER
1/4" = 1'-0"

4'-0"

4'-0"

1/2" PLYW.

1 x 3

12" SHELF

POLE

3/4" PLYW.

1/2" PLYWOOD

DADO

8" SHELF

BASE SHOE

ELEVATION

SHELF

3/4" PLYWOOD

PLAN

WARDROBE
EXPANDABLE DESIGN Ⓑ
1/2" = 1'-0"

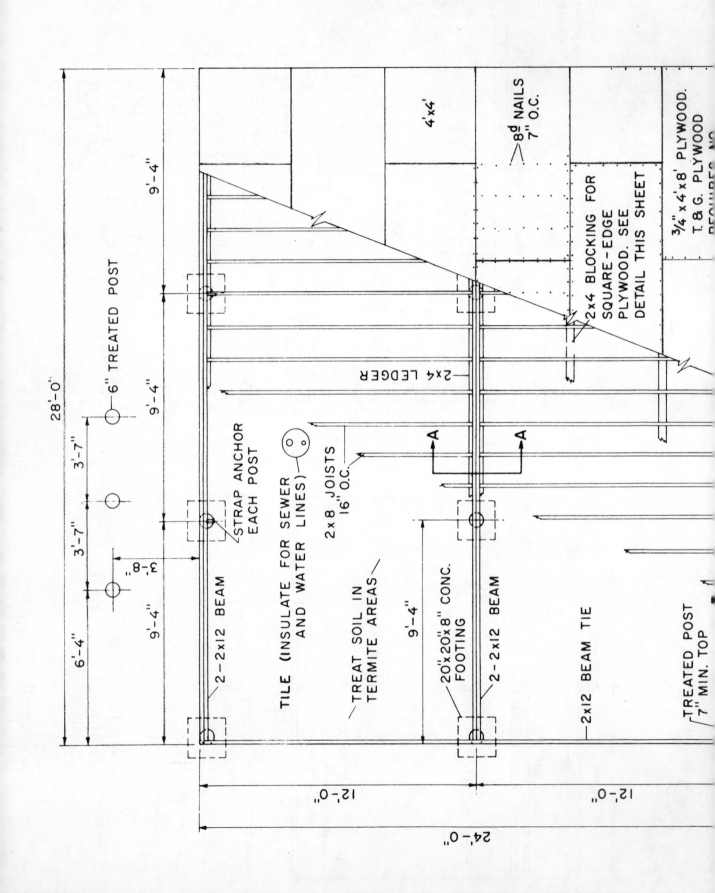

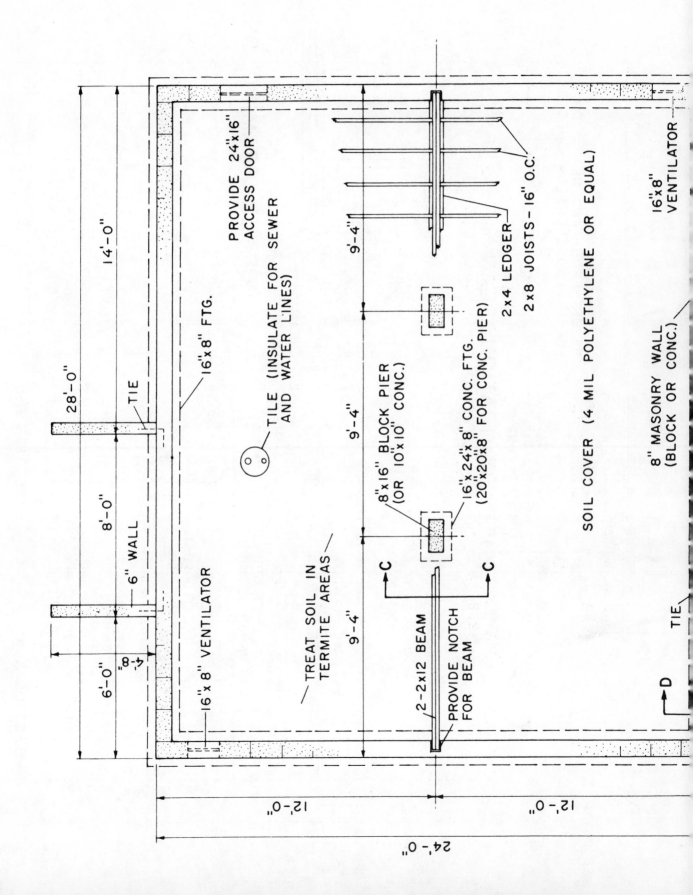

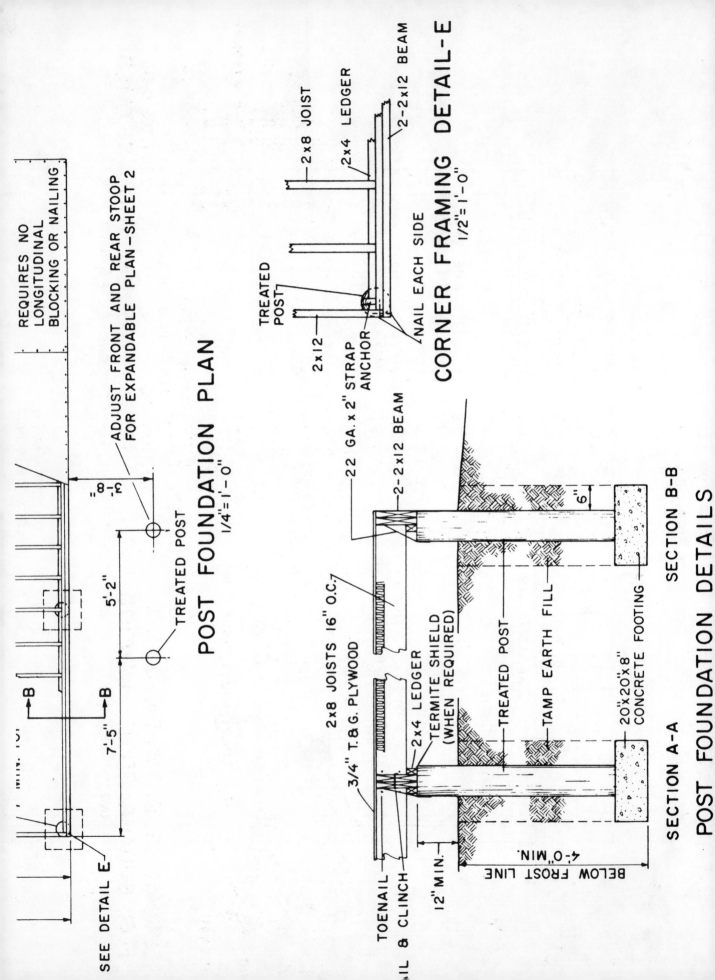

REQUIRES NO
LONGITUDINAL
BLOCKING OR NAILING

ADJUST FRONT AND REAR STOOP
FOR EXPANDABLE PLAN-SHEET 2

TREATED POST

3'-8"

5'-2"

7'-5"

B
B

SEE DETAIL E

POST FOUNDATION PLAN
1/4"=1'-0"

2x8 JOIST

2x4 LEDGER

2-2x12 BEAM

TREATED
POST

2x12

22 GA. x 2" STRAP
ANCHOR

NAIL EACH SIDE

CORNER FRAMING DETAIL-E
1/2"=1'-0"

2-2x12 BEAM

2x8 JOISTS 16" O.C.

3/4" T.&G. PLYWOOD

2x4 LEDGER

TERMITE SHIELD
(WHEN REQUIRED)

TREATED POST

TAMP EARTH FILL

20"x20"x8"
CONCRETE FOOTING

6"

TOENAIL

NAIL & CLINCH

12" MIN.

4'-0" MIN.

BELOW FROST LINE

SECTION A-A

SECTION B-B

POST FOUNDATION DETAILS

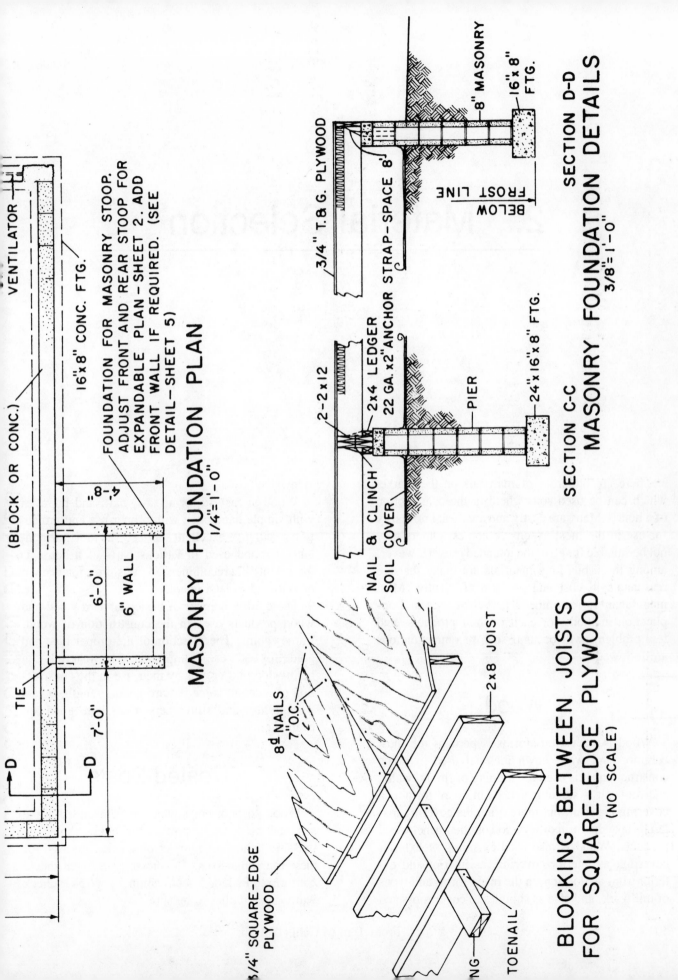

VENTILATOR

(BLOCK OR CONC.)

16"x8" CONC. FTG.

FOUNDATION FOR MASONRY STOOP.
ADJUST FRONT AND REAR STOOP FOR
EXPANDABLE PLAN—SHEET 2. ADD
FRONT WALL IF REQUIRED. (SEE
DETAIL—SHEET 5)

4'-8"

6'-0"

6" WALL

TIE

7'-0"

D

D

MASONRY FOUNDATION PLAN
1/4"=1'-0"

3/4" T.&G. PLYWOOD

8" MASONRY

16"x8" FTG.

FROST LINE
BELOW

SECTION D-D

2-2x12

2x4 LEDGER

22 GA. x2" ANCHOR STRAP—SPACE 8'

NAIL & CLINCH
SOIL COVER

PIER

24"x16"x8" FTG.

SECTION C-C

MASONRY FOUNDATION DETAILS
3/8"=1'-0"

3/4" SQUARE-EDGE
PLYWOOD

8d NAILS
7" O.C.

2x8 JOIST

TOENAIL

BLOCKING BETWEEN JOISTS
FOR SQUARE-EDGE PLYWOOD
(NO SCALE)

2. Material Selection

There are hundreds of materials on the market which can be used somewhere in the construction of a house. Many are costly and are meant primarily for use in the most expensive homes. Others may not be suitable for all of the intended uses. However, among these building materials are many that are reasonable in cost and perform efficiently. Most manufacturers recommend particular uses and application methods for each of their products, and few problems will occur if such recommendations are followed.

Wood

Wood in its various forms is perhaps the most common and well-known material used in home construction. It is used for framing of floors, walls, and roofs. It is sometimes used in board form as a covering material, but more often the covering materials take the form of plywood or other panel wood products. Wood is also used as siding or exterior covering, as interior covering, as interior and exterior trim, as flooring, in the many forms and types of millwork, and also as shingles to cover roofs and sidewalls.

Wood is easy to form, saw, nail, and fit, even with simple handtools; with proper use and protection it will give excellent service. The moisture content of wood used in various parts of a house is important, and recommended moisture contents will be outlined in later chapters.

There are a number of basic standard wood and wood products used in the construction of wood-frame cabins. The selection of the proper type and grade for each use is important. The materials can be divided into groups by their use in the construction of a cabin: some require good strength, others workability, and still others necessitate good appearance.

Treated Posts

Wood posts or poles which are embedded in the soil and used for support of the house should be pressure treated. A number of species are used for these round members. The pressure treatment should conform to Federal Specification TT-W-571; check with your supplier to be sure.

Dimension Material

Dimension lumber 2 to 4 inches thick and other wood parts are not full size as they are received from the *lumber yard*. For example, a nominal 2 by 4 may have a finished thickness of 1½ to 1⁹⁄₁₆ inches and a width of 3½ to 3⁹⁄₁₆ inches, depending on the moisture content. These materials are sawn from green logs and must be surfaced as well as dried to a usable moisture content. These processes account for the difference in size between a finished dry member and a rough green member.

The following tabulation of sizes is being recommended to the American Lumber Standards Committee by the Southern Pine Inspection Bureau, West Coast Lumber Inspection Bureau, and Western Wood Products Association.

Nominal (inches)	Dry (inches)	Green (inches)
1	¾	²⁵⁄₃₂
2	1½	1⁹⁄₁₆
4	3½	3⁹⁄₁₆
6	5½	5⅝
8	7¼	7½
10	9¼	9½
12	11¼	11½
14	13¼	13½
16	15¼	15½

The green-dry size relationship should hold for dimension lumber up to 4 inches in nominal thickness.

The first materials to be used, after the foundation is in place, are the floor *joists* and *beams* upon which the joists rest. These require adequate strength in bending and moderate stiffness. The sizes used depend on a number of factors; the *span*, spacing, species, and grade. Recommended sizes are listed in the working plans. The second grade of a species, such as southern pine, western hemlock, or Douglas-fir, is commonly selected for these uses. But, the third grade is usually acceptable.

For best performance, the moisture content of most dimension materials should not exceed 19 percent.

Wall studs (the structural members making up the wall framing) are usually nominal 2 by 4 inches in size and spaced 16 or 24 inches apart. Their strength and stiffness are not as important as for the floor joists, and for lower costs, third grade of a species such as Douglas-fir or southern pine is satisfactory. Slightly higher grades of other species, such as white fir, eastern white pine, spruce, the western white pines, and others, are, however, often used.

Members used for trusses, rafters, beams, and ceiling joists in the roof framing have about the same requirements as those listed for floor joists. For lower cost, the second grade can be used for trusses if the additional strength reduces the amount of material required.

Covering Materials

Floor *sheathing* (subfloor) consists of *board lumber* or *plywood*. Here, too, the spacing of the joists, the species of boards or plywood, and the intended use determine thickness of the subfloor. A single layer may serve both as subfloor and top surface material; for example, ⅝-inch or thicker tongued-and-grooved plywood of Douglas-fir, southern pine, or other species in a slightly greater thickness can be used when joists are spaced no more than 20 inches on center. While Douglas-fir and southern pine plywoods are perhaps the most common, other species are equally adaptable for floor, wall, and roof coverings. The "Identification Index" system of marking each sheet of plywood indicates the allowable rafter or roof truss and floor joist spacing for each thickness of a standard grade suitable for this purpose. A nominal 1-inch board subfloor normally requires a top covering of some type.

Roof sheathing, like the subfloor, usually consists of plywood or *board lumber*. Where exposed wood beams spaced 2 to 4 feet apart are used for low-pitched roofs, for example, wood decking, fiberboard roof deck, or composition materials in 1- to 3-inch thicknesses might be used. The thickness varies with the spacing of the supporting rafters or beams. These sheathing materials often serve as an interior finish as well as a base for roofing.

Wall sheathing, if used with a siding or secondary covering material, can consist of plywood, lumber, structural insulating board, or gypsum board. The type and method of sheathing application normally determine whether *corner bracing* is required in the wall. When 4- by 8-foot sheets of $^{25}/_{32}$-inch regular or ½-inch-thick, medium-density, insulating fiberboard or $^{5}/_{16}$-inch or thicker plywood are used vertically with proper nailing all around the edge, no bracing is required for the rigidity and strength needed to resist windstorms. There are plywood materials available with grooved or roughened surfaces which serve both as sheathing and finishing materials. Horizontal application of plywood, insulating fiberboard, lumber, and other materials usually requires some type of diagonal *brace* for rigidity and strength.

Exterior Trim

Some exterior trim, such as *facia* boards at cornices or gable-end overhangs, is placed before the roofing is applied. Using only those materials necessary to provide good utility and satisfactory appearance results in a cost saving. These trim materials are usually wood and, if relatively clear of *knots*, can be painted without problems. Lower grade boards with a rough-sawn surface can be stained.

Roofing

One of the lowest cost roofing materials which provides satisfactory service for sloped roofs is mineral-surfaced *asphalt roll roofing*. Asphalt shingles also give good service. Both are available in a number of colors. The material cost of asphalt *shingles* is about twice that of surfaced roll roofing. However, an asphalt shingle would normally last longer and have a better appearance than the roll roofing.

Wood shingles have a pleasing appearance for sloped roofs. Although they are usually more costly than composition roofing, they could be used where availability, cost, and application conditions were favorable.

Window and Door Frames

Double-hung, casement, or awning wood windows normally consist of prefitted sash in assembled frames ready for installation. A double-hung window is one in which the upper and lower sash slide vertically past each other. A *casement sash* is hinged at the side and swings in or out. An awning window is hinged at the top and swings out. A low-cost, factory-built unit which requires only fastening in place may be the most economical. A fixed sash or a large window glass can be fastened by stops to a prepared frame and generally costs less than a movable-type window. It is normally more economical to use one larger window unit than two smaller ones. Screens should ordinarily be supplied for all operable windows and for doors. In the colder climates, if you want year round use of your casing, storm windows and storm or combination doors are also desirable. Combination units, with screen and storm inserts, are commonly used.

Exterior Coverings

Exterior coverings such as horizontal wood siding, vertical boards, boards and battens, and similar forms of siding usually require some type of backing in the form of sheathing or nailers between studs. In mild climates, nominal 1-inch and thicker sidings are often used over a waterproof paper applied directly to the braced stud wall. There are many sidings of this type on the market in both wood and nonwood materials.

Combination sheathing usually consists of 4-foot-wide sheets of plywood, exterior particleboard, or hardboard. Applied vertically before installation of window and door frames, such materials serve very well for exteriors. Plywood may be stained or painted, and the other materials should be painted. Paper-over-laid plywood also serves as a dual-purpose exterior covering material and takes paint well. Wood shingles and *shakes* and similar materials normally require a solid backing or spaced boards of some type.

Insulation

Most cabins, even those of lowest cost, should have some type of *insulation* to resist the cold and to increase comfort during hot weather. There are various types of insulation, from insulating fiberboard to fill types, which can be used in the construction of a cabin. Perhaps the most common *thermal insulations* are the flexible (blanket and batt) and the fill types.

A blanket insulation might be used between the floor joists or studs. Batt insulation of various types might be used between floor joists or in the ceiling areas. Most flexible insulations are supplied with a vapor barrier which resists movement of water vapor through the wall and minimizes *condensation* problems. A friction-type batt insulation is also available for use in floors, walls, or ceilings. Fill-type insulation is most commonly used in attic-ceiling areas.

The structural insulating board often serves as sheathing in the wall or as a fair insulating material under a plywood floor. Each material has its place, and selection should be based on climate as well as on cost and utility.

Interior Coverings

Many *dry-wall* (unplastered) interior coverings

are available, from gypsum board to prefinished plywood. Perhaps the most economical are the gypsum board products. They are normally applied vertically in 4- by 8-foot sheets or horizontally in room-length sheets with the joint at midwall heights. They are also used for ceilings. Thicknesses range from ⅜ to ⅝ inch. *Butt joints* and corners require the use of tape and joint compound, or a *corner bead*, and require somewhat more labor than prefinished materials. Plastic-covered gypsum board is also available at additional cost, but must usually be installed with adhesive. Hardboards, insulation board, plywood, and other sheet materials are available, as are wood and fiberwood paneling. The choice must be based on overall cost of material, ease of installation, intended use of cabin, as well as on ease of maintenance.

Interior Finish and Millwork

Interior finish and millwork consist of doors and door frames, base moldings, window and door trim, kitchen and other cabinets, flooring, and similar items. The type and grade selected determine the cost to a great extent. Selection of simple moldings, lower cost species for jambs and other wood members, simple kitchen shelving, low-cost floor coverings, and the elimination of doors where practical will often make a difference of hundreds of dollars in the total cost of the house.

The most commonly used doors are the flush-type and the panel-type. The flush-type consists of thin plywood or similar facings with a solid or hollow core. The panel door consists of solid side stiles and *crossrails* with plywood or other panel fillers. For exterior types, both may be supplied with openings for glass. Exterior doors are usually 1¾ inches thick and interior doors 1⅜ inches thick.

Door jambs, casings, moldings, and similar millwork of a number of wood species can be obtained. Select the lower cost materials, yet those that will still give good service. Some species in this class are the pines, the spruces, and Douglas-fir.

Factory-built kitchen cabinets are expensive and can cost several hundred dollars in a moderate-size cabin. The use of open shelving which can be curtained and a good counter is almost a must in a low-cost cabin. Doors can be added at a later date.

Wood strip flooring or wood tile of hardwood species might be too costly to consider in the original construction, but could be installed at a future time. Softwood floorings or the lower cost hardwood floorings might be within the original budget. The use of lower cost asphalt tile or even a painted finish may be the best initial choice. However, when a woodboard subfloor is used, some type of underlayment is required under the tile. Particleboard, hardboard, and plywood are the most common materials for this use.

Nails and Nailing

In a wood-frame cabin, nailing is the most common method of fastening the various parts together. Nailing should be done correctly because even the highest grade member often does not serve its purpose without proper nailing. Thus, it is well to follow established rules in nailing the various wood members together. While most of the nailing will be described in future sections, the following table lists recommended practices used for framing and application of covering materials. Figure 3 shows the sizes of common nails. Most finish and siding nails have the same equivalent lengths. For example, an *eightpenny* common nail is the same length as an eightpenny galvanized siding nail, but not necessarily the same diameter.

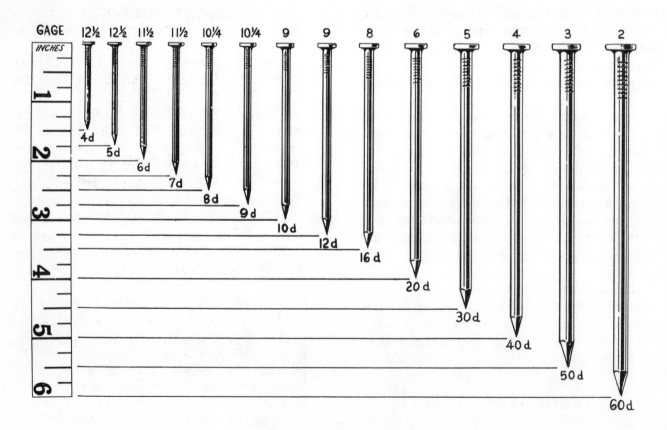

Figure 3—Nail size table.

From Tent to Cabin

Painting and Finishing

There are many satisfactory *paints* and finishes for exterior use. *Pigmented stain* is one of the easiest types to apply and is also long lasting. It is available in many colors from light to dark and is generally one of the best finishes for rough or sawn wood surfaces. Exterior paints used on smooth-surfaced siding and trim or on the trim as an accent for stained walls should be applied in several coats for best service. The first may consist of a nonporous linseed oil *primer*. Following coats can consist of latex, alkyd, or oil-base exterior paints. A *water-repellent preservative* provides a natural clear finish for wood surfaces.

Many interior paints are suitable for walls and ceilings. Latex and alkyd types are perhaps the most common, but the oil types are also suitable. Floor and *deck paints* provide long wearing surfaces. One of the most common finishes for wood floors is the floor *sealer*, which provides a natural transparent surface.

Chimney

Some type of chimney will be required for the fireplace or wood stove. A masonry chimney requires a rigid concrete base, bricks or other masonry, *flue lining*, plus labor to erect it. A manufactured chimney which is supported by the ceiling joists or rafters may be the best choice from the standpoint of overall cost.

Utilities

Cost of the heating, plumbing, and wiring phases of construction is usually a high percentage of total cost. These costs can be reduced to a great extent by careful selection and planning. Electricity is readily available in many areas and should be included in most cabins. A minimum number of circuits and few switched outlets will aid in reducing the overall installation cost.

Heating units might consist of a low-cost space heater for wood, oil, or gas, or a small, central forced-air system with a minimum amount of duct work. The difference between the two may amount to several hundred dollars. The space heater may be more than sufficient for cabins constructed in the milder climates.

Water supply and sewage disposal systems are often the most costly and difficult to install of all the utilities. When municipal or other systems are available for water and sewer service, there are no problems except the cost of installation. When good water can be obtained from a shallow well, a pump and pressure tank will provide a water supply at a low cost. However, in areas where a deep well is needed, costs may be great. Wells should ordinarily be located a minimum of 50 feet from a septic tank and 100 feet from an absorption field.

Disposal of sewage in areas where public systems are not available requires the use of a septic tank and absorption system. The satisfactory performance of such a system depends on drainage, soil types, and other factors. It is sometimes necessary, when costs are critical, to provide for future installation of a disposal system. Roughed-in connections for plumbing facilities can and should be made in the cabin during its construction and a portable or chemical system can be used until more complete plumbing is installed.

Water supply and sewage disposal systems are specialized phases of construction. Advice and guidance of a local health officer and engineer from your county office should be requested.

3. Cabin Specifications and Materials

Excavation—Grading

Sod, growing plants, shrubs, stumps, and trees shall be removed and ground smoothed in building area and 2 feet outside of building line. Excavate footings to required depth and size shown in plans. No forms are required if soil is stable. Locate excavated soil conveniently for backfilling around treated wood posts.

Concrete Work

Footings shall be poured over undisturbed soil in excavations to indicated thickness and size as shown on plan. Top surface to be level.

Mix concrete to a 1:2½:3½ mix. If premixed concrete is available, use 5-bag mix.

Treated Wood Posts

Pressure-treated wood posts with 7-inch minimum top diameter shall be treated to conform to Federal Specification TT-W-571.

Carpentry

GENERAL

This branch of the work comprises all rough and finish carpentry necessary to complete the cabin, as shown on the plans and as specified. This includes layout, cutting and fitting framing, and other carpentry items. Any phase which is necessary for the completion of the house and not specifically covered in the plans or specifications shall be included as required.

WOOD FRAMING

Dimension material for studs to be Standard (third grade); and for floor joists and framing, ceiling joists, rafters, beams, and trusses construction (second grade) in Douglas-fir, southern pine, or equivalent, unless otherwise noted on the plans. All floor and ceiling joists, studs, and rafters shall be spaced 16 inches on center. Moisture content of framing lumber not to exceed 19 percent.

SUBFLOOR

The subfloor shall be plywood to serve as a floor alone or as a base for resilient tile and shall consist of ¾-inch C-C plugged Exterior grade, touch-sanded, and with matched edges in Douglas-fir, southern pine, or equivalent. When matched-edge plywood is not obtainable, square-edged plywood in the same grade and thickness can be substituted but 2- by 4-inch blocking shall be used for all longitudinal joints. Toenail 2- by 4-inch blocks flatwise in each joist space.

ROOF SHEATHING

Roof sheathing shall be ⅜-inch Douglas-fir or southern pine plywood or equal in Standard sheathing grade or nominal 1- by 6- or 1- by 8-inch boards in No. 3 Douglas-fir, southern pine, or equivalent. Boards shall be square edge, shiplap, or dressed and matched, and laid up tight at a moisture content of not more than 15 percent.

INSULATION

Floors and walls of the first floor, walls and ceiling of the second floor, and the second floor area outside of the knee walls to be insulated with standard batt- or blanket-type flexible insulation with vapor barrier placed toward the inside of the building. Unless otherwise specified, minimum insulation thicknesses in the central and northern tiers of states shall be: Ceiling, 3 inches; wall and floor, 2 inches. Vapor barrier shall be placed toward the inside of the building. Vapor barrier to have a maximum perm value of 0.30.

SIDING

Panel siding shall be ⅝-inch thick and 4-foot wide exterior grade plywood in rough-sawn pattern. Remaining walls shall be panel siding of ⅝ inch by 4 by 9 foot exterior grade plywood in texture 1-11 (4-inch grooves). Pattern shall be reverse board and batten, channel groove, or equivalent. Edges of the sheets shall be dipped or brush coated with a water-repellent preservative before installation. A pigmented stain finish is recommended. Plywood shall be nailed at each stud and at ends of panels with galvanized or other rust-resistant nails spaced 7 to 8 inches apart. Use eightpenny nails for the ⅝-inch plywood.

EXTERIOR MILLWORK

(a) *Exterior finish.*—Exterior trim and similar materials shall be No. 2 ponderosa pine or equivalent suitable for staining.

(b) *Window frames and sash.*—Complete double-hung windows shall be used with upper and lower sash cut to two horizontal lights, glazed with single-strength glass. Units to be treated with water-repellent preservative as outlined in Commercial Standard CS 190-64. Sash to be furnished fully balanced and fitted and with outside casing in place. Set in openings, plumb, and square. Screens shall be furnished, and storms when required.

(c) *Exterior door frames and doors.*—Exterior door frames shall have 1⅜-inch rabbeted jambs and 1⅝-inch oak sill or softwood sill with metal edge, all assembled. Set in openings, plumb, and square.

Exterior doors to be standard 1¾-inch with solid stiles and rails; panel type with glazed openings as shown on plans. Screen doors shall be furnished, or combinations when required.

(d) *Screens.*—Galvanized fly screen shall be used for gable end outlet ventilators and for inlet ventilators located in the plywood frieze board, as shown on plans.

(a) *Interior door frames and doors.*—Interior door frames and cased openings shall be nominal 1-inch ponderosa pine or equal in "D" Select. Stops shall be installed only where doors are specified.

Interior doors shall be 1⅜ inches thick, five-cross-panel style with solid stiles and rails.

(b) *Interior trim*.—Interior trim shall be ponderosa pine or equal in "D" Select in ranch pattern in the following sizes:

Casings	—	$^{11}/_{16}$ by $2^{1}/_{4}$ inches
Stops	—	$^{7}/_{16}$ by $1^{3}/_{8}$ inches or wider
Base	—	$^{7}/_{16}$ by $2^{1}/_{4}$ inches
Base shoe	—	$^{1}/_{2}$ by $^{3}/_{4}$ inch (when required)

Note: (1) Casing to be used at bottom of windows in place of stool and apron.

(2) Base shoe used along free-standing plywood wardrobes.

(c) *Walls and ceilings*.—All ceilings shall be finished with $^{3}/_{8}$-inch gypsum board with recessed edges and with the length applied across the ceiling joists. End joints shall be staggered at least 16 inches. Walls shall be finished with $^{3}/_{8}$-inch gypsum board with recessed edges and applied vertically. Application and joint treatment shall follow accepted practices. Install prefinished plywood in wall areas shown on plans.

Walls of tub recess shall be covered with plastic-finished hardboard panels over gypsum board. Install with mastic in accordance with manufacturer's directions. Inside corners, edges, and tub edges shall be finished with plastic moldings.

(d) *Flooring*.—Finish flooring throughout shall be $^{1}/_{8}$-inch-thick asphalt tile in 9- by 9-inch size, "B" quality. Combination plywood subfloor shall be cleaned, nails driven flush, and joints sanded smooth where required. Tile shall be applied in accordance with manufacturer's recommendations. Rubber baseboard shall be furnished and installed in the bathroom, wood base in the remainder of the house.

(e) *Hardware*.—Furnish and install all rough and finish hardware complete as needed for perfect operation. Locks shall be furnished for all outside doors. Outside doors to be hung with three 4- by 4-inch loose-pin butt hinges and inside doors with two 3-$^{1}/_{2}$ by 3-$^{1}/_{2}$-inch loose-pin butt hinges. Bathroom five-cross-panel door shall be furnished with standard bathroom lock set. Standard screen door latches, hinges, and door closers shall be furnished and installed. Furnish and install semiconcealed cabinet hinges, pulls, and catches where required for cabinet or closet doors. All finish hardware to be finished in dull brass.

Sheet Metal Work and Roofing

SHEET METAL

Sheet metal flashing, when required for the prefabricated chimney and vent stack, shall be 28-gauge galvanized iron or painted terneplate.

ROOFING

Roofing shall be a minimum of 210-pound square-tab 12- by 36-inch asphalt shingles. A minimum of four $^{7}/_{8}$-inch galvanized roofing nails shall be used for each 12- by 36-inch shingle strip. Any defects or leaks shall be corrected.

Electrical Work

The work shall include all materials and labor necessary to make the systems complete as shown on the plans. All work and materials shall comply with local requirements or those of the National Electrical Code. All wiring shall be concealed and carried in BX or other approved conduit to each outlet, switch, fixture, and appliance or electrical equipment such as furnace, hot water heater, and range when required, and as shown on the plan. Panel shall be 100 amp. capacity with overload cutout. Wall fixtures to consist of the following:

Two outside wall fixtures with crystal glass.

Two overhead (wall) fixtures, for kitchen and bath.

Heating

Heater and prefabricated chimney shall be installed as shown on the plans with supply ducts located in furred-down ceiling of hall. Heater shall be for LP or natural gas with a 100,000 minimum B.t.u. input or as required by design for each specific area. Cold air return at furnace base and from each corner of the house. Cold air duct shall consist of ⅛-inch transite-covered joist spaces along outside walls and connection to 10-inch-diameter or 6-inch by 12-inch rectangular galvanized or aluminum ducts to heater.

Plumbing

All plumbing shall be installed in accordance with local or National plumbing codes. Hot- and cold-water connections shall be furnished to all fixtures as required. Sewer and water and gas lines (when required) shall extend to building line with water shutoff valve. Framed and insulated box shall be used to protect water and sewer lines from freezing in crawl space where required. Cover with ⅛-inch transite or equal and insulate with 3 inches of fiberglass or styrofoam when required. Use a 16-by 16-inch vitrified tile or equal below groundline.

Furnish and install the following fixtures:
  One kitchen sink—21 by 15 inches, self rim, steel, white, with fixtures.
  One bathtub—5 foot, cast iron, white, left-hand drain, complete with shower rod and shower head, with fixtures.
  One water closet—Reverse trap, white, with seat, fixtures, and shutoff valve.
  One lavatory—19 by 17 inches, steel, white, and with fixtures and shutoff valves.
  One hot water heater—50-gallon (minimum), gas or electric.
  Washing machine connection with hot and cold water and drain.

Painting and Finishing

EXTERIOR

Exterior plywood panel siding, facia, shutters, and soffit areas shall be stained with pigmented stain as required. Use light gray, yellow or another light color stain for the trim and shutters and a darker stain (brown, olive, gray, etc.) for the panel siding or a reverse color selection as desired by owner. (Optional shutters to be stained on faces and edges.)

Window and door frames, window sash, screen doors, and similar millwork shall be painted a light color, or as owners request. Types of paint and procedures to comply with recommended practices and materials.

INTERIOR

All woodwork shall be painted in semigloss. Walls and ceilings finished in latex flat, bathroom woodwork and ceiling shall be finished with semigloss.

Termite Protection

Termite protection shall be provided in termite areas by means of soil treatment or termite shields or both as required by local practices and regulations.

Concrete Blocks

Concrete blocks (used as an alternate to foundation of treated wood posts) shall comply with ASTM C-90, Grade U-II, for standard size and quality.

Concrete blocks shall be laid over concrete footings, as shown on the foundation plan. Footings shall be level and laid out to conform to the building line. Blocks shall be laid up with ⅜-inch-thick mortar joints, tooling the joints on all exposed exterior surfaces. Anchor straps, when used, shall be embedded to a depth of at least 12 inches.

4. List of Materials Needed

The following material is required for construction of the cabin; quality of material and treatments are given in the specifications.

FOUNDATION

The foundation of treated posts set on concrete footings requires:

1 cubic yard concrete

12 treated foundations posts, 5 feet long or longer as required by slope, with 7-inch minimum top diameter.

FLOOR FRAMING

Floor framing consisting of floor joists supported on ledgers nailed to the anchored floor beams requires:

4 — 2 × 12's	12 feet long
9 — 2 × 12's	20 feet long
40 — 2 × 8's	12 feet long
12 — 2 × 4's	10 feet long

FLOOR

Requirements of floor tile and subfloor, including attic subfloor are:

42 — 4- × 8-foot sheets of ¾-inch tongued-and-grooved plywood

2600 — 9- by 9-inch asphalt tile (10 pct. waste) (with adhesive)

WALL AND PARTITION FRAMING

Framing material for walls and partitions (studs and plates) includes:

182 — 2 × 4's	8 feet long
80 — 2 × 4's	12 feet long
10 — 2 × 6's	12 feet long

CEILING AND ROOF FRAMING

Materials for rafters and joists are:

20 — 2 × 4's	8 feet long
44 — 2 × 6's	20 feet long
20 — 2 × 8's	12 feet long
20 — 2 × 8's	14 feet long
3 — 1 × 8's	10 feet long

ROOF

Roofing and sheathing requirements are:

38 — 4- by 8-foot sheets of ⅜-inch plywood, sheathing grade (standard) (CD)

12 squares — 210-pound asphalt shingles

SIDING

The following siding or equivalent alternates are required:

26 — 4- by 9-foot sheets rough-textured, ⅝-inch channel groove plywood

10 — 4- by 9-foot sheets rough-textured, ⅝-inch reverse board and batten plywood siding

WINDOWS

All windows are double-hung and purchased treated and complete with screens, and storms when required. Quantity of each size is:

2 — $^{36}/_{20}$
4 — $^{32}/_{20}$
3 — $^{24}/_{20}$
1 — $^{24}/_{16}$

EXTERIOR DOORS

Doors are 1¾ inches thick, glazed; and frame, trim and hardware are required for each. Screen doors shall be furnished, or combinations when required. Sizes are:

Front—3 feet 0 inches wide and 6 feet 8 inches high

Rear—2 feet 8 inches wide and 6 feet 8 inches high

INSULATION

Blanket insulation with aluminum foil vapor barrier on one side is required for ceiling, walls, and floor.

1500 square feet—2 inches thick or as required, 16 inches wide

100 square feet—3 inches thick or as required, 16 inches wide

ROOF VENTILATORS

Requirements for ventilating the roof are:

2 —Peak-type vent

14 square feet—Screen for inlet vent slots

FRIEZE BOARD

Material required for frieze board is:

6 — ⁶⁄₄ × 6's   10 feet long

INTERIOR WALL AND CEILING FINISH

Gypsum board is used for all interior finish except one accent wall in living area. The bathroom has plastic-coated hardboard above the bathtub. Requirements are:

106 — 4- by 8-foot sheets of ⅜-inch gypsum board

3 — 4- by 8-foot sheets of plastic-coated hardboard with corner and edge moldings (bath)

6 — 4- by 8-foot sheets of ¼-inch prefinished plywood paneling

5 — 250-foot rolls of joint tape

10 — 25-pound bags of joint compound

STAIRS

Materials for stairs are:

2 — 1 × 10's   14-foot long stringers
2 — 2 × 4's   10 feet long
2 — 2 × 12's   14 feet long
3 — 1 × 8's   10 feet long
11 — Treads ⁵⁄₄ × 10½ × 2 feet 6 inches
16 board feet of 1 × 4 fir flooring (platform)

INTERIOR DOORS

Interior door requirements are:

1 set—2-foot 4-inch × 6-foot 8-inch hollow-core door with jambs, stops, and hardware

3 sets—Jambs for 2-foot 6-inch × 6-foot 8-inch doors

2 sets—Jambs for 2-foot 6-inch × 6-foot 6-inch doors

2 — 4- by 8-foot sheets of ½-inch plywood, interior AC

INTERIOR TRIM

Trim for windows, doors, and base includes:
295 feet—⁹⁄₁₆- × 2⅛-inch casing
285 feet—½- × 3-inch base

CABINETS

Material requirements for wood-frame and plywood cabinets are:

3 — 4- × 8-foot sheets of ¾-inch plywood, interior AC	
1 — 1 × 3	8 feet long
6 — 1 × 4's	8 feet long
2 — 1 × 8's	8 feet long

WARDROBES

Wardrobes consisting of closet poles with a shelf over require:

3 — 4- × 8-foot sheets of ¾-inch plywood, interior AA
2 — 4- × 8-foot sheets of ½-inch plywood, interior AA
4 — Closet poles, 1⁵⁄₁₆-inch diameter × 8 feet long
6 pair — Pole sockets for 1⁵⁄₁₆-inch poles

FRONT STOOP

The front stoop, consisting of planks laid across 2 × 4 framing supported by treated posts, has the following material requirements:

2 — Treated posts, 5 feet long with 6-inch minimum top diameter	
3 — 2 × 4's	8 feet long
10 — 2 × 6's	6 feet long
4 — ½-inch galvanized carriage bolts, 8 inches long	

REAR STOOP

Material requirements for the rear stoop are:

3 —Treated posts, 5 feet long, with 6-inch minimum top diameter	
4 — 2 × 4's	8 feet long
9 — 2 × 6's	8 feet long
6 — ½-inch galvanized carriage bolts, 8 inches long	

NAILS

50 pounds—Eightpenny common
26 pounds—Sixteenpenny common
2 pounds—Twentypenny common
3 pounds—Tenpenny common, galvanized
2 pounds—Sixteenpenny common, galvanized
2 pounds—Fourpenny finish
12 pounds—Eightpenny finish
16 pounds—¾-inch galvanized roofing
25 pounds—Fourpenny cooler

PAINT AND FINISH

Quantities required for one coat of paint inside, two on exterior (windows and doors), and one coat of stain outside are:

10 gallons—Walls and ceiling (interior)
3 gallons—Interior trim
7 gallons—Exterior siding and trim (use different body and trim color, as desired)
1 gallon—Exterior paint (windows, doors, and frames)

ELECTRICAL

In addition to rough wiring and 100-amp. service, the following items are required:

17—Duplex outlets
2—Wall-mounted interior lights
2—Wall-mounted exterior lights
3—Ceiling lights
5—Switches, single pole
2—Switches, 3-way

HEATING

The heating system requires a 100,000 B.t.u. gas furnace with nine registers, six cold-air returns, duct, a prefab chimney, controls, and other items required for a complete system.

PLUMBING

Complete plumbing must be provided for the following required fixtures:

1—5-foot bathtub
1—Water closet
1—Lavatory
1—Kitchen sink
1—50-gallon water heater (undercounter type)
1—16- by 16- × 24-inch vitrified tile or equal (at sewer and water entrance)

UNFINISHED SECOND FLOOR

When the second floor is left unfinished, the following materials can be deducted from the bill of materials.

37	4- by 8-ft. sheets of ⅜-in. gypsum board
4	4- by 8-ft. sheets of ¼-in. prefinished plywood paneling
2	250-ft. roll of joint tape
4	25-lb. bags of joint compound
65 ft.	⁹⁄₁₆- by 2⅛ in. casing
85 ft.	½- by 3-inch base
2 sets	jambs for 2-ft. 6-in. by 6-ft. 6-in. doors
2	4- by 8-ft. sheets of ¾-in. plywood, interior AA
2	4- by 8-ft. sheets of ½-in. plywood, interior AA
2	closet poles, 1⅝-in. diameter by 8 ft. long
3 pair	pole sockets for 1⁵⁄₁₆-inch poles
1300	9- by 9-in. asphalt tile (with adhesive)

Alternates or Options

FLOOR (SQUARE-EDGE PLYWOOD)

When tongued-and-grooved plywood is not available, square-edge plywood with all edges blocked can be used. Material requirements for flooring and subfloor are:

DESIGN A

21 — 4- by 8-foot sheets of ¾-inch plywood
20 — 2 × 4's   12 feet long
1300 — 9- × 9-inch asphalt tile (10 pct. waste) (with adhesive)

DESIGN B

42 — 4- × by 8-foot sheets of ¾-inch plywood
20 — 2 ×   12 feet long
1300 — 9- × 9-inch asphalt tile (10 pct. waste) (with adhesive)

SHUTTERS (OPTIONAL)

2 — 4- × 8-foot sheets of ⅝-inch plywood, exterior grade, textured surface

FOUNDATION (CONCRETE BLOCK)

The foundation of concrete blocks on poured concrete footings, plus masonry front and rear stoops, requires: (Note: Based on 4-ft. foundation depth.)

6 cubic yards of concrete (footings and stoops)
462 — 8- × 8- × 16-inch concrete blocks
78 — 4- × 8- × 16-inch concrete solid-cap blocks
72 — 8- × 6- × 16-inch concrete blocks
24 — 8- × 6- × 8-inch concrete blocks (stoops)
18 sacks prepared mortar
2 cubic yards mason's sand
60 square feet 6- × 6-inch mesh reinforcing (stoops)
4 — ½-inch reinforcing rods, 5 feet long (step)

4 — ½-inch reinforcing rods, 7 feet long (step)
700 square feet 4-mil polyethylene film (soil cover)
2 — 8- × 16-inch foundation vents
1 — 16- × 16-inch (minimum) access door and frame

FLOOR FRAMING (FOR CONCRETE-BLOCK FOUNDATION)

3 — 2 × 12's	20 feet long
46 — 2 × 12's	12 feet long
6 — 2 × 4's	10 feet long

40 lineal feet of 22-gauge × 2-inch anchor strap

SECOND-FLOOR BATHROOM

A second bathroom could be added in a second-floor dormer. The dormitory-type bedroom is expanded into a portion of the dormer. Materials required for constructing the dormer and providing bathroom fixtures are: (Note: As a less costly addition, a lavatory could be installed in one or both upstairs bedrooms.)

49 — 2 × 4's	8 feet long
26 — 2 × 4's	16 feet long
12 — 2 × 6's	8 feet long

6 — 4- × 8-foot sheets of rough-textured, ⅝-inch reverse board and batten plywood siding
15 — 4- × 8-foot sheets of ⅜-inch gypsum board

96 — 9- × 9-inch asphalt tile (with adhesive)
2 — $^{24}/_{16}$ treated double-hung windows (storm and screen)
1 set. — 2-foot 4-inch × 6-foot 6-inch hollow-core door with jambs, stops, and hardware
1 — Wall-mounted interior light
1 — Switch
1 — Hot-air register with duct
1 — 30- × 30-inch shower stall
1 — Lavatory
1 — Water closet

FRONT PORCH

Materials required for the front porch are:

3	Treated posts, 5 ft. long, with 6-inch minimum top diameter
1	2 × 4, 12 feet long
12	2 × 6's, 8 feet long
12	2 × 6's, 10 feet long -24-
1	2 × 6, 14 feet long
4	2 × 8's, 14 feet long
3	4 × 4's, 8 feet long
140 bd. ft.	Fir flooring
5	4- by 8-ft. sheets ⅜-inch plywood, sheathing grade (standard) (CD)
300 sq. ft.	65-lb. roll roofing (surfaced)

5. Foundation

After the site for the house has been selected, all plant growth and sod should be removed. The area can then be raked and leveled slightly for staking and location of the supporting posts or piers.

The foundation plan in the working drawings for the cabin shows all the measurements necessary for construction. The first step in locating the house is to establish a baseline along one side with heavy cord and solidly driven stakes located well outside the end building lines (stakes 1 and 2, fig. 4). This baseline should be at the outer faces of the posts, piers, or foundation walls. When a post foundation is used with an overhang, the post faces will be 13½ inches in from the building line when a 12-inch overhang is used. (fig. 5). When masonry piers or wood posts are located at the edge of the foundation, the outer faces are the same as the building line. These details are included in the working drawings. A second set of stakes (3 and 4) should now be established parallel to stakes 1 and 2 at the opposite side according to the measurements shown in the foundation plan of the working drawing. When measuring across, be sure that the tape is at right angles to the first baseline. Just as the 1–2

baseline does, this line will locate the outer edge of posts or piers. A third set of stakes, 5 and 6, should then be established at one end of the building line (fig. 4).

A square 90° corner can be established by laying out a distance of 12 feet at line 1–2 and 9 feet along line 5–6. Short cords can be tied to the lines to mark these two locations. Now measure between the two marks and when the diagonal measurement is 15 feet, the two corners at stakes 1–5 and 3–6 are square (fig. 4). The length of the house is now established by the fourth set of stakes, 7 and 8. Finally, the centerline along the length of the house can be marked by stakes 9 and 10. A final check of the alignment for a true rectangular layout is made by measuring the diagonals from one corner to the opposite corner (fig. 4). Both diagonals should be the same length.

In some areas of the country, building regulations might restrict the use of treated wood foundation posts. A masonry foundation fully enclosing the crawl space may be necessary or preferred. For such houses, the details shown in the Appendix to this book can be used. Details of skirtboard enclosures for post foundations are also included in the appendix.

Footings

The holes for the post or masonry pier *footings* can now be excavated to a depth of about 4 feet or as required by the depth of the *frostline*. They should be spaced as shown in the foundation plan of the working plans and in figure 5. The embedment depth should be enough so that the soil pressure keeps the posts in place.

Place the dirt a good distance away from the holes to prevent its falling back in. Size of the holes for the wood post and the masonry piers should be large enough for the footings. When posts or piers are spaced 8 feet apart in one direction and 12 feet in the other, a 20- by 20-inch or 24-inch-diameter footing is normally sufficient (fig. 5). In softer soils or if greater spacing is used, a 24- by 24-inch footing may be required.

Posts alone without footings of any type, but with good embedment, are being used for pole-type buildings. However, because the area of the bottom end of the pole against the soil determines its load capacity, this method is not normally recommended in the construction of a cabin where uneven settling could cause problems. Where soil capacities are very high and posts are spaced closely, it is likely that a footing support under the end of the post would not be required. However, because a good,

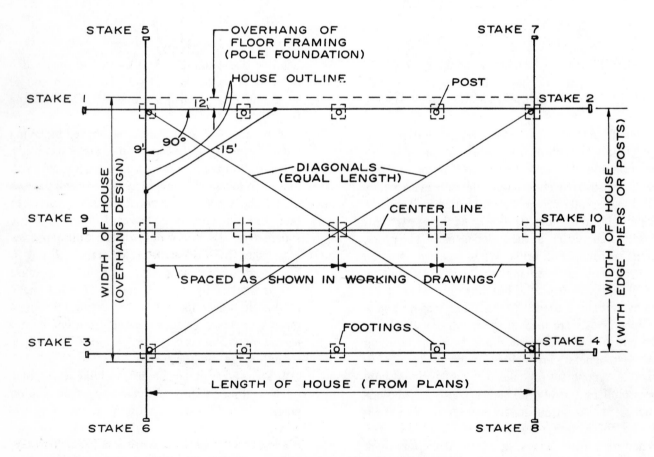

Figure 4—House and footing layout.

From Tent to Cabin

stable foundation is important, the use of adequate footings of some type must be considered.

After the holes have been dug to the recommended depth and cleared of loose dirt, an 8-inch-thick or thicker concrete footing should be poured (fig. 5). If premixed *concrete* is not available, it can be mixed by hand or by a small on-the-job mixer. Tops of the footings should be leveled by measuring down a constant distance from the level line. A 5- or 6-bag mix (premixed concrete) or a 1 to 2½ to 3½ (cement:sand:gravel) job-mixed concrete should be satisfactory. The footings for the post and pier foundations should be located as shown on the working drawings.

Post Foundations—With Side Overhang

Treatment of the foundation posts should conform to Federal Specification TT-W-571. Check these specifications with the lumber supplier. Penetration of the preservative for foundation posts should be equal to one-half the radius and not less than 90 percent of the sapwood thickness. The selection of posts should be governed also by final finish and appearance. When cleanliness, freedom from odor, or paintability is essential, waterborne preservative-treated posts should be used. The important principle is not to use untreated posts in contact with the soil.

Treated posts having a top diameter as shown on the plans should be selected for each of the footing locations. The length can be determined by setting the layout strings to the level of the top of the beams and posts. Select the corner with the highest ground elevation and move the string on this stake to about 18 to 20 inches above the ground level at this point. The minimum clearance under joists or beams should be 12 inches. However, 18 to 24 inches or more is preferred when accessibility is desired. Then with the aid of a lightweight string or line level (fig. 6), adjust the cord on the other stakes so that the layout strings around the edge of the build-

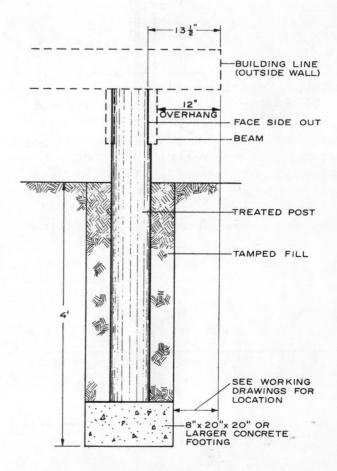

Figure 5—Post embedment and footing alinement (overhang design)

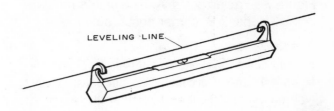

Figure 6—Line level. Locate line level midway between building corners when leveling.

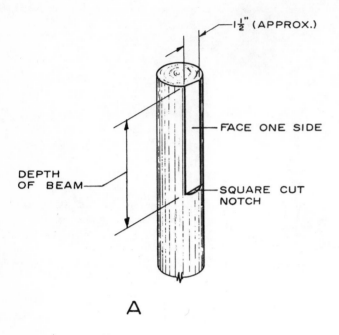

A

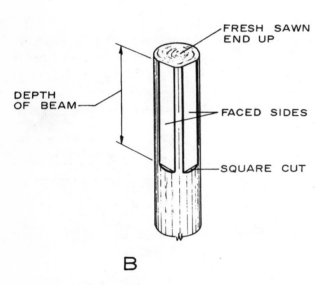

B

Figure 7—Facing posts. A, Side or intermediate post; B, corner post (use largest).

ing and down the center are all truly level and horizontal. To insure accuracy, the line must be tight with no sag and the level located at the center. (If available, a surveyor's level will serve even better.) Thus, the distance from the string to the top of concrete footings will now be the length of the posts needed at each location. A manometer-type level can also be used in establishing a constant elevation

for the posts. This type of level consists of a long, clear plastic tube partly filled with water or other liquid. The water level at each end establishes the correct elevation.

If pressure-treated posts are not available in the lengths just determined, use poles more than twice as long as required. Saw them in half and use *with the treated end down*. Now with a saw and a hand ax or drawknife, slightly *notch* and face one side for a distance equal to the depth of the beams(fig. 7A). The four largest diameter posts should be used for the corners and notched on two adjacent sides (fig. 7B). Facing should be about 1½ inches wide, except for corners or when beam joints might be made where 2½ inches is preferable.

Treated 6- by 6-inch or 8- by 8-inch posts can be used in place of the round posts when available. Although they may cost somewhat more and do *not* have the resistance of treated round posts, square posts will reduce on-site labor time.

Locate the notched and faced posts on the concrete footings using the cord on the stakes as a guide for the faced sides. Place and tamp 8 to 10 inches of dirt around them initially to hold them in place. Posts should be vertical and the faced side aligned with the cord from the stakes along each side, the center, and the ends of the house outline. When posts are aligned, fill in the remaining dirt. Fill and tamp no more than 6 inches in the hole at one time to insure good, solid embedment.

Select *beams* the size and length shown in the foundation plan of the working drawings. Moisture content should normally not exceed 19 percent. These beams are usually 2 by 10 or 2 by 12 inches in size and the lengths conform to the spacing of the posts. For example, posts spaced 8 feet apart will require 8- and 16-foot-long beams. The outside beam can now be nailed in place. Starting along one side at the corner, even with the leveling string, nail one beam to the corner post and each crossing post (fig. 8A). Initially, use only one twentypenny nail at the top of each beam, and don't drive it in fully. (The center should be left free to allow for a carriage bolt.) Side beam ends should project be-

From Tent to Cabin

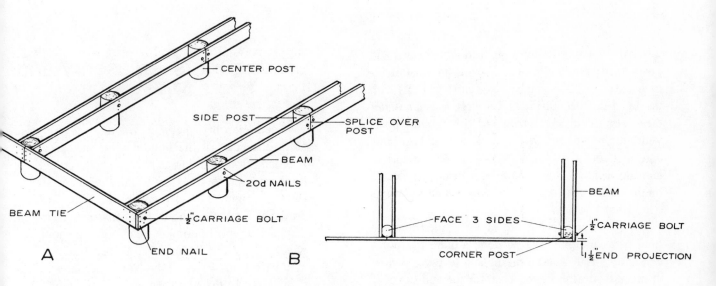

Figure 8—Beam installation. A, Overall view; B,
plan view.

yond the post about 1½ inches or the thickness of the end header (fig. 8B). When all outside beams and those along the center row of posts are erected, all final leveling adjustments should be made. In addition to the leveling cord from the layout stakes, use a carpenter's level and a straightedge to insure that each beam is level, horizontal, and in line with the cord. Final nailing can now be done on the first set of beams. Posts extending over the tops of the beams can now be trimmed flush.

The second set of beams on the opposite sides of the posts should now be installed. Because round posts vary in diameter, the facing on the second side has been delayed until this time. Use a strong cord or string and stretch along the length of the side of the foundation on the inside of the posts and parallel to the outside beams (fig. 9A). This will establish the amount of notching and facing to be done for each post. Use a saw to provide a square notch to support the second beam. All posts can be thus faced and the second beams nailed in place level with, and in the same way as, the outside beams. This facing is usually unnecessary when square posts are used (fig. 9B). However, additional bolts are required when the beam does not bear on a notch. Joints of the *headers* should be made over

the center of the posts and staggered. For example, if an 8- and a 16-foot length beam are used on the outside of the posts, stagger the joints by first using a 16-foot, then an 8-foot length, on the inside. Only one *joint* should be made at each support.

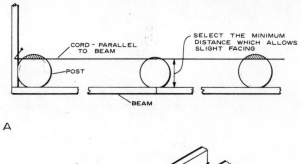

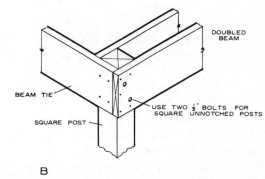

Figure 9—Facing and fastening posts. A, Round
posts; B, square post.

Drill ½-inch holes through the double beams and posts at the midheight of the beam, and install ½-by 8-, 10-, or 12-inch galvanized carriage bolts with the head on the outside and a large washer under the nut on the inside. Use two bolts for square posts without a notch (fig. 9B). At splices, use two bolts and stagger (fig. 10A). When available at the correct moisture content, single nominal 4-inch-thick beams might be used to replace the two 2-inch members (fig. 10B).

All poles and beams are now installed and the final earth tamping can be done around the poles where required. A final raking and leveling is now in order to insure a good base for the soil cover if required. There is now a solid level framework upon which to erect the floor joists.

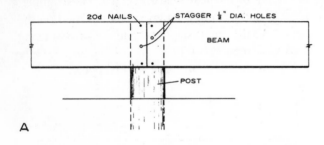

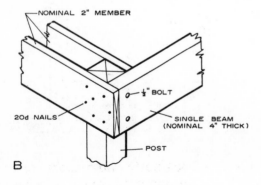

Figure 10—Fastening beams to posts. A, Bolting; B, single beam.

Edge Piers—Masonry and Posts

When masonry piers or wood posts are used along the edge of the building line instead of for overhang floor framing as previously described, the 8-inch poured footings are usually the same size as shown in figure 11A. However, check the working drawings for the exact size. For masonry piers, the distance to the bottom of the footings should be governed by the depth of frost penetration. This may vary from 4 feet in the Northern States to less than 1 foot in the Southern areas. The wood posts normally require a 3- to 4-foot-deep hole. The masonry piers or posts should be aligned so that the outside edges are flush with the outside of the buidling line (fig. 11,A,B). The foundation plan in the working drawings covers these details further.

Concrete block, brick, or other masonry, or poured concrete piers can now be constructed over the footings. Concrete block piers should be 8 by 16 inches in size, brick, or other masonry 12 by 12 inches, and poured concrete 10 by 10 inches. The tops of the piers should all be level and about 12 to 16 inches above the highest corner of the building area. Use any of the previously described leveling methods. Use a 22-gage by 2-inch-wide galvanized perforated or plain anchor strap for nailing into the beams. It should extend through at least two courses, filling the core when hollow masonry is used (fig. 11A). A prepared mortar mix with 3 or 3½ parts sand and ¼ part cement to each part of mortar or other approved mixes should be used in laying up the masonry units. The wood post installation details are shown in figure 11B. Anchor straps are nailed to each post and beam with twelve-penny galvanized nails.

Beams consisting of doubled 2 by 10 or 2 by 12 members (check the foundation plan of the working drawings) can now be assembled. Place them on the posts or piers and make the splices at this location. Make only one splice at each pier. Nominal 2-inch members can be nailed together with ten-

From Tent to Cabin

penny nails spaced 16 inches apart in two rows. Fabrication details at the corner and intersection with the center beam and fastening of the beam tie (*stringer*) are shown in figure 11C.

Ledgers, used to support the floor joists, should be nailed to the inside of the nailed beams. The sizes are 2 by 2, 2 by 3, or 2 by 4 as indicated in the foundation plan of the working drawings. Ledgers should be spaced so that the top of the joists will be flush with the top of the edge and center beams when bearing on the ledgers (fig. 11A,B). Use sixteenpenny nails spaced 8 inches apart in a staggered row to fasten the ledger to the beam.

The foundation and beams are now in place ready for the assembly of the floor system.

An alternate method of providing footings for the treated wood foundation posts involves the use of temporary braces to position the posts while the concrete is poured (fig. 12). After the holes are dug, posts of the proper length are positioned and temporary braces nailed to them (fig. 12A). A minimum of 8 inches should be allowed for footing depth (fig. 12B). When posts are aligned and set to the proper elevation, concrete is poured around them. After the concrete has set, holes are filled (*backfilled*) and earth tamped firmly around the posts. Construction of the floor framing can now begin.

This system of setting posts and pouring the concrete footings can also be used when a beam is located on each side of the posts (fig. 8). Posts are placed in the holes, the beams nailed in their proper position, and the beams aligned and blocked to the correct elevation. After the concrete has set and the fill has been tamped in place, the beams can be bolted to the posts.

Termite Protection

In areas of the South and in many of the Central and Coastal States, *termite* protection must be considered in construction of crawl-space cabins. Pressure-treated lumber or poles are not affected by termites, but these insects build passages to and can

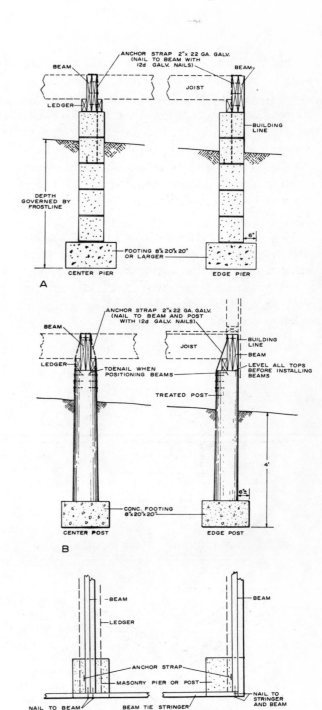

Figure 11—Edge posts and masonry piers. A, Masonry edge piers; B, edge post foundation; C, corner and edge framing of beam.

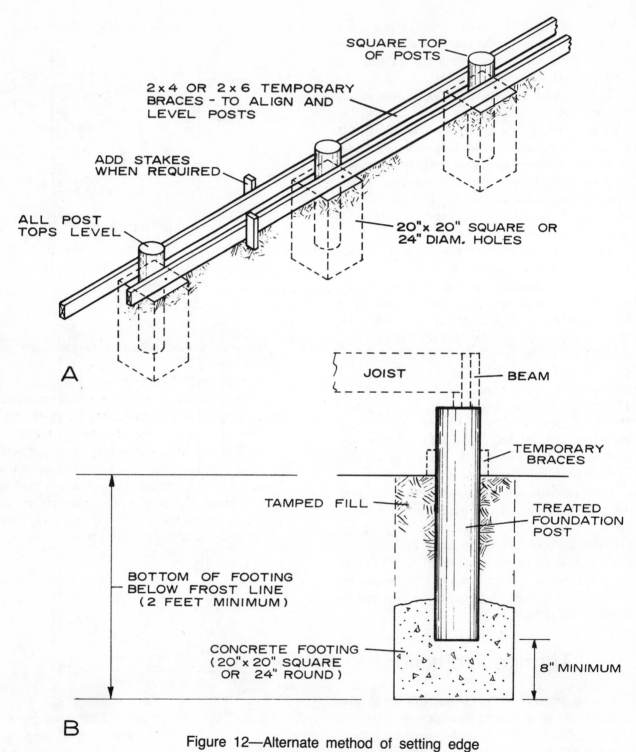

SQUARE TOP
OF POSTS

2 x 4 OR 2 x 6 TEMPORARY
BRACES - TO ALIGN AND
LEVEL POSTS

ADD STAKES
WHEN REQUIRED

ALL POST
TOPS LEVEL

20"x 20" SQUARE OR
24" DIAM. HOLES

A

JOIST

BEAM

TEMPORARY
BRACES

TAMPED FILL

TREATED
FOUNDATION
POST

BOTTOM OF FOOTING
BELOW FROST LINE
(2 FEET MINIMUM)

CONCRETE FOOTING
(20"x 20" SQUARE
OR 24" ROUND)

8" MINIMUM

B

Figure 12—Alternate method of setting edge
foundation posts. A, Temporary
bracing; B, footing position.

From Tent to Cabin

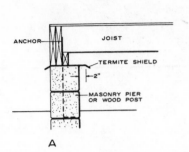
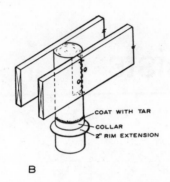
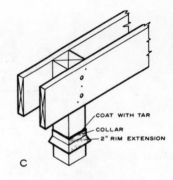

Figure 13—Termite shields. A, On top of masonry or wood post; B, round posts; C, square posts.

damage untreated wood. Perhaps the most common and effective present-day method of protection is by the use of soil poisons. Spraying soil with solutions of approved chemicals such as aldrin, chlordan, dieldrin, and heptachlor using recommended methods will prove protection for 10 or more years.

A physical method of preventing entry of termites to untreated wood is by the use of *termite shields*. These are made of galvanized iron, aluminum, copper, or other metal. They are located over continuous walls (fig. 13A) or over or around treated wood foundation posts (fig. 13B and C). They are not effective if bent or punctured during or after construction.

Crawl spaces should have sufficient room so that an examination of poles and piers can be made easily each spring. These inspections normally provide safeguards against wood-destroying insects. Termite tubes or water-conducting fungus should be removed and destroyed and the soil treated with poison. Caution should be used in soil treatment, however, since the effective chemicals are often toxic to animal life and should not be used where individual water systems are present.

6. Joists

The beams, or beams and ledger strips, and the foundations are now in place and joists can be installed. Size and lengths of the floor joists, as well as the species and spacing, are shown in the floor framing layout in the working plans for the cabin being built. The joists may vary from nominal 2 by 8 inches in size to 2 by 10 inches or larger where spans are long. Moisture content of floor joists and other floor framing members should not exceed 19 percent when possible. Spacing of joists is normally 16 or 24 inches on center so that 8-foot lengths of plywood for subfloor will span six or four joist spaced.

In low-cost cabins, savings can be made by using plywood for subfloor which also serves as a base for resilient tile or other covering. This can be done by specifying tongued-and-grooved edges in a plywood grade of C-C plugged Exterior Douglas-fir, southern pine, or similar species. Regular Interior Underlayment grade with exterior glue is also considered satisfactory. The *matched* edges provide a tight lengthwise joint, and end joints are made over the joists. If tongued-and-grooved plywood is not available, use square edged plywood and block between joists with 2 by 4's for edge nailing. Plywood subfloor also serves as a tie between joists over the center beam. Insulation should be used in the floor in some manner to provide comfort and reduce heat loss. It is generally used between or over the joists. These details are covered in the working drawings.

Single-floor systems can also include the use of nominal 1- by 4-inch matched finish flooring in species such as southern pine and Douglas-fir and the lower grades of oak, birch, and maple in $25/32$-inch thickness. To prevent air and dust infiltration, joists should first be covered with 15-pound asphalt felt or similar mateirals. The flooring is then applied over the floor joists and the flood insulation added when the cabin is enclosed. When this single-floor system is used, however, some surface protection from weather and mechanical damage is required. A full-width sheet of heavy plastic or similar covering can be used, and the walls erected directly over the film. When most of the exterior and interior work is done, the covering can be removed and floor sanded and finished.

Post Foundation—With Side Overhang

The joists for a low-cost cabin are usually the third grade of such species as southern pine or Douglas-fir and are often 2 by 8 inches in size for spans of approximately 12 feet. If an overhang of about 12 inches is used for 12-foot lengths, the joist spacing normally can be 24 inches. Sizes, spacing, and other details are shown in the plans for each individual cabin.

The joists can now be cut to length, suing a *butt joint* over the center beam. Thus, for a 24-foot-wide

cabin, each pair of joists should be cut to a 12-foot length, less the thickness of the end header joist which is usually 1½ inches. The edge or stringer joists should be positioned on the beams with several other joists and the pre-marked headers nailed to them with one sixteenpenny nail (or just enough to keep them in position). The frame, including the edge (stringer) joists and the header joists, is now the exact outline of the cabin. Square up this framework by using the equal diagonal method (fig. 4). The overhang beyond the beams should be the same at each side of the cabin. Now, with eightpenny nails, *toenail* the joists to each beam they cross and the stringer joists to the beam beneath (fig. 14) to

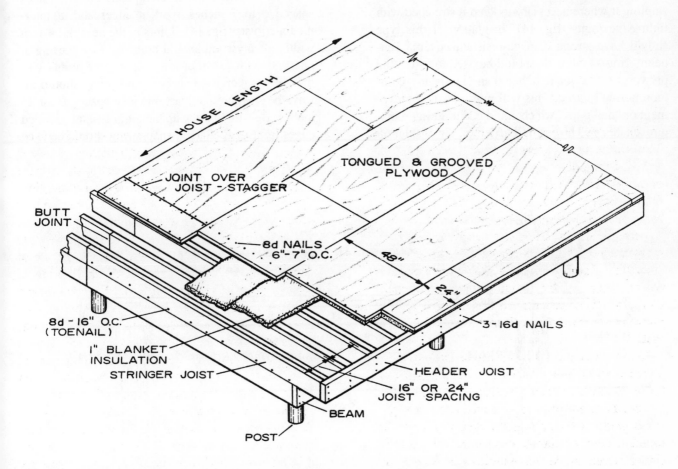

Figure 14—Floor framing (post foundation with side overhang).

hold the framework exactly square. Add the remaining joists and nail the headers into the ends with three sixteenpenny nails. Toenail the remaining joists to the headers with eightpenny nails. When the center of a parallel partition wall is more than 4 inches from the center of the joists, add solid blocking between the joists. The blocking should be the same size as the joists and spaced not more than 3 feet apart. Toenail blocking to the joists with two tenpenny nails at each side.

In moderate climates, 1-inch blanket insulation may be sufficient to insulate the floor of crawl-space cabins. It is usually placed between the joists in the same way that thicker insulation is normally installed. Another method consists of rolling 24-inch-wide 1-inch insulation, across the joists, nailing or stapling it where necessary to keep it stretched with tight edge joints (fig. 14). Insulation of this type should have strong damage-resistant covers. Tenpenny ring-shank nails should be used to fasten the plywood to the joists rather than eightpenny common normally used. This will minimize nail movement or "nail pops" which could occur during moisture changes. The vapor barrier of the insulation should be on the upper side toward the subfloor. Two-inch and thicker blanket or batt insulation is placed between the joists and should be applied any time after the floor is in place, preferably when the cabin is near completion.

When the cabin is 20, 24, 28, or 32 feet wide, the first row of tongued-and-grooved plywood sheets should be 24 inches wide, so that the butt-joints of the joists at the center beam are reinforced with a full 48-inch-wide piece (fig. 15). This plywood is usually ⅝- or ¾-inch thick when it serves both as subfloor and underlayment. Rip 4-foot-wide pieces in half and save the other halves for the opposite side. Place the square, sawed edges flush with the header and nail the plywood to each crossing joist and header with eightpenny common nails spaced 6 to 7 inches apart at edges and at intermediate joists (fig. 14). Joints in the next full 4-foot widths of plywood should be broken by starting at one end with a 4-foot-long piece. End joints will thus be staggered 48 inches. End joints should always be staggered at least one joist space, 16 or 24 inches. Be sure to draw up the tongued-and-grooved edges tightly. A chalked snap-string should be used

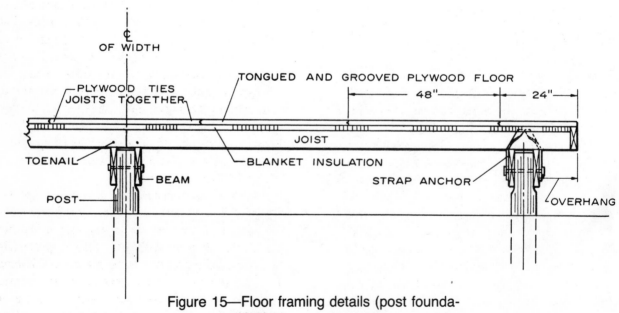

Figure 15—Floor framing details (post foundation).

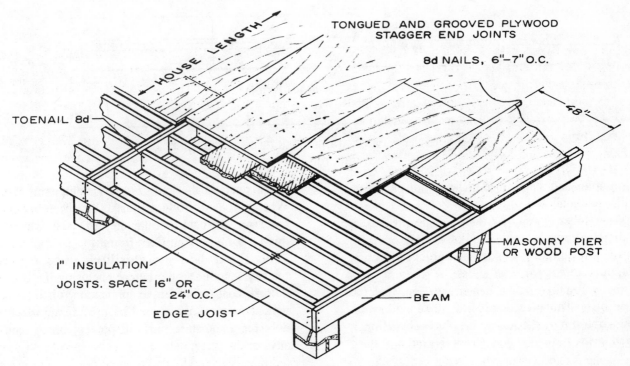

TONGUED AND GROOVED PLYWOOD STAGGER END JOINTS

HOUSE LENGTH

8d NAILS, 6"–7"O.C.

48"

TOENAIL 8d

MASONRY PIER OR WOOD POST

1" INSULATION

JOISTS. SPACE 16" OR 24"O.C.

EDGE JOIST

BEAM

Figure 16—Floor framing for edge foundation
(masonry piers or wood posts).

to mark the position of the joists for nailing.

Edge Foundation—Masonry Pier or Wood Post

When edge piers or wood posts are used with edge support beams, the joists can be cut to length to fit snugly between the center and outside beams so that they rest on the ledger strips. Sizes of header, joists, and other details are shown on the working drawings for each individual cabin. Toenail each end to the beams with two eightpenny nails on each side (fig. 16). In applying the plywood subfloor to the floor framing, start with full 4-foot-wide sheets rather than the 2-foot-wide pieces used for the side overhang framing (fig. 17). The nail-laminated center beam provides sufficient reinforcing between the ends of joists. Apply the insulation and nail the plywood the same way as outlined in the previous section.

Insulation Between Joists

Thicker floor insulation than the 1-inch blanket is usually required for cabins in colder areas. This will be indicated in the floor framing details of the working drawings or in the specifications. This type is normally used between the joists. Thus, the subfloor is nailed directly to the joists and the insulation placed between the joists after the subfloor is in place. Friction-fit (or similar insulating batts) 15 inches wide should be used for joists spaced 16 inches on center. Use 23-inch-wide batts for joists spaced 24 inches on center.

Friction-fit batts need little support to keep them in place. Small "dabs" of asphalt roof cement on the upper surfaces when installing against the bottom of the plywood will keep them in place (fig. 18). Standard batts can also be placed in this manner, but somewhat closer spacing of the cement might be required in addition to stapling along the edges. The use of a vapor barrier under the subfloor

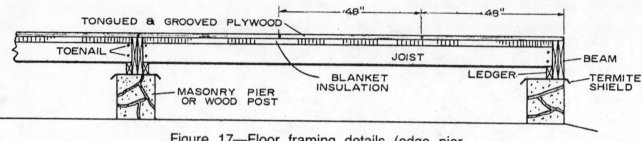

TONGUED & GROOVED PLYWOOD

TOENAIL

48"   48"

JOIST   BEAM

BLANKET   LEDGER   TERMITE
INSULATION   SHIELD

MASONRY PIER
OR WOOD POST

Figure 17—Floor framing details (edge pier foundation).

is important and is described in the section on "Thermal Insulation".

When other types of subfloor are specified, such as diagonal boards, some kind of overlay or finish is usually required. If tongued-and-grooved flooring is applied directly to and across the joists, a tie is normally required at the center butt joints of the floor joists. This is accomplished with a metal strap across the top of the joists or 1- by 4- by 20-inch wood strips (*scabs*) nailed across the faces of each

set of joists at the joint with six eightpenny nails. When plywood subfloor is used, the sheets are centered over the center beam and joist ends to provide this tie for overhang floor framing.

Finally, if the plywood is likely to be exposed for any length of time before enclosing the cabin, a brush coat (or squeegee application) of water-repellent preservative should be used. This will not only repel moisture but will prevent or minimize any surface degradation.

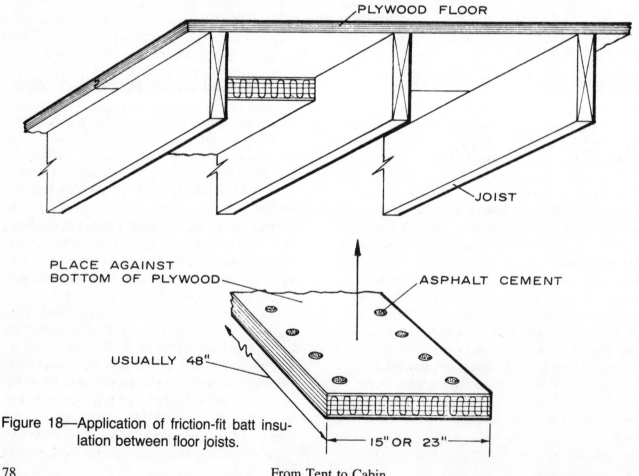

PLYWOOD FLOOR

JOIST

PLACE AGAINST
BOTTOM OF PLYWOOD

ASPHALT CEMENT

USUALLY 48"

15" OR 23"

Figure 18—Application of friction-fit batt insulation between floor joists.

7. Framing

Exterior sidewalls, and in some designs an interior wall, normally support most of the roof-loads as well as serving as a framework for attaching interior and exterior coverings. When roof trusses spanning the entire width of the cabin are used, the exterior sidewalls carry both the roof and ceiling loads. Interior partitions then serve mainly as room dividers. When ceiling joists are used, interior partitions usually sustain some of the ceiling loads.

The exterior walls of a wood-frame cabin normally consist of *studs*, interior and exterior coverings, windows and doors, and insulation. Moisture content of framing members usually should not exceed 19 percent.

The framework for a conventional wall consists of nominal 2- by 4-inch members used as top and bottom *plates*, as studs, and as partial (cripple) studs around openings. Studs are generally cut to lengths for 8-foot walls when subfloor and finish floors are used. This length depends on the thickness and number of wall plates (normally single bottom and double top plates). Studs can often be obtained from lumber dealers in a precut length. Double headers over doors and windows are generally larger than 2 by 4's when the width of the opening is greater than 2½ feet. Two 2- by 6-inch members are used for spans up to 4½ feet and two 2- by 8-inch members for openings from 4½ to about 6½ feet. Headers are normally cut 3 inches (two 1½-inch stud thicknesses) longer than the rough opening width unless the edge of the opening is near a regular spaced stud.

Framing of Sidewalls

The exterior framed walls, when erected, should be flush with the outer edges of the plywood subfloor and floor framing. Thus, the floor can be used both as a layout area and for horizontal assembly of the wall framing. When completed, the entire wall can be raised in place in "tilt-up" fashion, the plates nailed to the floor system, and the wall *plumbed* and braced.

The two exterior sidewalls of the cabin can be framed first and the exterior end walls later. Cut two sets of plates for the entire length of the house, using 8-, 12-, or 16-foot lengths, staggering the joints. Joints should be made at the centerline of a stud (*on center*). Starting at one end, mark each 16 or 24 inches, depending on the spacing of the studs, and also mark the centerlines for windows, doors, and partitions. These measurements are given on the working drawings. These are centerline (*o.c.*) markings, except for the ends. With a small square, mark the location of each stud with a line about ¾ inch on each side of the centerline mark (fig. 19).

Studs can now be cut to the correct length. When a low-slope roof with wood decking (which also serves as a ceiling finish) is used, the stud length for an 8-foot wall height with single plywood flooring should be 95½ inches, less the thickness of three plates. Thus for plates 1½ inches thick, this will mean a stud length of 91 inches. When ceiling joists or trusses are used with the single plywood floor, this length can be about 92⅛ inches. These measurements are primarily to provide for the vertical use of 8-foot lengths of dry-wall sheet materials for the walls with the ceiling finish in place. Cornerposts can be made up beforehand by nailing two short 2- by 4-inch blocks between two studs (fig. 20). Use two twelvepenny nails at each side of each block.

Begin fabrication of the wall by fastening the

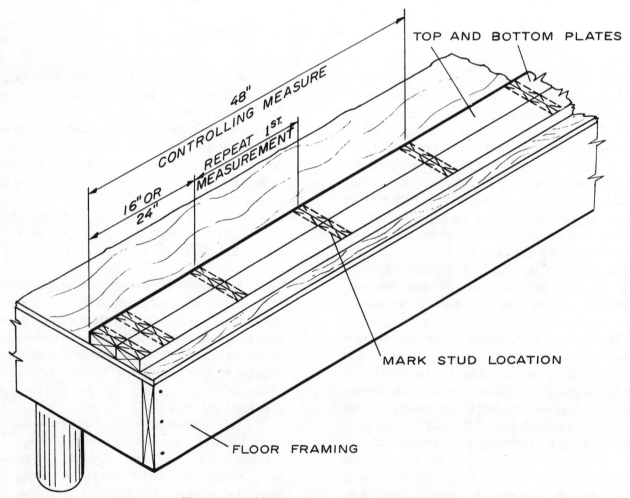

Figure 19—Marking top and bottom plates.

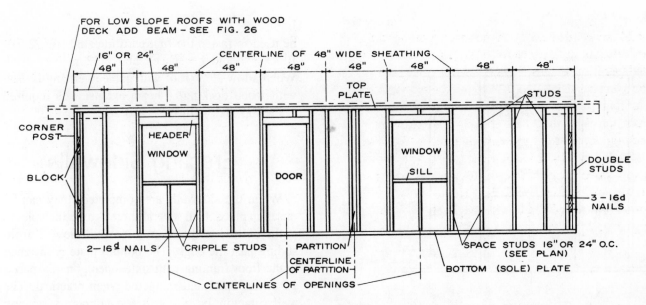

Figure 20—Framing layout of typical wall.

bottom plate and the first top plate to the ends of each cornerpost and stud (with two sixteenpenny nails) into each member. As studs are nailed in place, provisions should be made for framing the openings for windows and floors (fig. 20). Studs should be located to form the rough openings, the sizes of which vary with the types of windows selected. The rough openings are framed by studs which support the window and door headers or *lintels*. A full-length stud should be located at each side of these framing studs (fig. 21).

The following allowances are usually made for rough opening widths and heights for doors and windows. Half of the given width should be marked on each side of the centerline of the opening, which has previously been marked on top and bottom plates.

A. *Double-hung window (single unit)*
Rough opening width = glass width *plus* 6 inches
Rough opening height = total glass height *plus* 10 inches

B. *Casement window (two sash)*
Rough opening width = total glass width plus 11¼ inches

Rough opening height = total glass height *plus* 6⅜ inches

C. *Exterior doors*
Rough opening width = width of door *plus* 2½ inches
Rough opening height = height of door *plus* 3 inches

Clearances, or rough-opening sizes, for typical double-hung windows, for example, are shown in table 2.

Table 2.—*Frame opening sizes for double hung windows*

Window glass size (each sash)		Rough frame opening size	
Width *Inches*	Height *Inches*	Width *Inches*	Height *Inches*
24	16	30	42
28	20	34	50
32	24	38	58
36	24	42	58

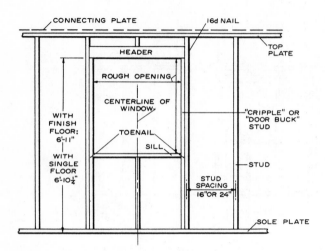

CONNECTING PLATE   16d NAIL

HEADER

ROUGH OPENING

CENTERLINE OF WINDOW

WITH FINISH FLOOR: 6'-11"

TOENAIL

SILL

WITH SINGLE FLOOR 6'-10¼"

TOP PLATE

"CRIPPLE" OR "DOOR BUCK" STUD

STUD

STUD SPACING 16" OR 24"

SOLE PLATE

Figure 21—Framing at window opening and height of window and door headers.

The height of the window and door headers above the subfloor when doors are 6 feet 8 inches high and finish floor is used is shown in figure 21. When only resilient tile is used over flooring made up of a single layer of material, the framing height for windows and doors should be 6 feet 10¼ inches for 6-foot 8-inch doors. The sizes of the headers should be the same as those previously outlined. Framing is arranged as shown in figure 21. Doubled headers can be fastened in place with two sixteenpenny nails through the stud into each member. Cripple (door *buck*) studs supporting the header on each side of the opening are nailed to the full stud with twelve-penny nails spaced about 16 inches apart and staggered. The sill and other short (cripple) studs are toenailed in place with two eightpenny nails at each side when end-nailing is not possible.

Doubled studs should normally be used on exterior walls where intersecting interior partitions are located. This is often accomplished with spaced studs, (fig. 22A) and provides nailing surfaces for interior covering materials. Blocking with 2- by 4-inch members placed flatwise between studs spaced 4 to 6 inches apart in the exterior wall might also

be used to fasten the first partition stud (fig. 22B). Blocks should be spaced about 32 inches apart. When a low-slope roof with gable overhang is used with wood decking, a beam extension is required at the top plates (figs. 20 and 26).

Erecting Sidewalls

When the sidewalls are completed, they can be raised in place. Nail several short 1- by 6-inch pieces to the outside of the beam to prevent the wall from sliding past the edge. The bottom plate is fastened to the floor framing with sixteenpenny nails spaced 16 inches apart and staggered when practical. The wall can now be plumbed and temporary bracing added to hold it in place in a true vertical position. Bracing may consist of 1- by 6-inch members nailed to one face of a stud and to a 2 by 4 block which has been nailed to the subfloor. Braces should be at about a 45° angle. If the wall framing is squared and braced, the panel siding or exterior covering can be fastened to the studs while the walls are still on the subfloor. In addition, window frames can be installed before erection of the wall. These processes are covered in following sections on "Exterior Wall Coverings" and "Exterior Frames".

End Walls—Moderate-Slope Roof

The exterior end walls for a gable-roofed cabin may be assembled on the floor in the same general manner as the sidewalls with a bottom plate and single top plate. However, the total length of the wall should be the exact distance between the inside of the exterior sidewalls already erected. Furthermore, only one end stud is used rather than the doubled cornerposts (fig. 23). Window and door openings are framed as outlined for the exterior sidewalls. When 48-inch-wide panel siding is used for the exterior, serving both as sheathing and siding, for example, the stud spacing should conform

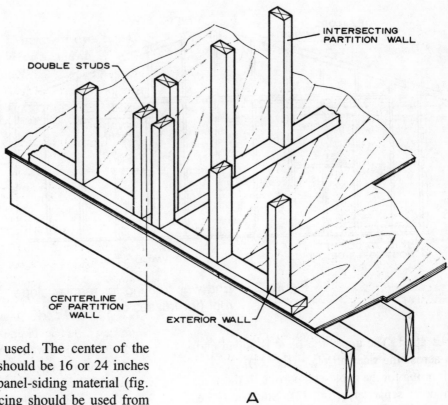

DOUBLE STUDS

INTERSECTING
PARTITION WALL

CENTERLINE
OF PARTITION
WALL

EXTERIOR WALL

A

to the type of covering used. The center of the second stud in this wall should be 16 or 24 inches from the outside of the panel-siding material (fig. 24). This method of spacing should be used from each corner toward the center, and any adjustments required because of sheet-material width should be made at a center window or door.

End walls are erected in the same manner as the sidewalls with the bottom plate fastened to the floor framing. These walls also must be plumbed and braced. The end studs should be nailed at each side to the cornerposts with sixteenpenny nails spaced

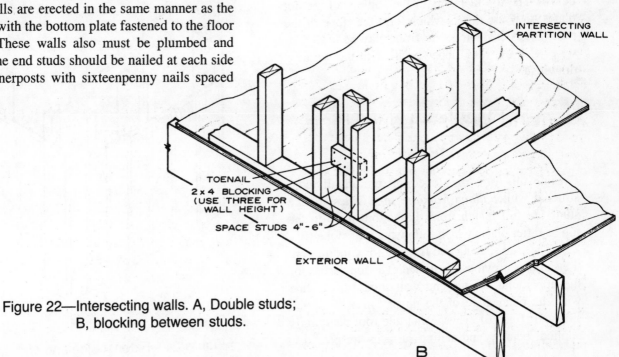

INTERSECTING
PARTITION WALL

TOENAIL
2 x 4 BLOCKING
(USE THREE FOR
WALL HEIGHT)

SPACE STUDS 4"- 6"

EXTERIOR WALL

B

Figure 22—Intersecting walls. A, Double studs;
B, blocking between studs.

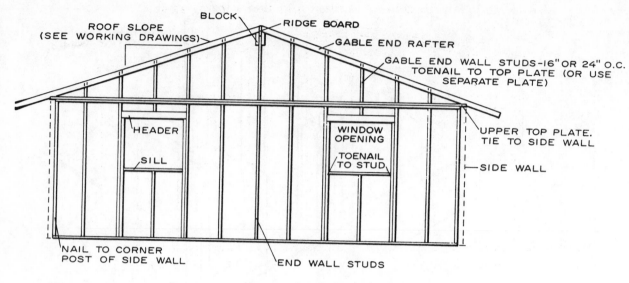

Figure 23—End wall framing for regular slope roof (for trusses or rafter-type).

16 inches apart. The upper top plate is added and extends across the sidewall plate (fig. 23).

The framing for the gable-end portion of the wall is often done separately (fig. 23). Studs may be toenailed to the upper top wall plate, or an extra 2-by 6-inch bottom plate can be used, which provides a nailing surface for ceiling material in the rooms below. The top members of the gable wall are not plates; they are rafters which form the slope of the roof. Studs are notched to fit or may be used flatwise. Use the roof slope specified in the working drawings.

End Walls—Low-Slope Roof

End walls for a low-slope roof are normally constructed with *balloon framing*. In this design, the studs are full length from the bottom plate to the top or rafter plates which follow the roof slope (fig. 25). The stud spacing and framing for windows are the same as previously outlined. The top surface of the upper plate of the end wall should be in line with the outer edge of the upper top plate of the sidewall (fig. 26). Thus, when the roof decking is applied, bearing and nailing surfaces are provided

at end and sidewalls. A beam extension beyond the end wall is provided to support the wood decking when a *gable*-end overhang is desired. This can be a 4- by 6-inch member which is fastened to the second sidewall stud (fig. 26).

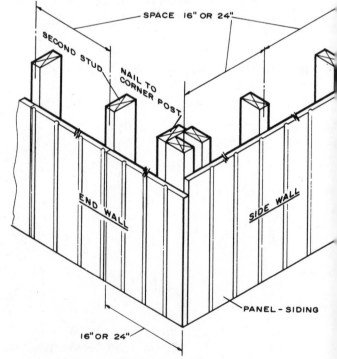

Figure 24—Exterior side and end wall intersection.

From Tent to Cabin

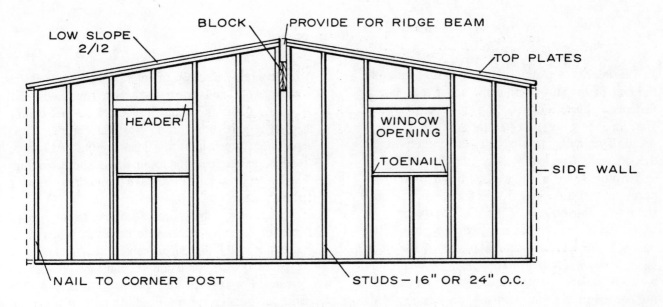

Figure 25—Framing for end wall (low-slope
roof).

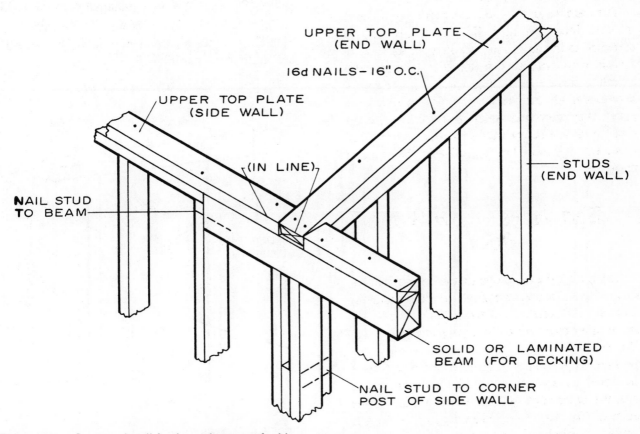

Figure 26—Corner detail for low-slope roof with
wood decking.

The lower top plate of the end wall is nailed to the end of the studs before the upper top plate is fastened in place. For attaching the upper plate, use sixteenpenny nails spaced 16 inches apart and staggered. Two nails are used over the cornerposts of the sidewalls (fig. 26).

To provide for a center *ridge* beam which supports the wood decking inside the cabin, the area should be framed (fig. 27). After the beam is in place, twelvepenny nails are used through the stud on each side of the beam. The size of the ridge beam is shown on the working plans for each cabin which is constructed using this method. When decking is used for a gable overhang, the beam extends beyond the end walls.

Interior Walls

Interior walls in conventional construction (with ceiling joists and rafters) are erected in the same manner and at the same height as the outside walls.

In general, assembly of interior stud walls is the same as outlined for exterior walls. The center load-bearing partition should be located so that ceiling joists require little or no wasteful cutting. Cross partitions are usually not load-bearing and can be spaced as required for room sizes. These spacings and other details are covered in the working drawing floor plan.

Studs should be spaced according to the type of interior covering material to be used. When studs are spaced 24 inches on center, the thickness of gypsum board, for example, must be ½ inch or greater. For 16-inch stud spacing, a thickness of ⅜ inch or greater can be used. Details of a typical intersection of interior walls are shown in figure 28. Load-bearing partitions should be constructed with nominal 2- by 4-inch studs, but 2- by 3-inch studs may be used for nonload-bearing walls. Doorway openings can also be framed with a single member on each side in nonload-bearing walls (fig. 28). Single top plates are commonly used on nonload-bearing interior partitions.

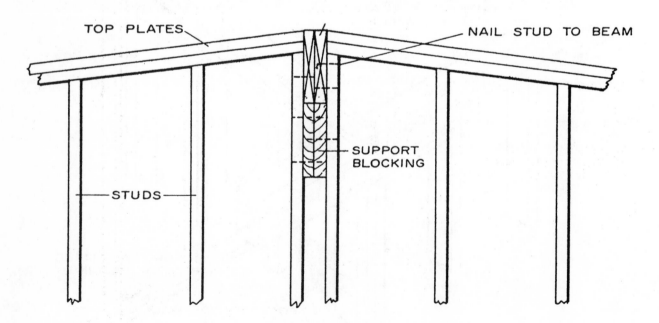

Figure 27—Framing detail at ridge (end wall for low-slope roof).

From Tent to Cabin

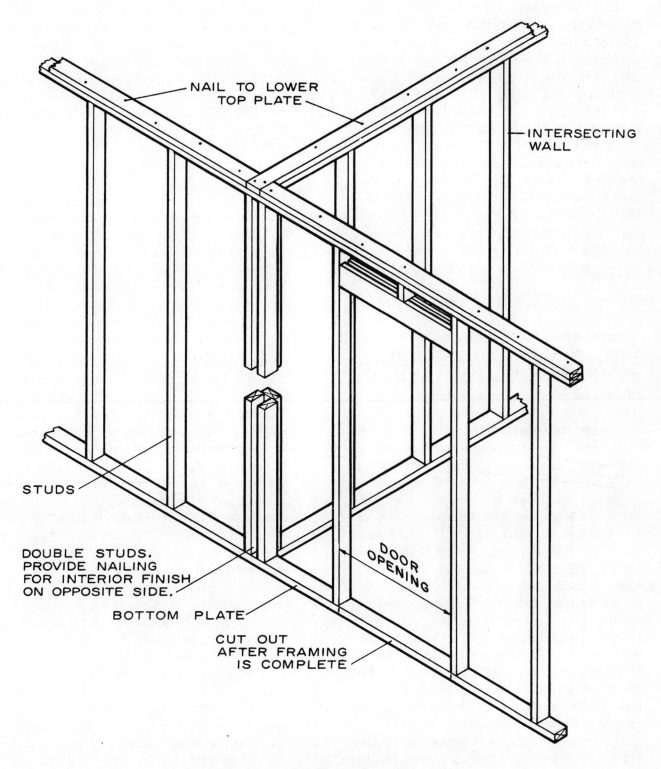

NAIL TO LOWER
TOP PLATE

INTERSECTING
WALL

STUDS

DOUBLE STUDS.
PROVIDE NAILING
FOR INTERIOR FINISH
ON OPPOSITE SIDE.

BOTTOM PLATE

CUT OUT
AFTER FRAMING
IS COMPLETE

DOOR
OPENING

Figure 28—Intersection of interior walls.

From Tent to Cabin

8.   Roof Systems

Roof trusses require no load-bearing interior partitions, so location of the walls and size and spacing of studs are determined by the cabin design and by the type of interior finish. The bottom chords of the trusses are often used to tie in with crossing partitions where required. Details of stud location at the intersection of an interior partition with an exterior wall are shown in figure 22A and B.

When a low-slope roof is used with wood decking, a full-height wall or a ridge beam is required for support at the center (fig. 29). The ridge beam may span from an interior center partition to an outside wall, forming a clear open area beneath. Cross or intersecting walls are full height with a sloping top plate. In such designs, one method uses the following sequence: (a) Erect exterior walls, center wall, and ridge beam; (b) apply roof decking; and (c) install other partition walls. Size and spacing of the studs in the cross walls are usually based on the thickness of the covering material, as no roof load is imposed on them. These spacings and sizes are part of the working drawings.

The upper top plates (connecting plates) are used to tie the wall framing together at corners, at intersections, and at crossing walls. The upper plate crosses and is nailed to the plate below (figs. 26 and 28). Two sixteenpenny nails are used at each intersection. The remainder of the upper top plate is nailed to the lower top plate with sixteenpenny nails spaced 16 inches apart in a staggered pattern.

The primary function of a roof is to provide protection to the cabin in all types of weather with a minimum of maintenance. A second consideration is appearance; a roof should add to the attractiveness of the cabin, as well as being practical. Happily, a roof with a wide overhang at the cornice and the gable ends not only enhances appearance, but provides protection to side and end walls. Thus, even in lower cost cabins, when the style and design permit, wide overhangs are desirable. Though they add slightly to the initial cost, savings in future maintenance usually merit this type of roof extension. Wood members used for roof framing should normally not exceed 19 percent moisture content.

As briefly described in the section on "Major Cabin Parts", the two types of roofs commonly used for cabins are (a) the low-slope and (b) the *pitched* roof. The flat or low-slope roof combines ceiling and roof elements as one system, which allows them to serve as interior finish, or as a fastening surface

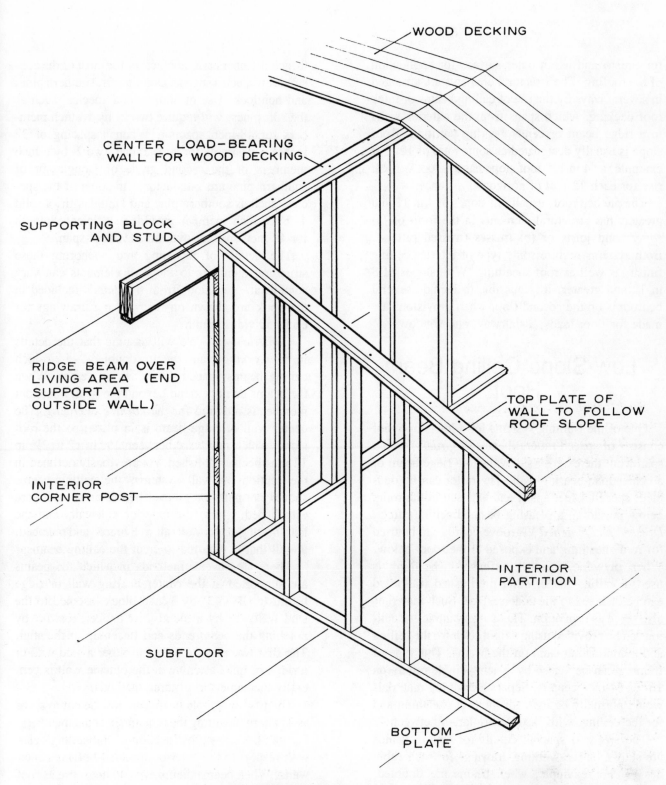

WOOD DECKING

CENTER LOAD–BEARING
WALL FOR WOOD DECKING

SUPPORTING BLOCK
AND STUD

RIDGE BEAM OVER
LIVING AREA (END
SUPPORT AT
OUTSIDE WALL)

TOP PLATE OF
WALL TO FOLLOW
ROOF SLOPE

INTERIOR
CORNER POST

INTERIOR
PARTITION

SUBFLOOR

BOTTOM
PLATE

Figure 29—Ridge beam and center wall for low-
slope roof.

for finish, and as an outer surface for application of the roofing. The structural elements are arranged in several ways by the use of ceiling beams or thick roof decking, which spans from the exterior walls to a ridge beam or center bearing partition. Roof slope is usually designated as some ratio of 12. For example, a "4 in 12" roof slope has a 4-foot vertical rise for each 12 feet of horizontal distance.

The pitched roof, usually in slopes of 4 in 12 and greater, has structural elements in the form of (a) *rafters* and joists or (b) trusses (trussed rafters). Both systems require some type of interior ceiling finish, as well as roof sheathing. With slopes of 8 in 12 and greater, it is possible to include several bedrooms on the second floor when provisions are made for floor loads, a stairway, and windows.

Low-Slope Ceiling Beam Roof

One of the framing systems for a low-slope roof consists of spaced rafters (beams or *girders*) which span from the exterior sidewalls to a ridge beam or a center load-bearing wall. The rafter can be doubled, spaced 4 feet apart, and exposed in the room below providing a pleasing beamed ceiling effect. *Dressed and matched* V-groove boards can be used for roof sheathing and exposed to the room below. When plywood or other unfinished sheathing is used, a ceiling tile or other prefinished wallboard can be fastened to the undersurface. Such materials also serve as insulation. Thus, a very attractive ceiling can be provided using a light color for the ceiling and a contrasting stain on the beams. This type of framing can be varied by spacing single rafters on 16- or 24-inch centers. Separate covering materials would normally be used for the roof sheathing and for the ceiling, with flexible insulation between.

The size and spacing details for ceiling beams are shown on the working drawings for each cabin design. For example, when beams are doubled, spaced 48 inches apart, and the distance from outer wall to interior wall is about 11½ feet, two 2- by

8-inch members are satisfactory for most of the construction species such as Douglas-fir, southern pine, and hemlock. Use of some wood species, such as the soft pines, will require two 2- by 10-inch members for 48-inch spacing. When a spacing of 32 inches is desirable for appearance, two 2- by 6-inch members of the second grade of Douglas-fir or southern pine are satisfactory. In some of the species, such as southern pine and Douglas-fir, a solid 4- by 6-inch member provides sufficient strength for 48-inch spacing over an 11½ foot-span.

The details of fastening and anchoring these structural members to the wall elements can vary somewhat. Variations from the details included in the book are shown on the working drawings for each individual cabin.

Construction.—We will assume that the details in the working plans specify doubled 2- by 8-inch ceiling beams spaced 48 inches on center. When the beams do not extend beyond the wall, a lookout member is required for the *cornice* overhang. The center wall or ridge beam is in place, so the roof slope, which may vary between 1½ in 12 to 2½ in 12, has been established. As previously outlined in the section on wall systems, the ceiling beams should normally be erected before cross walls are established. Thus, the exterior sidewalls and the load-bearing center wall, all well braced and plumbed, are all that is required to erect the ceiling beams.

There are several methods in which the beams are supported at the center bearing wall or ridge beam: (a) By a 2- by 3-inch block fastened to the stud wall; (b) by a metal joist hanger; and (c) by notching the beam ends and fastening to the stud. The first two may be used for either a stud wall or a ridge beam. Fastening at the outside wall is generally the same for all three methods.

The first or sample beam can now be cut to serve as a pattern in cutting the remainder of the members. Figure 30A shows the location of the ceiling beam with respect to the exterior and load-bearing center walls. When beams themselves do not serve as roof extensions, they can be assembled by nailing a 2- by 6-inch *lookout* (roof extension) at the outer wall

From Tent to Cabin

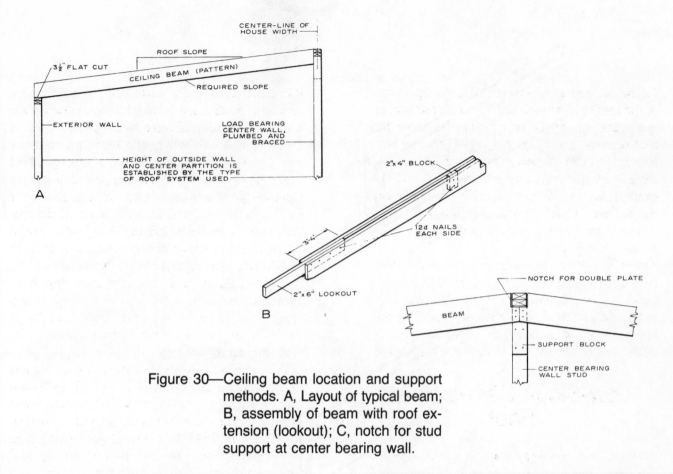

Figure 30—Ceiling beam location and support methods. A, Layout of typical beam; B, assembly of beam with roof extension (lookout); C, notch for stud support at center bearing wall.

and a 2- by 4-inch spacer block at the interior center wall (fig. 30B). Use two twelvepenny nails on each side of the block and twelvepenny nails spaced 6 inches apart for the 2- by 6-inch lookout member. When a block nailed to the stud is used to support the interior beam end, the ends should be notched (fig. 30C).

Details at center wall or beam.—The first system of connecting the inside end of the ceiling beam is most adaptable to ridge-beam construction. It consists of fastening a nominal 2- by 3-inch block to the beam with 4½ lag screws (fig. 31A). The 2 by 3 should be the same depth as the ceiling beam. The beam ends are then bolted to the 2- by 3-inch block with ⅜- by 5-inch carriage bolts.

Using joist hangers (fig. 31B) to fasten the inside end of the ceiling beams in another method most adaptable to a ridge-beam face, the ceiling beams dropped in place, and the hangers nailed to the beam. Eight- or tenpenny nails are commonly used for nailing. Hangers will be exposed, but can be painted to match the color of the beams.

A third method which can be used at a center bearing wall includes notching the ends of the ceiling beams (figs. 30C and 31C). When the beam is in place it is face-nailed to the stud at each side with two twelvepenny nails. Short 2- by 4-inch support blocks are then nailed at each side of the stud with twelvepenny nails (fig. 31C).

When solid 4- by 6-inch or larger members are used as ceiling beams in place of the doubled members, the joist hanger is probably the most suitable method of supporting the inside ends of the beams. If the solid or laminated beams are to be stained, care should be taken to prevent hammer marks.

Nailing ceiling beams at exterior walls.—The ceiling beams are normally fastened to the top plate of the outside walls by nailing. In windy areas, some type of strapping or metal bracket is often desirable (fig. 41B). The ceiling beams are toe-nailed to the top of the outside wall with two eight-penny nails at each side and a tenpenny nail at the ends (fig. 32). To provide nailing for panel siding and interior finish, 2- by 4-inch nailing blocks are

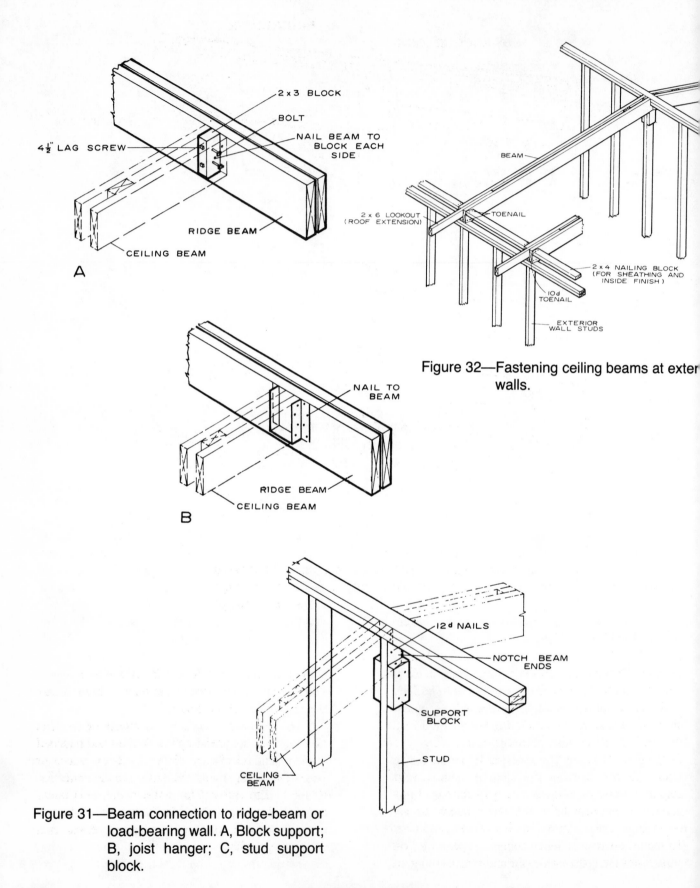

2 x 3 BLOCK

BOLT

NAIL BEAM TO BLOCK EACH SIDE

$4\frac{1}{2}''$ LAG SCREW

RIDGE BEAM

CEILING BEAM

A

BEAM

2 x 6 LOOKOUT (ROOF EXTENSION)

TOENAIL

2 x 4 NAILING BLOCK (FOR SHEATHING AND INSIDE FINISH)

10 d TOENAIL

EXTERIOR WALL STUDS

Figure 32—Fastening ceiling beams at exter walls.

NAIL TO BEAM

RIDGE BEAM

CEILING BEAM

B

12 d NAILS

NOTCH BEAM ENDS

SUPPORT BLOCK

STUD

CEILING BEAM

Figure 31—Beam connection to ridge-beam or load-bearing wall. A, Block support; B, joist hanger; C, stud support block.

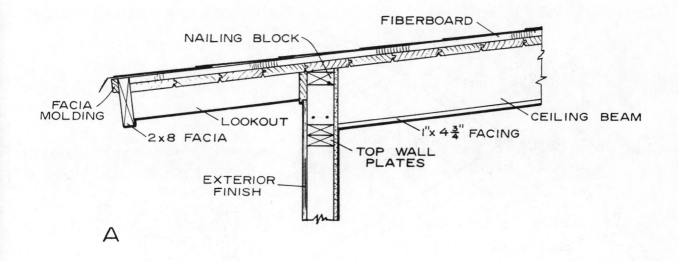

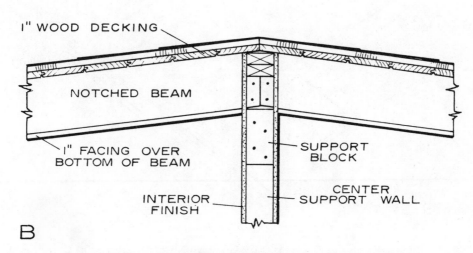

Figure 33—Cross sections of completed walls and roof framing. A, Section through exterior wall; B, section through center wall.

fastened between the ceiling beams (fig. 32). Toe-nailed with eightpenny nails at each edge and face.

Roof sheathing.—Ceiling beams and roof extensions are now in place and ready for installation of the roof sheathing. Roof sheathing can consist of 1- by 6-inch tongued-and-grooved V-groove lumber with $^{25}\!/_{32}$-inch fiberboard nailed over the top for insulation. Use two eightpenny nails for each board at each ceiling beam. The insulation fiberboard can be nailed in place with 1¼-inch roofing nails spaced 10 inches apart in rows 24 inches on center. Cross sections of the completed wall and roof framing are shown in figures 33 A and B. A nominal 1-inch member about 4¾ inches wide may be used to case the undersides of the beams.

A gable-end extension of 16 inches or less can be supported by extending the dressed and matched V-edge roof boards (fig. 34A). A 2- by 2-inch or larger member (*fly rafter*) is nailed to the underside of the boards and serves to fasten the facia board and molding (fig. 34B). The V-groove of the underside of the 1 by 6 roof sheathing serves as a decorative surface.

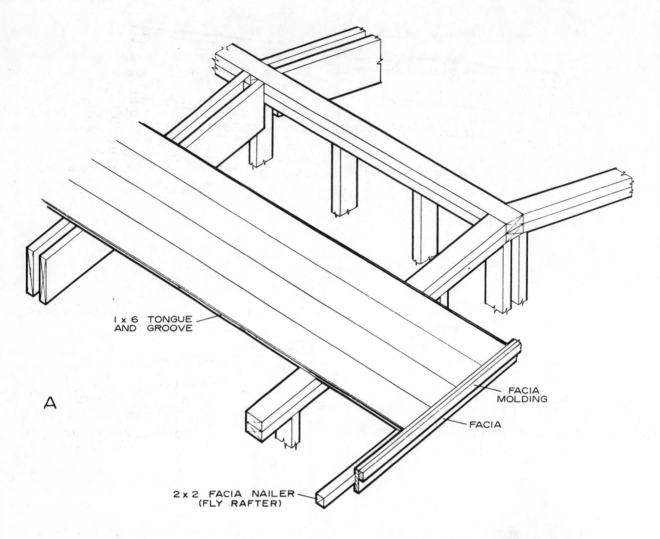

1 x 6 TONGUE
AND GROOVE

A

FACIA
MOLDING

FACIA

2 x 2 FACIA NAILER
(FLY RAFTER)

Figure 34—Gable end extension detail. A, Gable extension; B, fly rafter.

Rafter-Joist Roof

Another type of construction for low-slope roofs similar to the ceiling beam framing is the rafter-joist roof, in which the members are spaced 16 or 24 inches apart and serve both as rafters and ceiling joists (fig. 35A and B). Members may be 2 by 8 or 2 by 10 inches in size. Specific sizes are shown on the working drawings for each cabin plan. The space between joists is insulated, allowing space for a ventilating *airway*. Gypsum board or other types of interior finish can be nailed directly to the bottoms of the joists.

Rafter extensions can serve as nailing surfaces

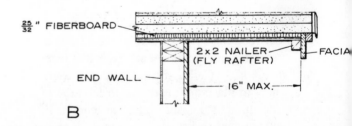

$\frac{25}{32}$ " FIBERBOARD

2 x 2 NAILER
(FLY RAFTER)

FACIA

END WALL

16" MAX.

B

for the *soffit* of a closed cornice (fig. 35A). When an open cornice is used, a nailing block is required over the wallplates and between rafters for the siding or *frieze* board.

The inside ends of the rafter-joists bear on an interior load-bearing wall (fig. 35B). Beams are

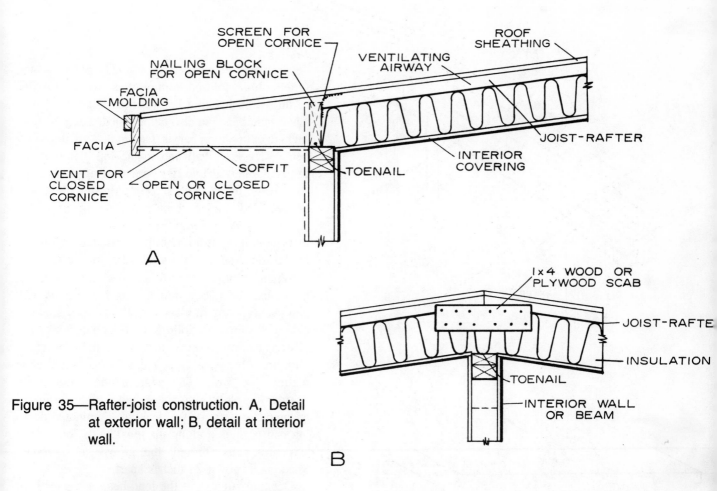

Figure 35—Rafter-joist construction. A, Detail at exterior wall; B, detail at interior wall.

toenailed to the plate with eightpenny nails on each side. A 1- by 4-inch wood or ⅜-inch plywood *scab* is used to connect opposite rafter-joists. This fastens the joists together and serves as a positive tie between the exterior sidewalls.

Low-Slope Wood-Deck Roof

A simple method of covering low-slope roofs is with wood decking. Decking should be strong enough to span from the interior center wall or beam to the exterior wall. Decking can also extend beyond the wall to form an overhang at the *eave* line (fig. 36A). This system requires dressed and matched nominal 2- by 6-inch southern pine or Douglas-fir decking or 3- by 6-inch solid or laminated decking (cedar or similar species) for spans of about 12 feet.

The proper sizes are shown in the working drawings. While this system requires more material than the beam and sheathing system, the labor involved at the building site is usually much less.

When gable-end extension is desired, some type of support is required beyond the end wall line at plate and ridge. This is usually accomplished by the projection of a small beam at the top plate of each sidewall (figs. 20 and 26) and at the ridge. Often the extension of the double top plate of the sidewall is sufficient. Depending on the type and thickness, the decking must sometimes be in one full-length piece without joints unless there are intermediate supports in the form of an interior partition. When such an interior wall is present, a butt joint can be made over its center. The working drawings cover these various details.

Figure 36 shows the method of applying wood decking. This type of wood decking usually has a

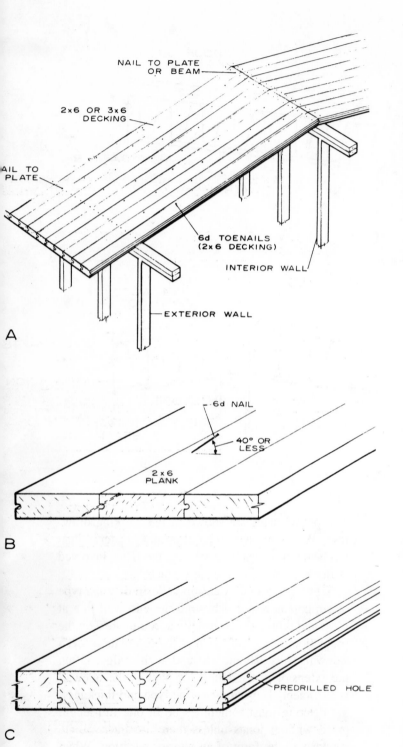

Figure 36—Wood-deck construction. A, Installing wood decking; B, toenailing horizontal joint; C, edge nailing 3- by
6-inch solid decking.

decorative V-edge face that should be placed down.
Often a light-colored stain or other finish is applied
to the wood decking before it is installed. Prefinished members can also be obtained. Each 2- by 6-
inch decking member is face-nailed to the ridge
beam or center wall and to the top plates of the
exterior wall with two sixteenpenny ring-shank nails
(fig. 36A). In addition, sixpenny finish nails should
be toenailed along each joint on 2- to 3-foot centers
(fig. 36B). A 40° angle or less should be used so
that the nail point does not penetrate the underside.
Nailheads should be driven flush with the surface.

When nominal 3- by 6-inch decking in solid or
laminated form is required, it is face-nailed with
two twentypenny ring-shank nails at center and outside wall supports. Solid 3- by 6-inch decking usually has a double tongue and groove and is provided
with holes between the tongues for horizontal edge
nailing (fig. 36C). This edge nailing is done with
7- or 8-inch long ring-shank nails, often furnished
by manufacturers of the decking. Laminated decking can be nailed along the lengthwide joints with
sixpenny nails through the groove and tongue.
Space nails about 24 inches apart.

Decking support at the load-bearing center wall
and at the ends of the sidewalls may also be provided
by an extension of the top plates (fig. 37). The sides
of the members can be faced later, if desired, with
the same material used for siding with 1- by 6- and
1- by 8-inch members.

Insulation for Low-Slope Roofs

It is considerably more difficult and costly to
provide the low-slope roof with adequate insulation,
except when the rafters-joist system is used with
both interior and exterior covering, and even then
the joists must have adequate depth to provide space
for insulation. Therefore, low-slope roofs are most
economical in extremely mild climates or in cabins
for seasonal use where both heating and air con-

From Tent to Cabin

ditioning requirements are quite minimal. Some insulation can be added economically by the use of $^{25}/_{32}$-inch insulating board sheathing placed over the wood decking. The use of expanded foam in sheet form as a base for the ½-inch insulation board or tile on the underside of the decking will provide increased resistance to heat loss. Rigid foam insulation can also be used on top of the decking, but ⅜-inch plywood is required over the foam to provide a nailing base for the shingles.

The "U" value of a building component is a measure of resistance to heat loss or gain and the lower the number is, the more effective the insulation. Figure 38 shows the value of adding various insulating materials to the basic wood decking.

The method of installing the $^{25}/_{32}$-inch insulating sheathing over the wood decking is relatively simple. The 4- by 8-foot sheets should be laid horizontally across the decking. Use the 1¼- or 1½-inch roofing nails spaced 10 inches apart in rows 24 inches apart along the length.

Insulating board or tile in ½-inch thickness and the expanded foam insulation are installed with wallboard adhesive designed for these materials. Manufacturers normally recommend the type and method of application. With ½- by 12- by 12-inch tile, for example, a small amount of adhesive in

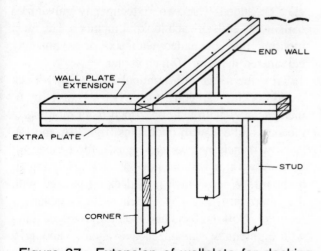

Figure 37—Extension of wallplate for decking support.

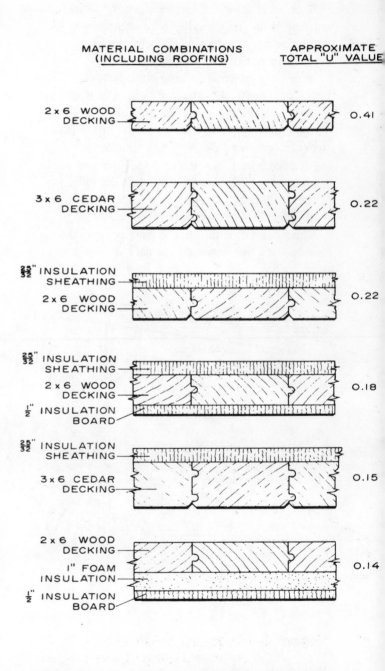

Figure 38—Insulating values of various materials and material combinations.

each corner and the use of hand pressure as the tile is placed is one system which is often used. When tile is tongued and grooved, stapling is the usual method of installation. Larger sheets of ½-inch insulating board may require a combination of glue and some nailing. Expanded foam insulation is ordinarily installed with approved adhesives.

When 1-inch wood decking is used over the joist-beam system (fig. 33A and B), the use of at least 25/32-inch insulating sheathing over the boards and ½-inch insulating board or tile on the inside is normally recommended. A 1-inch thickness of expanded foam insulation under the ½-inch tile would provide even better insulation. When the inner face of the decking is to be covered, lower grade 2- by 6-inch decking is commonly used.

Rigid foam over the deck is usually applied with roofing nails that penetrate the deck a minimum of

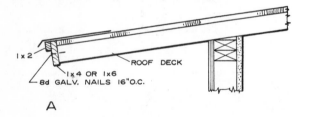

A

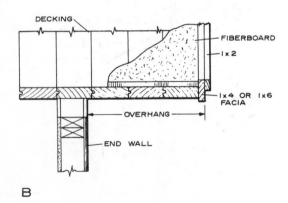

B

Figure 39—Facia for wood-deck roof. A, Side-wall overhang; B, end-wall overhang.

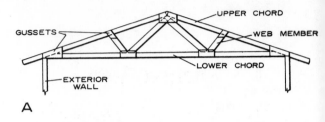

A

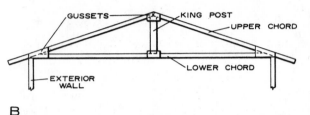

B

Figure 40—Trussed rafters. A, W-type truss; B, king-post truss.

¾ inch; however, foams vary in composition, so manufacturer's instructions should be followed. Plywood at least ⅜-inch thick can be applied over the foam as a nailing base for shingles.

Trim For Low-Slope Roofs

Simple trim in the form of facia boards can be used at roof overhangs and at side and end walls. When 2- by 6-inch lookouts are used in the ceiling-beam roof, a 2- by 8-inch *facia* member is usually required to span the 48-inch spacing of the beams (fig. 33A). In addition, a 1- by 2-inch facia molding may be added. Use two sixteenpenny galvanized nails in the ends of each lookout member. The facia molding may be nailed with six- or sevenpenny galvanized nails on 16-inch center.

Trim for roofs with nominal 2- by 3-inch-thick wood decking can consist of a 1- by 4- or 1- by 6-inch member with a 1- by 2-inch facia molding at the side and end-wall overhangs (fig. 39A and B). A 1- by 4-inch member can be used for 2-inch roof decking with or without the 25/32-inch insulating fiberboard. When 3-inch roof decking is used with the fiberboard, a 1- by 6-inch piece is generally required. Nail the facia and molding to the decking with eightpenny galvanized nails spaced about 16 inches apart. The roof deck is now ready for the roofing material.

Pitched Roof

A pitched-roof cabin is commonly framed by one of two methods: (a) With trussed rafters or (b) with conventional rafter and ceiling joist members. These framing methods are used most often for roof slopes of 4 in 12 and greater. The common W-truss (fig. 40A) for moderate spans requires less material than the joist and rafter system, as the members in the upper and lower chords are usually only 2 by 4 inches in size for spans of 24 to 32 feet. The king-post truss (fig. 40B) for spans of 20 to 24 feet uses even less material than the W-truss, but is perhaps more suitable for light to moderate roof loads. Low-slope roof trusses usually require larger members. In addition to lowering material costs, the truss has the advantage of permitting freedom in location of interior partitions because only the sidewalls carry the ceiling and roof loads.

The roof sheathing, trim, roofing, interior ceiling finish, and type of ceiling insulation used do not vary a great deal between the truss and the conventional roof systems. For plywood or lumber sheathing, 24-inch spacing of trusses and rafters and joists is considered a normal maximum. Greater spacing can be used, but it usually requires a thicker roof sheathing and application of wood stripping on the undersides of the ceiling joists and trusses to furnish a support for ceiling finish. Thus, most W-trusses are designed for 24-inch spacing and joist-rafter construction for 24- or 16-inch spacing. Trusses generally require a higher grade dimension material than the joist and rafter roof. However, specific details of the roof construction are covered in the working drawings for each cabin.

Trussed Roof

The common truss or trussed rafter is most often fabricated in a central shop. While some are constructed at the job site, an enclosed building provides better control for their assembly. These trusses are fabricated in several ways. The three most com-

mon methods of fastening members together are with (a) metal truss plates, (b) plywood gussets, and (c) ring connectors.

The metal truss plates, with or without prongs, are fastened in place on each side of member in-

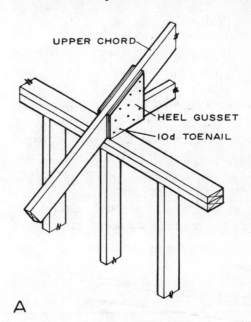

A

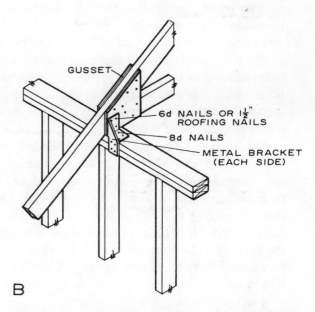

B

Figure 41—Fastening trusses to wallplate. A, Toenailing; B, metal bracket connector.

tersections. Some plates are nailed and others have supplemental nail fastening. Metal-plate trusses are usually purchased through a large lumber dealer or manufacturer and are not easily adapted to on-site fabrication. The trusses using fully nailed metal plates can usually be assembled at a small central shop.

The plywood-gusset truss may be a nailed or nailed-glued combination. The nailed-glued combination, with nails supplying the pressure, allows the use of smaller gussets than does the nailed system. However, if on-site fabrication is necessary, the nailed gusset truss and the ring connector truss are probably the best choices. Many adhesives suitable for trusses generally require good temperature control and weather protection not usually available on site. The size of the gussets, the number of nails or other connectors, and other details for this type of roof are included in the working drawings for each cabin.

Completed trusses can be raised in place with a small mechanical lift on the top plates of exterior sidewalls. They can also be placed by hand over the exterior walls in an inverted position, and then rotated into an upright position. The top plates of the two sidewalls should be marked for the location of each set of trusses. Trusses are fastened to the outside walls and to 1- by 4- or 1- by 6-inch temporary horizontal braces used to space and align them until the roof sheathing has been applied. Locate these braces near the ridge line.

Trusses can be fastened to the top wallplates by toenailing, but this is not always the most satisfactory method. The heel gusset in a plywood-gusset or metal plate truss is located at the wallplate and makes toenailing difficult. However, two tenpenny nails at each side of the truss can be used in nailing the lower chord to the plate (fig. 41A). Predrilling may be necessary to prevent splitting. A better system involves the use of a simple metal connector or bracket obtained from local lumber dealers. Brackets should be nailed to the wallplates at sides and top with eightpenny nails and to the lower chords of the truss with sixpenny or 1½-inch roofing

nails (fig. 41B) or as recommended by the manufacturer.

The gable-end walls for a pitched roof utilizing trusses are usually made the same way as those described in the section on "Wall Systems" and shown in figure 23.

Rafter and Ceiling Joist Roof

Conventional roof construction with ceiling joists and rafters (fig. 42) can begin after all load-bearing and other partition walls are in place. The upper top plate of the exterior wall and the load-bearing interior wall serve as a fastening area for ceiling joists and rafters. Ceiling joists are installed along premarked exterior top wallplates and are toenailed to the plate with three eightpenny nails. The first joist is usually located next to the top plate of the end wall (fig. 43). This provides edge-nailing for the ceiling finish. Ceiling joists crossing a center load-bearing wall are face-nailed to each other with three or four sixteenpenny nails. In addition, they are each toenailed to the plate with two eightpenny nails.

Angle cuts for the rafters at the *ridge* and at the exterior walls can be marked with a carpenter's square using a reference table showing the overall rafter lengths for various spans, roof slopes, and joist sizes. These tables can usually be obtained from your lumber dealer. However, if a rafter table is not available, a baseline can be laid out on the subfloor across the width of the house, marking an exact outline of the roof slope, ridge, board and exterior walls. Thus, a rafter pattern can be made, including cuts at the ridge, wall, and the overhang at the eaves.

Rafters are erected in pairs. The *ridge board* is first nailed to one rafter end with three tenpenny nails (fig. 44). The opposing rafter is then nailed to the first with a tenpenny nail at the top and two eightpenny nails toenailed at each side. The outside

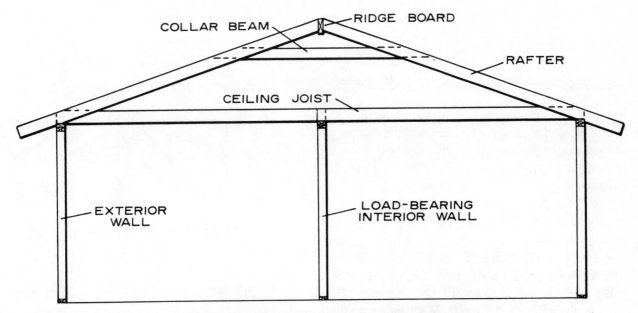

Figure 42—Rafter and ceiling joist roof framing.

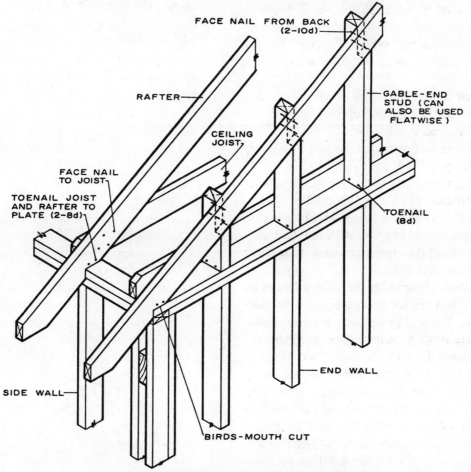

Figure 43—Fastening rafters and ceiling joists
to plate and gable-end studs.

rafter is located flush with and a part of the gable-end walls (fig. 43).

While the ridge nailing is being done, the rafters should be toenailed to the top plates of the exterior wall with two eightpenny nails (fig. 43). In addition, each rafter is face-nailed to the ceiling joist with three tenpenny nails. The remaining rafters are installed the same way. When the ridge board must be spliced, it should be done at a rafter with nailing at each side.

If gable-end walls have not been erected with the end walls, the gable-end studs can now be cut and nailed in place (fig. 43). Toenail the studs to the plate with eightpenny nails and face-nail to the end rafter from the inside with two tenpenny nails. In addition, the first or edge ceiling joist can be nailed to each gable-end stud with two tenpenny nails. Gable-end studs can also be used flatwise between the end rafter and top plate of the wall.

When the roof has a moderately low slope and the width of the cabin is 26 feet or greater, it is often desirable to nail a 1- by 6-inch *collar beam* to every second or third rafter (fig. 42) using four eightpenny nails at each end.

Framing for Flush Living-Dining Area Ceiling

A living-dining-kitchen group is often designed as one open area with a flush ceiling throughout. This makes the rooms appear much larger than they actually are. When trusses are used, there is no problem, because they span from one exterior wall to the other. However, if ceiling joists and rafters are used, some type of *beam* is needed to support the interior ends of the ceiling joists. This can be done by using a flush beam, which spans from an interior cross wall to an exterior end wall. Joists are fastened to the beams by means of joist hangers (fig. 45). These hangers are nailed to the beam with eightpenny nails and to the joist with sixpenny nails or 1½-inch roofing nails. Hangers are perhaps most easily fastened by first nailing to the end of the joist

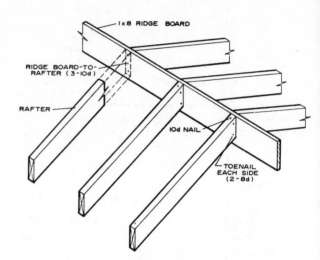

Figure 44—Fastening rafters at the ridge.

before the joist is raised in place.

An alternate method of framing utilizes a wood bracket at each pair of ceiling joists tying them to a beam which spans the open living-dining area (fig. 46). This beam is blocked up and fastened at each end at a height equal to the depth of the ceiling joists.

Roof Sheathing

Plywood or lumber roof sheathing is most commonly used for pitched roofs. Nominal 1-inch

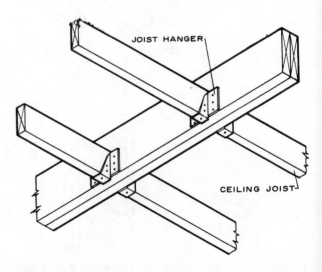

Figure 45—Flush beam with joist hangers.

boards no wider than 8 inches can be used for trusses or rafters spaced not more than 24 inches on center. Sheathing (standard) and other grades of plywood are marked for the allowable spacing of the rafters and trusses for each species and thickness used. For example, 1 "24/0" mark indicates it is satisfactory as roof sheathing for 24-inch spacing of roof members, but not satisfactory for subfloor.

Nominal 1-inch boards should be laid up without spacing and nailed to each rafter with two eight-penny nails. Plywood sheets should be laid across the roof members with staggered end joints. Use sixpenny nails for 3/8-inch and thinner plywood and eightpenny nails for 1/2-inch and thicker plywood. Space the nails 6 inches apart at the edges and 12 inches at intermediate fastening points.

When gable-end overhangs are used, extend the trim to the plywood or roofing boards when necessary before the 2- by 2- or 2- by 4-inch fly rafter (facia nailer) is nailed in place.

Roof Trim

Roof trim is installed before the roofing or shingles are applied. The cornice and gable (*rake*) trim for a pitched roof can be the same whether trusses or rafter-ceiling joist framing are used. In its simplest form, the trim consists of a facia board, some-

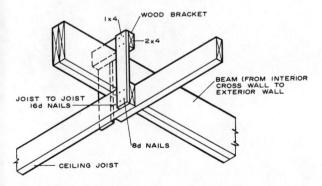

Figure 46—Framing for flush ceiling with wood brackets.

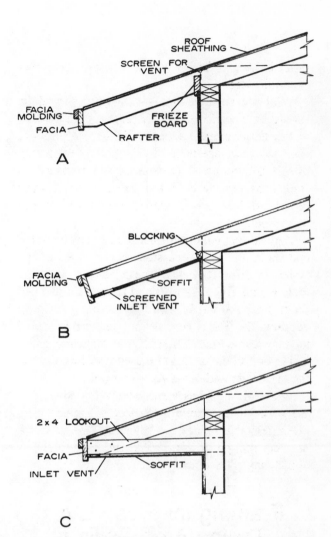

Figure 47—Cornice trim. A, Open cornice; B, sloped closed cornice; C, horizontal closed cornice.

times with molding added. The facia is nailed to the ends of the rafter extensions or to the fly rafters at the gable overhang. With more complete trim, a soffit is usually included at the cornice and gables.

CORNICE

The facia board at rafter ends or at the extension of the truss is often a 1- by 4- or 1- by 6-inch member (fig. 47A). The facia should be nailed to the end of each rafter with two eightpenny galvanized nails. Trim rafter ends when necessary for a

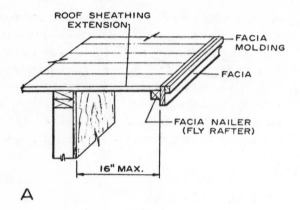

A

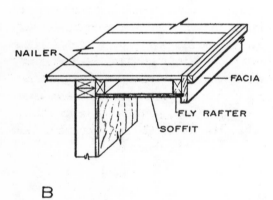

B

Figure 48—Gable-end trim. A, Open gable overhang; B, closed gable overhang.

straight line. Nail 1- by 2-inch facia molding with one eightpenny galvanized nail at rafter locations. In an open cornice, a frieze board is often used between the rafters, serving to terminate siding or siding-sheathing combinations at the rafter line (fig. 47A).

A simple closed cornice is shown in figure 47B. The soffit of plywood, hardboard, or other material is nailed directly to the underside of the rafter extensions. Blocking may be required between rafters at the wall line to serve as a nailing surface for the soffit. Use small galvanized nails in nailing the soffit to the rafters. When inlet attic ventilation is spec-

ified in the plans, it can be provided by a screened slot (fig. 47B), or by small separate ventilators.

When a horizontal closed cornice is used, *lookouts* are fastened to the ends of the rafter and to the wall (fig. 47C). They are face-nailed to the rafters and face- or toenailed to the studs at the wall. Use twelvepenny nails for the facenailing and eightpenny nails for the toenailing.

GABLE END

The gable-end trim may consist of a fly rafter, a facia board, and facia molding (fig. 48A). The 2- by 2- or 2- by 4-inch fly rafter is fastened by nailing through the roof sheathing. Depending on the thickness of the sheathing, use sixpenny or eightpenny nails spaced 12 inches apart. In this type of gable end, the amount of extension should be governed by the thickness of the roof sheathing. When nominal 1-inch boards or plywood thicker than ½ inch is used, the extension should generally be no more than 16 inches. For thinner sheathings, limit the extensions to 12 inches.

A closed gable-end overhang requires nailing surfaces for the soffit. These are furnished by the fly rafter and a nailer or nailing blocks located against the end wall (fig. 48B). An extension of 20 inches might be considered a limit for this type of overhang.

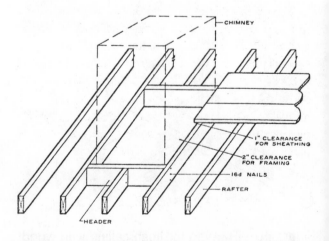

Figure 49—Roof framing at chimney.

From Tent to Cabin

FRAMING FOR CHIMNEYS

An inside chimney, whether of masonry or prefabricated, often requires that some type of framing be provided, where it extends through the roof. This may consist of simple headers between rafters below and above the chimney location, or require two additional rafter spaces (fig. 49). The chimney should have a 2-inch clearance from the framing members and 1 inch from roof sheathing. When nominal 2- or 3-inch wood decking is used, a small header can be used at each end of the decking at the chimney location for support.

Chimneys

Some type of chimney will be required for the heating unit, whether the cabin is heated by oil, gas, or solid fuel. It is normally erected before the roofing is laid but also can be installed after. Chimneys, either of masonry or prefabricated, should be structurally safe and provide sufficient draft for the heating unit and other utilities. Local building regulations often dictate the type to be used. A masonry chimney requires a stable foundation below the frostline and construction with acceptable brick or other masonry units. Some type of *flue lining* is included, together with a cleanout door at the base.

The prefabricated chimney may cost less than the full masonry chimney, considering both materials and labor, as well as providing a small saving in space. These chimneys are normally fastened to and supported by the ceiling joists and should be Underwriter Laboratory tested and approved. They are normally adapted to any type of fuel and come complete with roof flashing, cap assembly, mounting panel, piping, and chimney housing.

Roof Coverings

Roof coverings should be installed soon after the cornice and rake trim are in place to provide pro-

tection for the remaining interior and exterior work. For the low-cost cabin, perhaps the most practical roof coverings are roll roofing or asphalt shingles for pitched roofs and roll roofing in double coverage or *built-up roof* for flat or very low-slope roofs. A good maintenance-free roof is important from the standpoints of protection and the additional cost involved in replacing a cheaper roof after only a few years.

ASPHALT SHINGLES

Asphalt *shingles* may be used for roofs with slopes of 2 in 12 to 7 in 12 and steeper under certain conditions of installation. The most common shingle is perhaps the 3 in 1, which is a 3-tab strip, 12 by 36 inches in size. The basic weight may vary somewhat, but the 235-pound (per square of 3 bundles) is now considered minimum. However, many roofs with 210-pound shingles are giving satisfactory service. A small gable roof cabin uses about 10 squares of shingles, so use of a better shingle would mean about $10 to $20 more per cabin. Cost of application would be the same.

INSTALLATION

Underlay.—A single underlay of 15-pound saturated felt is used under the shingles for roof slopes of 4 in 12 to 7 in 12. A double underlay (double coverage) is required for slopes of 2 in 12 to 4 in 12. Roof slopes over 7 in 12 usually require no underlay. For single underlay, start at the eave line with the 15-pound felt, roll across the roof, and nail or staple the felt in place as required. Allow a 2inch head lap and install the second strip. This leaves a 34-inch exposure for the standard 36-inch-width rolls. Continue in this manner.

A double underlay can be started with two layers at the eave line, flush with the facia board or molding. The second and remaining strips have 19-inch head laps with 17-inch exposures (fig. 50). Cover the entire roof in this manner, making sure that all surfaces have double coverage. Use only enough

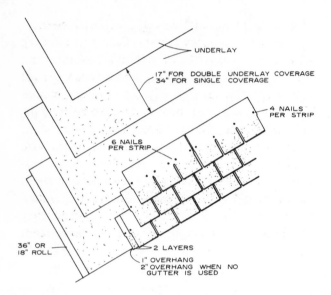

Figure 50—Installing asphalt shingles.

staples or roofing nails to hold the underlay in place. Underlay is normally not required for wood shingles.

Shingles.—Asphalt tab shingles are fastened in place with ¾- or ⅞-inch galvanized roofing nails or with staples, using at least four on each strip (fig. 50). Some roofers use six for each strip for greater wind resistance; one at each end and one at each side of each notch. Locate them above the notches so the next course covers them.

A starter strip and one or two layers of shingles are used at the eave line with a 1-inch overhang beyond the facia trim and ½- to ¾-inch extension at the gable end. When no gutters are used, the overhang should be about 2 inches. This will form a curve during warm weather for a natural drip. Metal edging or flashing is sometimes used at these areas. For slopes of 2 in 12 to 4 in 12, a 5-inch exposure can be used with the double underlay (fig. 50). For slopes of 4 in 12 and over, a 5-inch exposure may also be used with a single underlay.

RIDGE

A *Boston ridge* is perhaps the most common method of treating the ridge portion of the roof.

This consists of 12- by 12-inch sections cut from the 12- by 36-inch shingle strips. They are bent slightly and used in lap fashion over the ridge with a 5-inch exposure distance (fig. 51). In cold weather, be careful that the sections do not crack in bending. The nails used at each side are covered by the lap of the next section. For a positive seal, use a small spot of asphalt cement under each exposed edge.

ROLL ROOFING

When cost is a factor in construction of a cabin, the use of mineral-surfaced roll roofing might be considered. While this type of roofing will not be as attractive as an asphalt shingle roof and perhaps not as durable, it may cost up to 15 percent less for small cabin than standard asphalt shingles.

Roll roofing (65 pounds minimum weight in one-half lap rolls with a mineral surface) should be used over a double underlay coverage. Use a starter strip or a half-roll at the eave line with a 1-inch overhang and nail in place 3 to 4 inches above the edge of the facia (fig. 52). When *gutters* are not included initially, use a 2-inch extension to form a drip edge. Space roofing nails about 6 inches apart. Surface nailing can be used when roof slopes are 4 in 12 and greater.

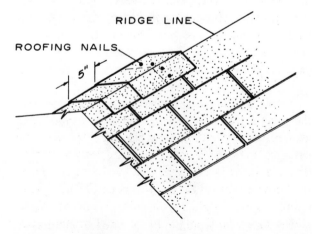

Figure 51—Boston ridge.

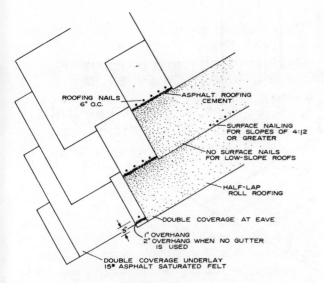

ROOFING NAILS 6" O.C.
ASPHALT ROOFING CEMENT
SURFACE NAILING FOR SLOPES OF 4:12 OR GREATER
NO SURFACE NAILS FOR LOW-SLOPE ROOFS
HALF-LAP ROLL ROOFING
DOUBLE COVERAGE AT EAVE
1" OVERHANG
2" OVERHANG WHEN NO GUTTER IS USED
DOUBLE COVERAGE UNDERLAY 15" ASPHALT SATURATED FELT

Figure 52—Installing roll roofing.

The second (full) roll is now placed along the eave line over a ribbon of asphalt roofing cement or lap-joint material. In low slopes, nailing is done above the lap, cement applied, and the next roll positioned so that the nails are covered. Edge overhang should be about ½ to ¾ inch at the gable ends. When vertical lap joints are required, nail the first edge, then use asphalt adhesive under a minimum 6-inch overlap. Use a sufficient amount of adhesive or lap-joint material to insure a tight joint. On steep slopes, surface nailing along the vertical edge is acceptable. The ridge can be finished with a Boston-type covering or by 12-inch-wide strips of the roll roofing, using at least 6 inches on each side.

CHIMNEY FLASHING

Flashing around the chimney at the junction with the roof is perhaps the most important flashed area in a simple gable roof. The Boston ridge over the shingles must be well installed to prevent wind-driven rain from entering, and the flashing around the chimney must also be well done. Prefabricated chimneys are supplied with built-in flashing which slides under the shingles above and over those below. A good calking or asphalt sealing compound around the perimeter completes the installation.

A masonry chimney requires flashing around the perimeter, which is placed as shingle flashing under the shingles at sides and top and extends at right angles up the sides (fig. 53). In addition, counter-flashing is used on the base of the chimney over the shingle flashing. This is turned in a masonry joint, wedged in place with lead plugs, and sealed with a calking material. Galvanized sheet metal, aluminum, and terneplate (coated sheet iron or steel) are the most common types used for flashing around the chimney. If they are not rust-resistant, they should be given a coat or two of good metal paint.

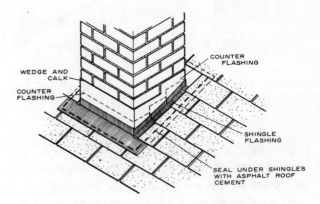

COUNTER FLASHING
WEDGE AND CALK
COUNTER FLASHING
SHINGLE FLASHING
SEAL UNDER SHINGLES WITH ASPHALT ROOF CEMENT

Figure 53—Chimney flashing.

Exterior Wall Coverings

Exterior coverings used over the wall framing commonly consist of a sheathing material followed by some type of finish siding. However, sheathing-siding materials (panel siding) serve as both sheathing and finish material. These materials are most often plywoods or hardboards. While they are somewhat higher in price than conventional sheathing alone, they make it possible to use only a single exterior covering material. Low-cost sheathing materials can be covered with various types of siding—from spaced vertical boards over plywood sheathing

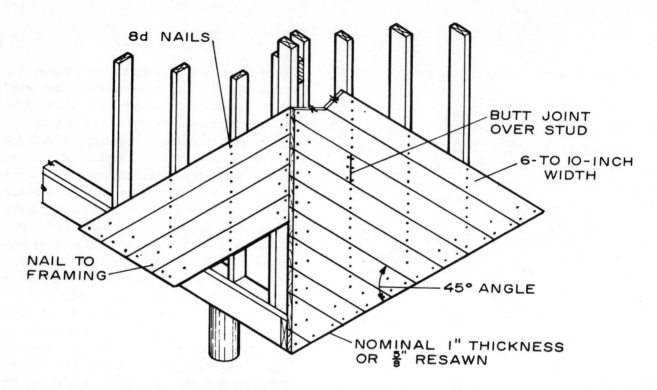

8d NAILS

BUTT JOINT
OVER STUD

6-TO 10-INCH
WIDTH

NAIL TO
FRAMING

45° ANGLE

NOMINAL 1" THICKNESS
OR $\frac{5}{8}$" RESAWN

Figure 54—Diagonal board sheathing.

to horizontal bevel siding over fiberboard, plywood, or other types of sheathing. All combinations should be studied so that cost, utility, and appearance are considered in the selection. The working drawings of the cabin indicate the most suitable siding materials.

SHEATHING

In a low-cost cabin, it is advisable to use a sheathing or a panel-siding material which will provide resistance to racking and thus eliminate the need for diagonal corner bracing on the stud wall. Notching studs and installing bracing can add substantially to labor cost. When siding material does not provide this rigidity and strength, some type of sheathing should be used. Materials which provide resistance to racking are (a) Diagonal board sheathing, (b) structural insulation board (fiberboard) sheathing in $^{25}/_{32}$-inch regular density or ½-inch intermediate fiberboard or nail-base fiberboard sheathing for direct application of shingles, and (c) plywood. The

fiberboard and plywood sheathing must be applied vertically in 4- by 8-foot or longer sheets with edge and center nailing to provide the needed racking resistance. Horizontal wood boards may also be used for sheathing but require some type of corner bracing.

DIAGONAL BOARDS

Diagonal wood sheathing should have a nominal thickness of ⅝ inch (resawn). Edges can be square, *shiplapped*, or tongued-and-grooved. Widths up to 10 inches are satisfactory. Sheathing should be applied at as near a 45° angle as possible as shown in figure 54. Use three eightpenny nails for 6- and 8-inch-wide boards and four eightpenny nails for the 10-inch widths. Also provide nailing along the floor framing or beam faces. Butt joints should be made over a stud unless the sheathing is end and side matched. Depending on the type of siding used, sheathing should normally be carried down over the outside floor framing members. This provides an

From Tent to Cabin

excellent tie between wall and floor framing.

STRUCTURAL INSULATION BOARD

Structural *insulating board* sheathing (fiberboard type) in 4-foot-wide sheets and in 25/32-inch regular-density or ½-inch intermediate fiberboard grades provides the required rigidity without bracing. It must be applied vertically in 8-foot and longer sheets with edge and center nailing (fig. 55). Nails should be spaced 3 inches apart along the edges and 6 inches apart at intermediate supports. Use 1¾-inch roofing nails for the 25/32-inch sheathing and 1½-inch nails for the ½-inch sheathing. Vertical joints should be made over studs. Siding is normally required over this type of sheathing.

PLYWOOD

Plywood sheathing also requires vertical application of 4-foot-wide by 8-foot or longer sheets (fig. 55). Standard (sheathing) grade plywood is normally used for this purpose. Use 5/16 inch minimum thickness for 16-inch stud spacing and ⅜ inch for 24-inch stud spacing. Nails are spaced 6 inches apart at the edges and 12 inches apart at intermediate studs. Use sixpenny nails for 5/16-inch ⅜-inch-thick plywood. Because the plywood sheathing in 5/16- or ⅜-inch sheets provides the necessary strength and rigidity, almost any type of siding can be applied over it.

Plywood and hardboard are also used as a single covering material without sheathing, but grades, thickness, and types vary from normal sheathing requirements. This phase of wall construction will be covered in the following section.

SHEATHING-SIDING MATERIALS—PANEL SIDING

Large sheet materials for exterior coverage (panel siding) can be used along and serve both as sheathing and siding. Plywood, hardboard, and exterior particleboard in their various forms are perhaps the most popular materials used for this purpose. The proper type and size of plywood and hardboard sheets with adequate nailing eliminate the need for bracing. Particleboard requires corner bracing.

These materials are quite reasonable in price, and plywood, for example, can be obtained in grooved, rough-sawn, embossed, and other surface variations as well as in a paper-overlay form. Hardboard can also be obtained in a number of surface variations. The plywood surfaces are most suitable for pigmented stain finishes in various colors. The medium-density, paper-overlay plywoods are an excellent base for exterior paints. Plywoods used for panel siding are normally exterior grades.

The thickness of plywood used for siding varies with the stud spacing. Grooved plywood, such as the "1-11" type, is normally ⅝ by inch thick with ⅜- by ¼-inch-deep grooves spaced 4 or 6 inches apart. This plywood is used when studs are spaced a maximum of 16 inches on center. Ungrooved plywoods should be at least ⅜ inch thick for 16-inch

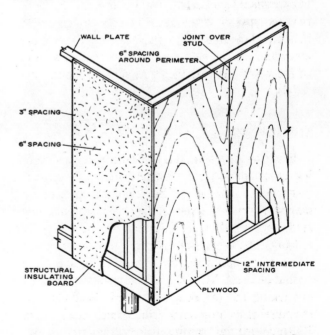

Figure 55—Sheathing with insulation board of plywood (vertical application).

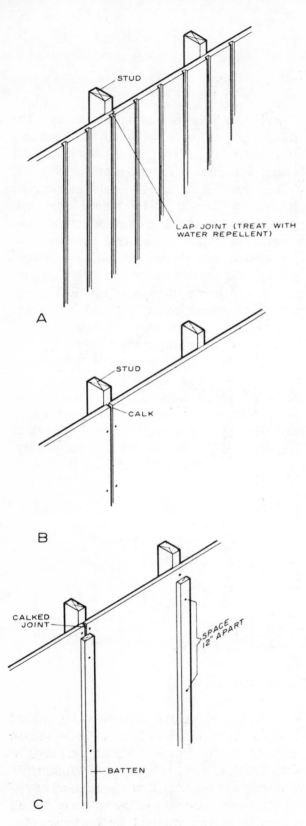

A

B

C

Figure 56—Joint treatment for panel siding. A,
Lap joint; B, calked butt joint; C, butt
joint with batten.

stud spacing and ½ inch thick for 24-inch stud spacing. Plywood panel siding should be nailed around the perimeter and at each intermediate stud. Use sixpenny galvanized siding or other rust-resistant nails for the ⅜-inch plywood and eightpenny for ½-inch and thicker plywood and space 7 to 8 inches apart. Hardboard must be ¼ inch thick and used over 16-inch stud spacing. Exterior particleboard with corner bracing should be ⅝ inch thick for 16-inch stud spacing and ¾ inch thick for 24-inch stud spacing. Space nails 6 inches apart around the edges and 8 inches apart at intermediate studs.

The vertical joint treatment over the stud may consist of a shiplap joint as in the "1-11" paneling (fig. 56A). This joint is nailed at each side after treating with a water-repellent preservative. When a square-edge butt joint is used, a sealant calk should be used at the joint (fig. 56B).

A square-edge butt joint may be covered with battens, which can also be placed over each stud as a decorative variation (fig. 56C). Joints should be calked and the batten nailed over the joint with eightpenny galvanized nails spaced 12 inches apart. Nominal 1- by 2-inch battens are commonly used.

A good detail for this type of siding at gable ends consists of extending the bottom plate of the gable ⅝ to ¾ inch beyond the top of the wall below (fig. 57). This allows a termination of the panel at the lower wall and a good drip section for the gable-end panel.

SIDING—WITH AND WITHOUT SHEATHING

There are a number of sidings, mainly for horizontal application, which might be suitable for walls with or without sheathing. The types most suitable for use over sheathing are: (a) The lower cost lap sidings of wood or hardboard, (b) wood or other type shingles with single or double coursing, (c) vertical boards, and (d) several nonwood materials. Initial cost and maintenance should be the criteria

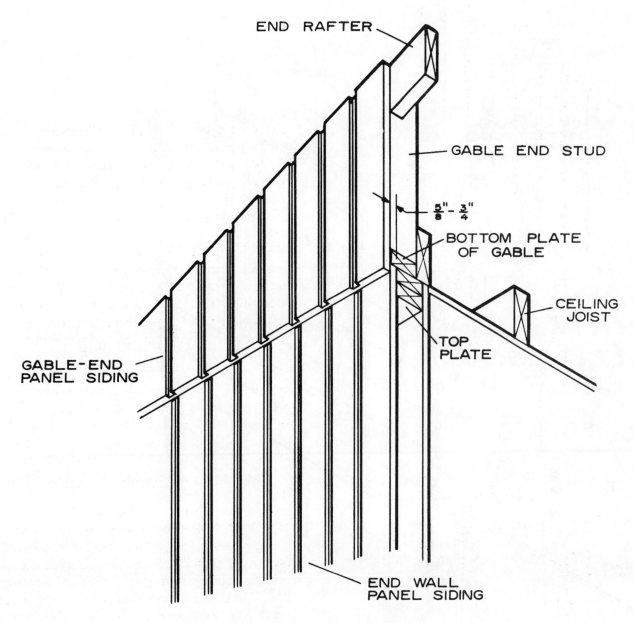

END RAFTER

GABLE END STUD

$\frac{5}{8}" - \frac{3}{4}"$

BOTTOM PLATE
OF GABLE

CEILING
JOIST

TOP
PLATE

GABLE-END
PANEL SIDING

END WALL
PANEL SIDING

Figure 57—Panel siding at gable end.

in the selection. *Drop siding* and nominal 1-inch paneling materials can be used without sheathing under certain conditions. However, such sidings require (a) a rigidly braced wall at each corner and (b) a waterproof paper over the studs before application of the siding.

APPLICATION

Bevel siding.—When siding is used over sheath-ing, window and door frames are normally installed first. This process will be discussed in the section entitled "Exterior Frames". The exposed face of sidings such as *bevel siding* in ½- by 6-inch, ½- by 8-inch, or other sizes should be adjusted so that the butt edges coincide with the bottom of the sill and the top of the *drip cap* of window frames (fig. 58). Use a sevenpenny galvanized siding nail or other corrosion-resistant nail at each stud crossing for the ½-inch-thick siding. The nail should be lo-

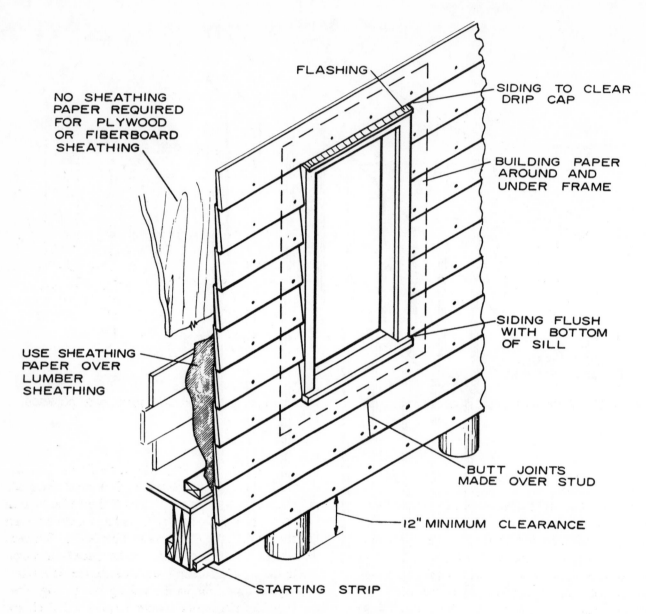

NO SHEATHING
PAPER REQUIRED
FOR PLYWOOD
OR FIBERBOARD
SHEATHING

FLASHING

SIDING TO CLEAR
DRIP CAP

BUILDING PAPER
AROUND AND
UNDER FRAME

SIDING FLUSH
WITH BOTTOM
OF SILL

USE SHEATHING
PAPER OVER
LUMBER
SHEATHING

BUTT JOINTS
MADE OVER STUD

12" MINIMUM CLEARANCE

STARTING STRIP

Figure 58—Installing bevel siding.

cated so as to clear the top edge of the siding course below. Butt joints should be made over a stud. Other horizontal sidings over sheathing should be installed in a similar manner. Nonwood sheathings require nailing into each stud.

Interior corners should butt against a 1½- by 1½-inch corner strip. This wood strip is nailed at interior corners before siding is installed. Exterior corners can be mitered, butted against *corner boards*, or covered with metal corners. Perhaps the corner board and metal corner are the most satisfactory for bevel siding.

Vertical siding.—In low-cost cabin construction, some vertical sidings can be used over stud walls without sheathings; others require some type of sheathing as a backer or nailing base. Matched (tongued-and-grooved) paneling boards can be used directly over the studs under certain conditions. First, some type of corner bracing is required for the stud wall. Second, nailers (blocking) between

From Tent to Cabin

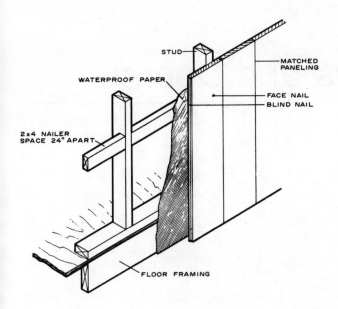

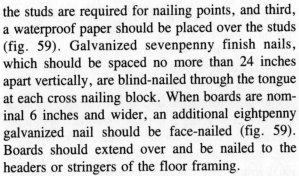

Figure 59—Vertical paneling boards over studs.

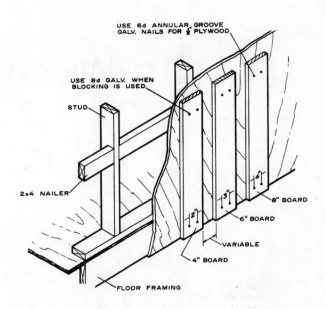

Figure 60—Vertical boards over plywood.

the studs are required for nailing points, and third, a waterproof paper should be placed over the studs (fig. 59). Galvanized sevenpenny finish nails, which should be spaced no more than 24 inches apart vertically, are blind-nailed through the tongue at each cross nailing block. When boards are nominal 6 inches and wider, an additional eightpenny galvanized nail should be face-nailed (fig. 59). Boards should extend over and be nailed to the headers or stringers of the floor framing.

Rough-sawn vertical boards over a plywood backing provide a very acceptable finish. The plywood should be an exterior grade or sheathing grade (standard) with exterior glue. It should be ½ inch thick or 5/16 inch thick with nailing blocks between studs (fig. 60). Rough-sawn boards 4 to 8 inches wide surfaced on one side can be spaced and nailed to the top and bottom wallplates and the floor framing members and to the nailing blocks (fig. 60). Use the surfaced side toward the plywood. A choice in the widths and spacings of boards allows an interesting variation between cabins.

9. Windows and Doors

Window and exterior door units, which include the frames as well as the *sash* or doors, are generally assembled in a manufacturing plant and arrive at the building site ready for installation. Doors may require fitting, however. Simple jambs and sill units for awning or hopper window sash can be made in a small shop with the proper equipment, the wood treated with a water-repellent preservative, and sash fitted and prehung. Only the sash would need to be purchased. However, this system of fabrication is practical only for the simplest units and only when a large number of the same type are required. Thus, for double-hung and sill units for awning or hopper window sash desirable to select the lower cost standard-size units and use a smaller number of windows. A substantial saving can be made, for example, by using one large double-hung window rather than two smaller ones.

Window frames are generally made with nominal 1-inch jambs and 2-inch sills. Sash for the most part are 1⅜ inches thick. Exterior door frames are made from 1½- to 1¾-inch stock. Exterior doors are 1¾ inches thick and the most common are the flush and the panel types.

As a general rule, the amount of natural light provided by the glass area in all rooms (except the kitchen) should be about 10 percent of the floor area. The kitchen can have natural or artificial light, but when an operating window is not available, ventilation should be provided. A bathroom usually is subject to the same requirements. From the standpoint of safety, cabins should have two exterior doors. Local regulations often specify any variations of these requirements. The main exterior door should be 3 feet wide and at least 6 feet 6 inches high; 6 feet 8 inches is a normal standard height for exterior doors. The service or rear door should be at least 2 feet 6 inches wide; 2 feet 8 inches is the usual width. These details are covered in the working drawings for each cabin.

Types of Windows and Doors

Perhaps the most common type of window used in cabins is the double-hung unit (fig. 61). It can be obtained in a number of sizes, is easily *weatherstripped*, and can be supplied with storms or screens. Frames are usually supplied with prefitted

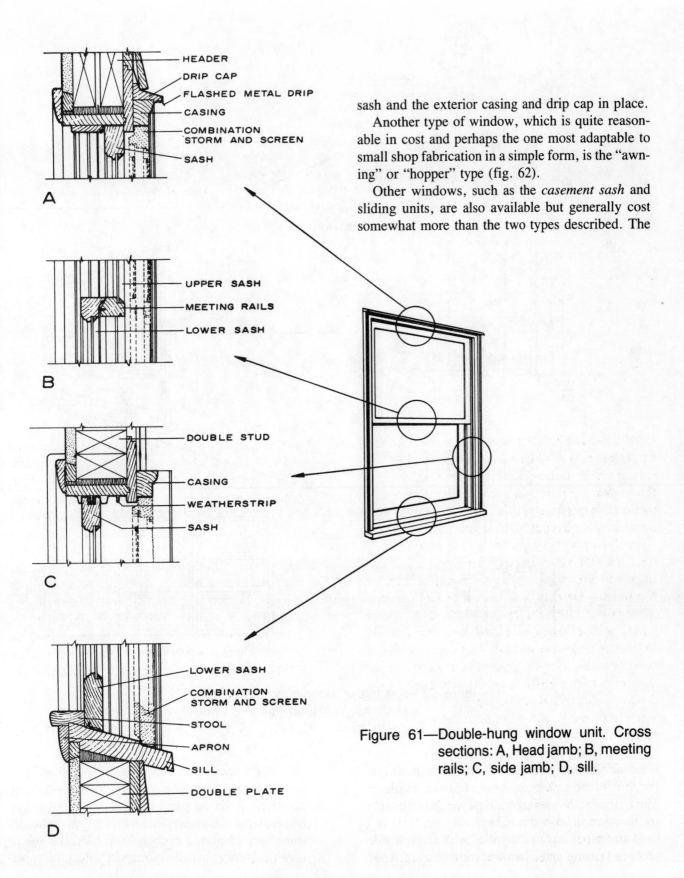

HEADER
DRIP CAP
FLASHED METAL DRIP
CASING
COMBINATION STORM AND SCREEN
SASH

A

UPPER SASH
MEETING RAILS
LOWER SASH

B

DOUBLE STUD
CASING
WEATHERSTRIP
SASH

C

LOWER SASH
COMBINATION STORM AND SCREEN
STOOL
APRON
SILL
DOUBLE PLATE

D

sash and the exterior casing and drip cap in place.

Another type of window, which is quite reasonable in cost and perhaps the one most adaptable to small shop fabrication in a simple form, is the "awning" or "hopper" type (fig. 62).

Other windows, such as the *casement sash* and sliding units, are also available but generally cost somewhat more than the two types described. The

Figure 61—Double-hung window unit. Cross sections: A, Head jamb; B, meeting rails; C, side jamb; D, sill.

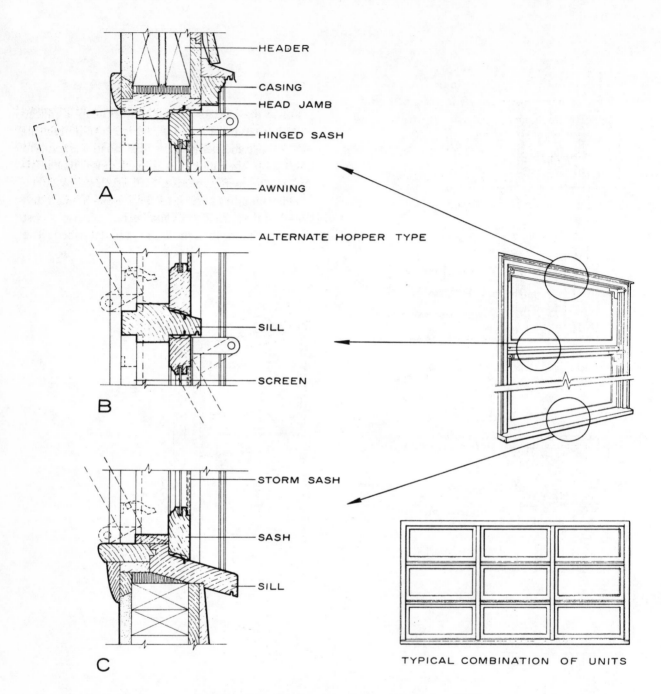

Figure 62—Awning or hopper window. Cross sections: A, Head jamb; B, horizontal mullion; C, sill.

fixed or stationary sash may consist of a simple frame with the sash permanently fastened in place. The frame for the awning window would be suitable for this type of sash (fig. 62).

Door frames are also supplied with exterior side and head casing and a hardwood sill or a softwood sill with a reinforced edge (fig. 63). Perhaps the most practical exterior door, considering cost and performance, is the panel type. A number of styles and patterns are available, most of them featuring some type of glazed opening (fig. 64). The solid-core flush door, usually more costly than the panel

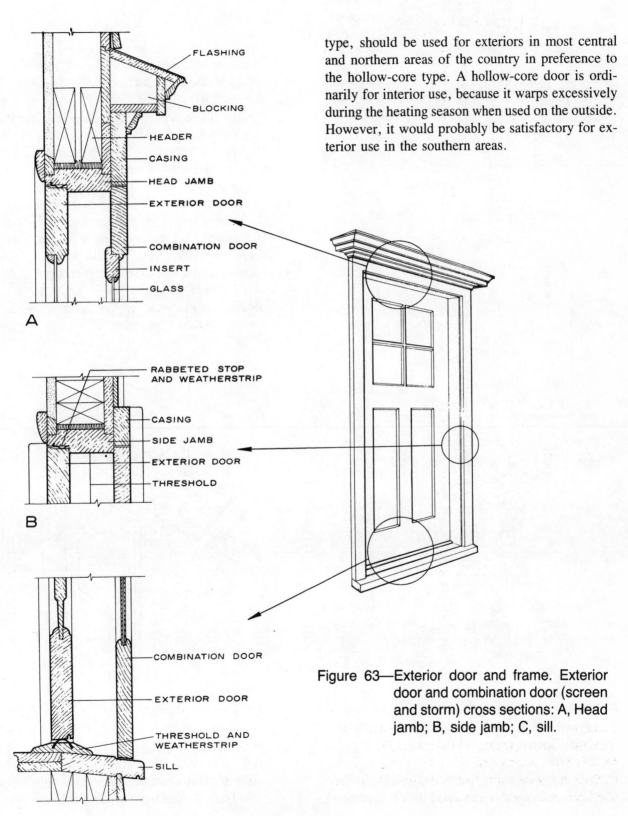

type, should be used for exteriors in most central and northern areas of the country in preference to the hollow-core type. A hollow-core door is ordinarily for interior use, because it warps excessively during the heating season when used on the outside. However, it would probably be satisfactory for exterior use in the southern areas.

A

FLASHING
BLOCKING
HEADER
CASING
HEAD JAMB
EXTERIOR DOOR
COMBINATION DOOR
INSERT
GLASS

B

RABBETED STOP AND WEATHERSTRIP
CASING
SIDE JAMB
EXTERIOR DOOR
THRESHOLD

COMBINATION DOOR
EXTERIOR DOOR
THRESHOLD AND WEATHERSTRIP
SILL

Figure 63—Exterior door and frame. Exterior door and combination door (screen and storm) cross sections: A, Head jamb; B, side jamb; C, sill.

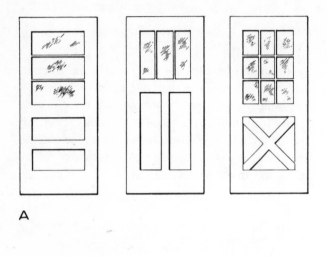

A

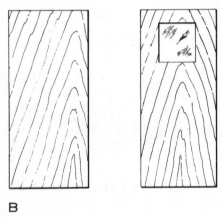

B

Figure 64—Exterior doors. A, Panel type; B, flush type.

Installation

WINDOW FRAMES

Preassembled window frames are easily installed. They are made to be placed in the rough wall openings from the outside and are fastened in place with nails. When a panel siding is used in place of a sheathing and siding combination, the frames are usually installed after the siding is in place. When horizontal siding is used with sheathing, the frames are fastened over the sheathing and the siding applied later.

To insure a water- and windproof installation for a panel-siding exterior, a ribbon of calking sealant (rubber or similar base) is placed over the siding at the location of side and head casing (fig. 65). When a siding material is used over the sheathing, strips of 15-pound asphalt felt should be used around the opening (fig. 58).

The frame is placed in the opening over the calking sealant (preferably with the sash in place to keep it square), and the sill leveled with a carpenter's level. Shims can be used on the inside if necessary. After leveling the sill, check the side casing and jamb with the level and square. Now nail the frame in place using tenpenny galvanized nails through the casing and into the side studs and the header over the window (fig. 66). While nailing, slide the sash up and down to see that they work freely. The nails should be spaced about 12 inches apart and both side and head casing fastened in the same manner. Other types of window units are installed

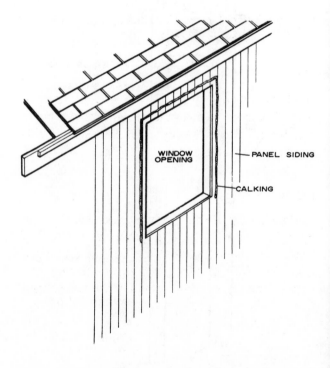

Figure 65—Calking around window opening before installing frame.

From Tent to Cabin

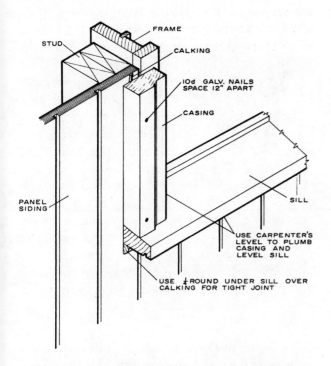

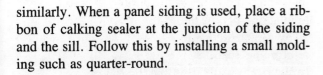

Figure 66—Installation of double-hung window frame.

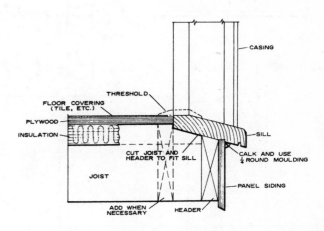

Figure 67—Door installation at sill.

similarly. When a panel siding is used, place a ribbon of calking sealer at the junction of the siding and the sill. Follow this by installing a small molding such as quarter-round.

DOOR FRAMES

Door frames are also fastened over panel siding by nailing through the side and head casing. The header and the joists must first be cut and trimmed (fig. 67). Use a ribbon of calking sealer under the casing. The top of the sill should be the same height as the finish floor so that the *threshold* can be installed over the joint. The sill should be shimmed when necessary to have full bearing on the floor framing. A *quarter-round* molding in combination with calking when necessary for a tight windproof joint should be used under the door sill when a panel siding or other single exterior covering is used. When joists are parallel to the plane of the door, headers and a short support member are necessary at the edge of the sill (fig. 67). The threshold is installed after the finish floor has been laid.

10. Framing Details for Plumbing and Electrical

In cold northern areas, installing plumbing in a basementless cabin requires some care. Some protection for the drain and supply piping in the form of an insulated box from subfloor to the ground is required. Thus, supply and drain lines should be located so as to eliminate long runs. Most plans for low-cost cabins will back the kitchen and bath against a common utility wall so that all plumbing lines can be concentrated there for lower cost installation. In those cabins which do not include all the facilities initially, plumbing lines should be roughed in so that connections can be made at a later date with little trouble.

Floor framing should be arranged so that little or no cutting of joists is required to install closet bends and other drainage and supply lines. This may require the use of a small header, for example, to frame out for the connections.

Plumbing Stack Vents

The utility wall between the kitchen and bath should be constructed so that connections can be made easily. This is usually done by using a nominal 2- by 6-inch plate and placing the studs flatwise at each side (fig. 68A). This will provide the needed wall thickness for the bell of a 4-inch cast-iron soil pipe, which is larger than the thickness of a 2- by 4-inch stud wall. It is also possible to furr out several studs to a 6-inch width at the *soil stack*, rather than thickening the entire wall. In areas where building regulations permit the use of a 3-inch vent pipe, a 2- by 4-inch stud wall may be used, but it requires reinforcing scabs at the top plate (fig. 68B). Use twelvepenny nails to fasten the scabs.

Bathtub Framing

The floor joists in the bathroom which support the tub or shower should be arranged so that no cutting is necessary in connecting the drainpipe. This usually requires only a small adjustment in spacing of joists (fig. 69). When joists are parallel to the length of the tub, they are usually doubled under the outer edge (fig. 69). Tubs are supported at the enclosing walls by hangers or by woodblocks. The wall at the fixtures should also be framed to allow for a small access panel.

Cutting Floor Joists

Floor joists should be cut, notched, or drilled only when there is little effect on their strength. While it is desirable to prevent cutting whenever possible, alterations are sometimes required. Joists should then be reinforced by nailing a 2- by 6-inch scab with twelvepenny nails to each side of the altered member. An additional joist adjacent to the cut joist can also be used.

Notching the top or bottom of the joist should only be done in the end quarter of the span and to not more than one-sixth of the depth. Thus, for a nominal 2- by 8-inch joist 12 feet long, the notch should be not more than 3 feet from the end support and no more than about 1¾ inches deep. When a joist requires more severe alteration, headers and tail beams can be used to eliminate the need for

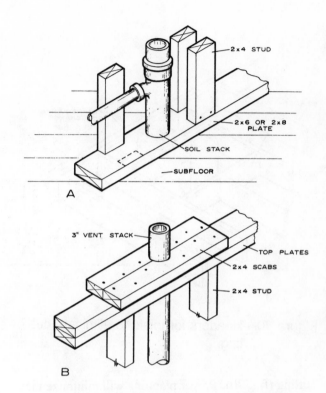

Figure 68—Framing for vent stack. A, 4-inch soil pipe; B, 3-inch stack vent.

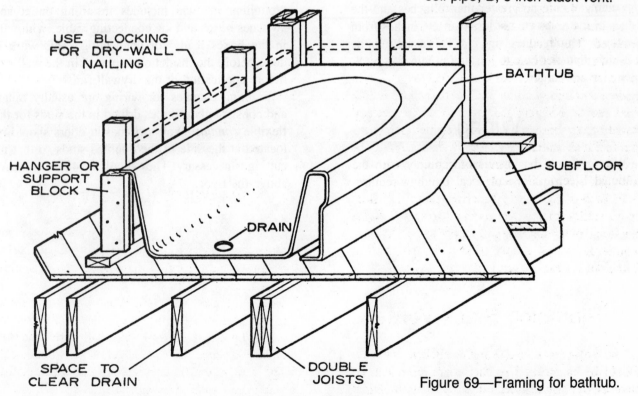

Figure 69—Framing for bathtub.

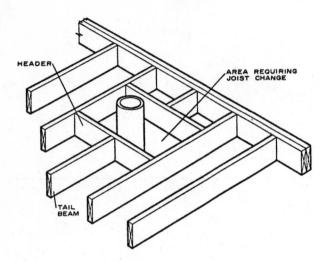

Figure 70—Headers for joists to eliminate cutting.

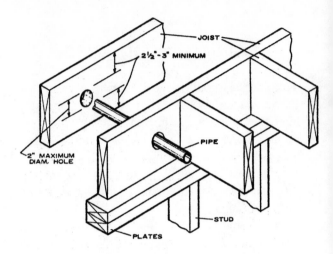

Figure 71—Boring holes in joists.

cutting (fig. 70). Proper planning will minimize the need for altering joists.

When necessary, holes may be bored in joists if the diameters are no greater than 2 inches and the edges of the holes are not less than 2½ inches from the top or bottom edges (fig. 71). This usually limits a 2-inch-diameter hole to joists of nominal 2- by 8-inch size and larger.

Wiring

Wiring should be installed to comply with the National Electric Code or local building require-ments. Interior wiring for electrical services is usu-ally started sometime after the cabin has been en-closed. The initial phase of wiring is termed "roughing in" and includes installing outlet and switches boxes and the connecting cable, with wire in the boxes ready for connecting. This work is done before the insulation is placed in the wall and before application of the drywall finish.

Framing changes for wiring are usually minor and consist only of holes drilled in the studs for the flexible *conduit*. Wall switches at doors should be located at the side of the doubled studs so that no cutting is necessary. They should be 48 to 54 inches above the floor.

11. Insulation and Ventilation

Thermal Insulation

Thermal insulation is used to minimize heat loss during the heating season and to reduce the inflow of heat during hot weather. Resistance to the passage of warm air is provided by materials used in wall, ceiling, and floor construction.

In constructing a crawl-space cabin, other factors must be considered in addition to providing insulation, such as: (a) Use of a *vapor barrier* with the insulation; (b) protection from ground moisture by the use of a vapor barrier ground cover (especially true if the crawl space is enclosed with a full foundation or skirt boards); and (c) use of both attic and crawl-space ventilation when required. Insulation and vapor barriers are discussed here. Ventilation is covered in the next section.

The amount of insulation used in walls, floor, and ceilings usually depends on the geographic location of the cabin. In all parts of the country, at least 3½-inch thick insulation is essential in walls, and where winters are severe, the addition of foam sheathing or the alternate 2 by 6 stud wall with 5½-inch thick insulation is often necessary. Ceilings

should have a "U" 0.05 or lower depending on the climate. Some codes allow slightly higher "U" values for roof decks, and requirements are greatly reduced for seasonal cabins that need little heating or cooling. Floors also require insulation. Many States now have minimum insulation requirements and a national mandatory standard for new construction is expected soon. Legal requirements should be checked with local code authorities during the planning stage for any cabin.

Types of Insulation

Commercial insulating materials which are most practical in the construction of low-cost cabins are: (a) Flexible types in blanket and batt forms, (b) loose-fill types, and (c) *rigid insulation* such as building boards or insulation boards. Others include reflective insulations, expanded plastic foams, and the like.

The common types of blanket and batt insulation, as well as loose-fill types, are made from wood and cotton fiber and mineral wool processed from rock, slag, or glass. Insulating or building board may be made of wood or cane fibers, of glass fibers, and of expanded foam.

In comparing the relative insulating values of various materials, a 1-inch thickness of typical blanket insulation is about equivalent to (a) 1½ inches of insulating board, (b) 3 inches of wood, or (c) 18 inches of common brick. Thus, when practical, the use of even a small amount of thermal insulation is good practice.

The insulating values of several types of flexible insulation do not vary a great deal. Most loose-fill insulations have slightly lower insulating values than the same material in flexible form. However, fill insulations, such as *vermiculite*, have less than 60 percent the value of common flexible insulations. Most lower density sheathing or structural insulating boards have better insulating properties than vermiculite.

Vapor Barriers

Vapor barriers are often a part of blanket or batt insulation, but they may also be a separate material which resists the movement of water vapor to cold or exterior surfaces. They should be placed as close as possible to the warm side of all exposed walls, floors, and ceiling. When used as ground covers in crawl spaces, they resist the movement of soil moisture to exposed wood members. In walls, they eliminate or minimize condensation problems which can cause paint peeling. In ceilings they can, with good *attic ventilation*, prevent moisture problems in attic spaces.

Vapor barriers commonly consist of: (a) Papers with a coating or lamination of an asphalt material; (b) plastic films; (c) aluminum or other metal foils; and (d) various paint coatings. Most blanket and batt insulations are supplied with a laminated paper or an aluminum foil vapor barrier. Friction-type batts usually have no vapor barriers. For such insulation, the vapor barrier should be added after the insulation is in place. Vapor barriers should generally be a part of all insulating processes.

Vapor barriers are usually classed by their *"perm"* value, which is a rate of water-vapor movement through a material. The lower this value, the greater the resistance of the barrier. A perm rating of 0.50 or less is considered satisfactory for vapor barriers. Two-mil (0.002-inch-thick) polyethylene film, for example, has a perm rating of about 0.25.

When the crawl space is enclosed during or after construction of the cabin, or the soil under the cabin is quite damp, a *soil cover* should be used. This vapor barrier should have a perm value of 1.0 or less and should be laid over the ground, using about a 4-inch lap along edges and ends. Stones or half-sections of brick can be used at the laps and around the perimeter to hold the material in place. The ground should be leveled before placing the cover. Materials such as polyethylene, roll roofing, and asphalt laminated barriers are satisfactory for ground covers.

Where and How to Insulate

Insulation in some form should be used at all exterior walls, floors, and at the ceiling as a separate material or as a part of the cabin structure in most climates.

FLOORS

Blanket insulation in 1-inch thickness can be installed under a tongued-and-grooved plywood subfloor as previously described and illustrated in figure 14. However, this type is most commonly applied between the joists. In applying insulation, be sure that the vapor barrier faces up, against the bottom of the plywood.

The use of friction or other types of insulating batts between joists has been shown in figure 18. This insulation can be installed any time after the cabin has been enclosed and roofing installed. When

From Tent to Cabin

friction-type insulation without a vapor barrier is used, a separate vapor barrier should be placed over the joists before the subfloor is nailed in place. Laminated or foil-backed kraft paper barriers or plastic films can be used. They should be lapped 4 to 6 inches and stapled only enough to hold the barriers in place until the subfloor is installed.

When batts are not the friction type, they usually require some support in addition to the adhesive shown in figure 18. This support can be supplied simply by the use of small, 3/16- by 3/4-inch or similar size, wood strips cut slightly longer than the joist space so that they spring into place (fig. 72). They can be spaced 24 to 36 inches apart or as needed. Wire netting nailed between joists may also be used to hold the batt insulation (fig. 72). The 1-inch-thick or thicker blanket insulation can also be installed in this way if desired.

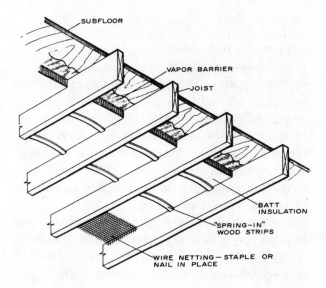

Figure 72—Installing insulating batts in floor.

WALL INSULATION

When blanket or batt insulation for the walls contains a vapor barrier, the barrier should be placed toward the room side and the insulation stapled in place (fig. 73A). An additional small strip of vapor barrier at the bottom and top plates and around openings will insure good resistance to vapor movements in these critical areas.

When friction or other insulation without a vapor barrier is used in the walls, the entire interior surface should be covered with a vapor barrier. This is often accomplished by the use of wall-height rolls of 2- or 4-mil plastic film (fig. 73B). Other types of vapor barriers extending from bottom plate to top plate are also satisfactory. The studs, the window and door headers, and plates should also be covered with the vapor barrier for full protection. The full-height plastic film is usually carried over the entire window opening and cut out only after the dry wall has been installed. Staple or tack just enough to hold the vapor barrier in place until the interior wall finish is installed.

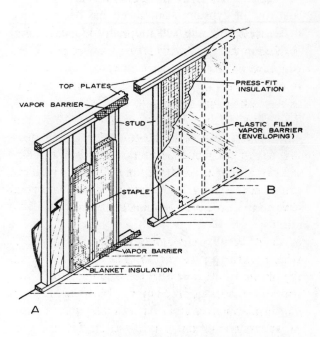

Figure 73—Wall insulating. A, Blanket insulating with vapor barrier; B, plastic film vapor barrier.

CEILING INSULATION

Loose-fill or batt-type ceiling insulation is often placed during or after the dry-wall ceiling finish is applied, depending on the roof design. In ceilings having no attic or joist space, such as those with wood roof decking, the insulation is normally a part of the roof construction and may include ceiling tile, thick wood decking, and structural insulating board in various combinations. This type of construction has been covered in the section on framing of low-slope roofs and figure 38.

Loose-fill insulation, blown or hand placed, can be used where there is an attic space high enough for easy access. It can be poured in place and leveled off (fig. 74A). A vapor barrier should be used under the insulation.

Batt insulation with attached vapor barrier can be used in most types of roof and ceiling constructions with or without an attic space. The batt insulation is made to fit between ceiling or roof members spaced 16 or 24 inches on center. After the first row of gypsum board sheets has been applied in a level ceiling, the batts (normally 48 inches long) are placed between ceiling joists with the vapor barrier facing down. The next row of gypsum board is applied and the batts added. At the opposite side of the room, the batts should be stapled lightly in place before the final dry-wall sheets are applied. When one set of members serves as both ceiling joists and rafters, an airway should be allowed for ventilation (fig. 74B).

Ventilation

Providing ventilation is an important phase of construction for all cabins regardless of their cost. This includes ventilation of attic areas, the spaces between combination joist-rafters, and the crawl space. Only a small amount of crawl-space ventilation is normally required when the crawl space is entirely enclosed and a soil cover is used. Good *attic ventilation* is important to prevent condensation of moisture which can enter from the heated rooms below. Furthermore, good attic ventilation means a cooler attic in the summertime and greater comfort in the living areas below.

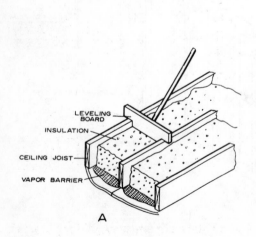

A

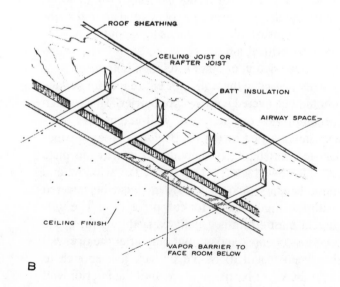

B

Figure 74—Ceiling insulation. A, Fill type; B, batt type.

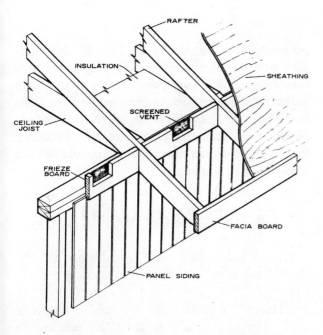

Figure 75—Inlet ventilators for open cornice.

ATTIC VENTILATION

The two types of attic ventilators used are the inlet and the outlet ventilator. Inlet ventilators are normally located in the soffit area of the cornice or at the junction of the wall and roof. They may be single ventilators or a continuous *vent*.

In some cabins, it is practical to use only the outlet ventilators usually in the gable end of a cabin that has no room for inlet ventilators.

Both inlet ventilators and outlet ventilators should be used whenever possible. In a cabin with an open cornice, inlet ventilators are usually most effective when installed in the frieze board which fits between the open rafters. Two saw cuts can be made in the top of the frieze board, the wood between removed, and screen installed on the back face (fig. 75). These openings are distributed along the sidewall to insure good ventilation. These details are ordinarily indicated in the working drawings for each cabin.

OUTLET VENTILATORS

Outlet ventilators should be located as near the ridge of a pitched roof as possible. In a gable-roofed cabin, the outlet ventilators are located near the top of the gable end (fig. 76A and B). Many types are available with wood or metal *louvers*. Some of the additional forms are shown in figure 76C, D and E. When ladder framing is used on a wide gable overhang, ventilators are often used along the soffit area (fig. 76F). Ladder framing is formed by lookout members which bear on an interior truss or rafter and on the end wall and extend beyond to a fly rafter. Roof ventilators are available in various forms. They consist of covered and screened metal units designed to fit most roof slopes. They are adapted to gable- or *hip-roof* cabins, and should be located on the rear slope of the roof as near the ridge as possible.

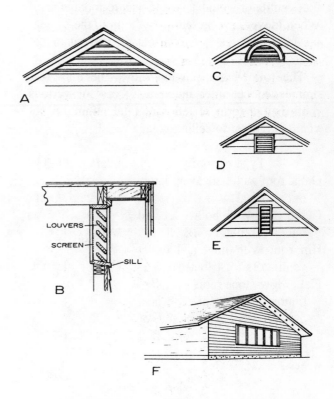

Figure 76—Outlet ventilators. A, Triangular; B, section through louvers; C, half circle; D, square; E, rectangular; F, gable overhang.

INLET VENTILATORS

Inlet ventilators installed in the soffit area of a closed cornice can consist of individual units spaced as required (fig. 77A). Another system of inlet ventilation consists of a narrow slot cut in the soffit (fig. 77B). All ventilators should be screened.

Amount of Ventilation

The net or face area of the ventilators required for a cabin is normally based on some ratio of the ceiling area. The net area is the total area of the ventilator with deductions made for the screening and louvers. When insect screen is used, the total area is reduced by half. In other words, a 1-square-foot ventilator would have a ½-square-foot net area. When louvers are present in addition to the screen, the total net area is only about 40 percent of the total.

The following tabulation shows the total recommended net inlet and outlet areas for various roofs in the form of ratios of total minimum net ventilating area to ceiling area:

Type of roof	Inlet	Outlet
Gable roof with outlet ventilators only		1/300
Gable roof with both inlet and outlet ventilators	1/900	1/900
Hip roof with inlet and outlet ventilators (distributed)	1/900	1/900
Flat or low-slope roofs with ventilators in soffit or eave area only (located at each side of house)		1/250

As an example, assume a cabin has 900 square feet of ceiling area and a gable roof with a soffit, so both inlet and outlet ventilators can be used. Screen reduces the area by half, so areas required are 1/450 of the ceiling. Thus 900 × 1/450 = 2 square feet. So use two outlet ventilators, each with 1 square foot. The total inlet area (well distributed) should also total 2 square feet.

Crawl-Space Ventilation

As previously mentioned, crawl-space ventilation is not required unless the space is entirely closed. When required, small ventilators can be located in the foundation walls on at least two opposite sides. The amount of ventilation depends on the presence of a ground cover or vapor barrier. When a vapor barrier is used, the total recommended net area of the ventilators is 1/1,500 of the floor area. Use at least two screened vents located on opposite ends of the cabin. When no vapor barrier is present, the total net area should be 1/150 of the floor area with the ventilators well distributed.

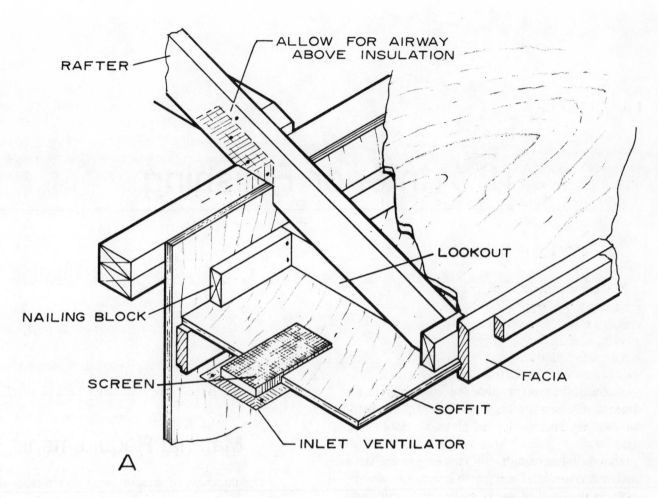

RAFTER

ALLOW FOR AIRWAY ABOVE INSULATION

LOOKOUT

NAILING BLOCK

SCREEN

FACIA

SOFFIT

INLET VENTILATOR

A

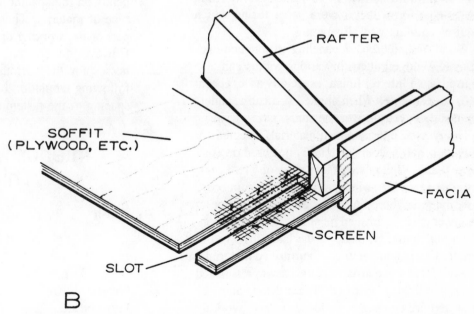

RAFTER

SOFFIT (PLYWOOD, ETC.)

FACIA

SCREEN

SLOT

B

Figure 77—Soffit inlet ventilators. A, Spaced
units; B, slot type.

From Tent to Cabin

12. Interior Finishing

Some of the most practical low-cost materials for interior finish are the gypsum boards, the hardboards, the fiberboards, and plywood. Hardboard, fiberboard, gypsum board, and plywood are often prefinished and require only fastening to the studs and ceiling joists. The gypsum boards can also be obtained prefinished, but in their most common and lowest cost form, they have a paper facing which requires painting or wallpapering.

Wood and fiberboard paneling in tongued-and-grooved V-edge pattern in various widths can also be used as an interior finish, especially as an accent wall, for example. When applied vertically, nailers are used between or over the studs.

The type of interior finish materials selected for a low-cost cabin should primarily be based on cost. These materials may vary from a low of 5 to 6 cents per square foot for ⅜-inch unfinished gypsum board to as much as three times this amount for some of the lower cost prefinished materials. However, consideration should be made of the labor involved in joint treatment and painting of unfinished materials. As a result, in some instances, the use of prefinished materials might be justified. These details and material requirements are included in the working drawings or the accompanying specifications for each cabin. Before interior wall and ceiling finish is applied, insulation should be in place and wiring,

heating *ducts*, and other utilities should be roughed in.

Material Requirements

The thickness of interior covering materials depends on the spacing of the studs or joists and the type of material. These requirements are usually a part of the working drawings or the specifications. However, for convenience, the recommended thicknesses for the various materials are listed in the following tabulation based on their use and on the spacing of the fastening members:

Interior Material Finish Thickness

Finish	Minimum material thickness (inches) when framing is spaced	
	16 inches	24 inches
Gypsum board	⅜	½
Plywood	¼	⅜
Hardboard	¼	....
Fiberboard	½	¾
Wood paneling	⅜	½

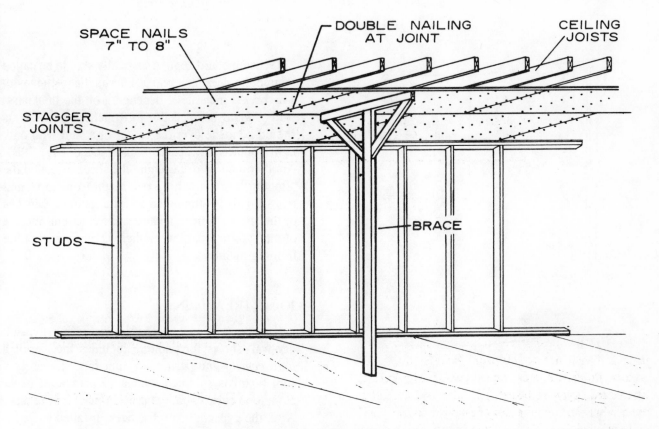

SPACE NAILS 7" TO 8"

DOUBLE NAILING AT JOINT

CEILING JOISTS

STAGGER JOINTS

STUDS

BRACE

Figure 78—Installing gypsum board on ceiling.

For ceilings, when the long direction of the gypsum board sheet is at right angles to the ceiling joists, use ⅜-inch thickness for 16-inch spacing and ½-inch for 24-inch joist spacing. When sheets are parallel, spacing should not exceed 16 inches for ½-inch gypsum board. Fiberboard ceiling tile in ½-inch thickness spacing of nailing strips.

Gypsum Board

APPLICATION

Gypsum board used for dry-wall finish is a sheet material composed of a gypsum filler faced with paper. Sheets are 4 feet wide and 8 feet long or longer. The edges are usually recessed to accommodate taped joints. The ceiling is usually covered before the wall sheets are applied. Start at one wall and proceed across the room. When batt-type ceil-

ing insulation is used, it can be placed as each row of sheets is applied. Use fivepenny (1⅝-inch-long) cooler-type nails for ½-inch gypsum and fourpenny (1⅜-inch) nails for ⅜-inch gypsum board. Ring-shank nails ⅛ inch shorter than these can also be used. Nailheads should be large enough so that they do not penetrate the surface.

Adjoining sheets should have only a light contact with each other. End joints should be staggered and centered on a ceiling joist or bottom chord of a truss. One or two braces slightly longer than the height of the ceiling can be used to aid in installing the gypsum sheets (fig. 78). Nails are spaced 6 to 8 inches apart and should be very lightly dimpled with the hammerhead. Do not break the surface of the paper. Edge or end joints should be doubled-nailed. Minimum edge nailing distance is ⅜ inch.

Vertical or horizontal application can be used on the walls. Horizontal application of gypsum board is often used when wall-length sheets eliminate ver-

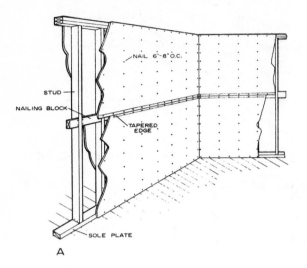

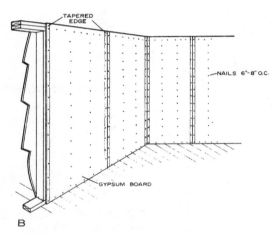

Figure 79—Installing gypsum board on walls. A, Horizontal application; B, vertical application.

tical joints. The horizontal joint thus requires only taping and treating. For normal application, horizontal joint reinforcing is not required. However, nailing blocks may be used between studs for a damage-resistant joint for the thinner gypsum sheets (fig. 79A). Horizontal application is also suitable to the laminated system in which 3/8-inch gypsum sheets are nailed vertically and room-length sheets are applied horizontally with a wallboard or contact adhesive. While this results in an excellent wall, it is much more costly than the single application.

Gypsum board applied vertically should be nailed around the perimeter and at intermediate studs with 1 3/8- or 1 5/8-inch nails, depending on the thickness. Nails should be spaced 6 to 8 inches apart. Joints should be made over the center of a stud with only light contact between adjoining sheets (fig. 79B). Another method of fastening the sheets is called the "floating top". In this system, the top horizontal row of nails is eliminated and the top 6 or 8 inches of the sheet are free. This is said to prevent fracture of the gypsum board when there is movement of the framing members.

JOINT TREATMENT

The conventional method of preparing gypsum dry-wall sheets for painting includes the use of a *joint cement* and perforated joint tape. Some gypsum board is supplied with a strip of joint paper along one edge, which is used in place of the tape. After the gypsum board has been installed and each nail driven in a "dimple" fashion (fig. 80A), the walls and ceiling are ready for treatment. Joint cement ("spackle" compound), which comes in powder or ready-mixed form, should have a soft putty consistency so that it can be easily spread with a trowel or wide putty knife. Some manufacturers provide a joint cement and a finish joint compound which is more durable and less subject to shrinkage than standard fillers. The procedure for taping (fig. 80B) is as follows:

1. Use a wide spackling knife (5-inch) to spread the cement over the tapered and other butt edges, starting at the top of the wall.

2. Press the tape into the recess with the knife until the joint cement is forced through the small perforations.

3. Cover the tape with additional cement to a level surface, feathering the outer edges. When edges are not recessed, apply tape in the normal manner, but feather out the cement farther so that the joint is level.

4. When dry, sand lightly and apply a thin second coat, feathering the edges again. A third coat

From Tent to Cabin

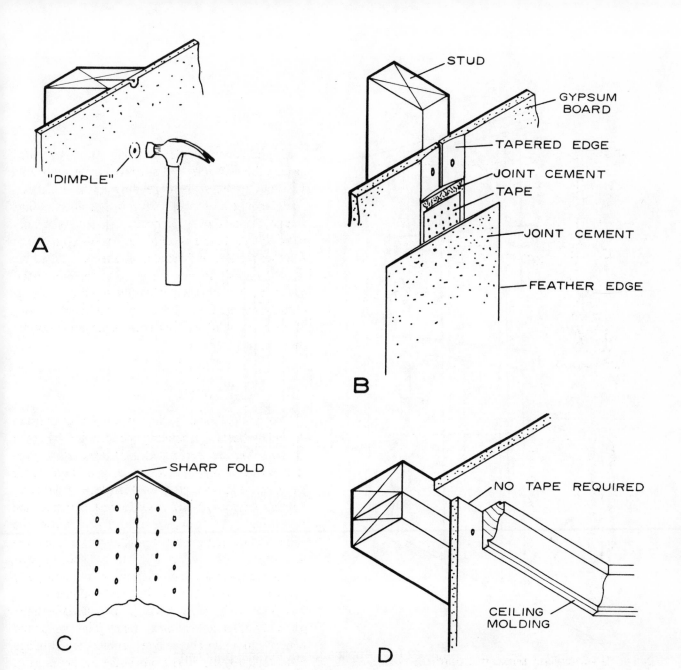

Figure 80—Preparing gypsum dry-wall sheets for painting. A, Drive nails in "dimple" fashion; B, detail of joint treatment; C, corner tape; D, ceiling moldings.

may be required after the second has dried.

5. After cement is dry, sand smooth.

6. For hiding nail indentations at members between edges, fill with joint cement. A second coat is usually required.

Interior and exterior corners may be treated with perforated tape. Fold the tape down the center to a right angle (fig. 80C). Now, (a) apply cement on each side of the corner, (b) press tape in place with the spackle or *putty* knife, and (c) finish with joint cement and sand when dry. Wallboard corner beads of metal or plastic also can be used to serve as a corner guide and provide added strength. They are nailed to outside corners and treated with joint ce-

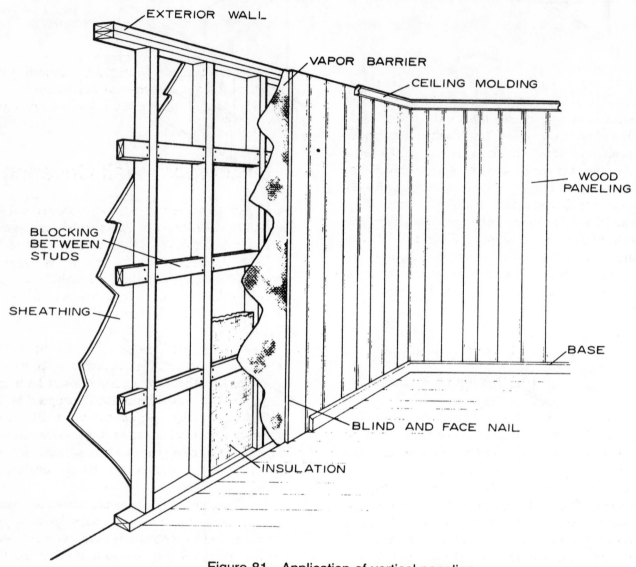

Figure 81—Application of vertical paneling.

ment. The junctions of the wall and ceiling can also be finished with a wood molding in any desired shape, which will eliminate the need for joint treatment (fig. 80D). Use eightpenny finish nails spaced about 12 to 16 inches apart and nail into the wallplate behind.

Treatment around window and door openings depends on the type of casing used. When a casing bead and trim are used instead of a wood casing, the jambs and the beads may be installed before or during application of the gypsum wall finish. These details will be covered in the section on "Interior Doors, Frames, and Trim".

Plywood and Hardboard

The application of prefinished 4-foot-wide hardboard and plywood sheets is relatively simple. They are normally used vertically and can be fastened with small finish nails (brads). Use nails 1½ inches long for ¼- or ⅜-inch-thick materials and space about 8 to 10 inches apart at all edges and intermediate studs. Edge spacing should be about ⅜ inch. Set the nails slightly with nail set. Many prefinished materials are furnished with small nails that require no setting because their heads match the color of the finish.

The use of panel and contact adhesives in applying prefinished sheet materials is becoming more popular and usually eliminates nails, except those used to align the sheets. Manufacturer's directions should be followed in this method of application.

In applying sheet materials such as hardboard or plywood paneling, it is good practice to insure dry, warm conditions before installing. Furthermore, place the sheets in an upright position against the wall, lined up about as they will be installed, and allow them to take on the condition of the room for at least 24 hours. This is also true for wood or fiberboard paneling covered in the following paragraphs.

Wood or Fiberboard Paneling

Tongued-and-grooved wood or fiberboard (insulating board) paneling in various widths may be applied to walls in full lengths or above the wainscot. Wood paneling should not be too wide (nominal 8-inch) and should be installed at a moisture content of about 8 percent in most areas of the country. However, the moisture content should be about 6 percent in the dry Southwest and about 11 percent in the Southern and Coastal areas of the country. In this type of application, wood strips should be used over the studs or nailing blocks placed between them (fig. 81). Space the nailers not more than 24 inches apart.

For wood paneling, use a 1½- to 2-inch finishing or casing nail and blind-nail through the tongue. For nominal 8-inch widths, a face nail may be used near the opposite edge. Fiberboard paneling (planking) is often supplied in 12- and 16-inch widths and is applied in the same manner as the wood paneling. In addition to the blind nail or staple at the tongue, two face nails may be required. These are usually set slightly unless they are color-matched. A 2-inch finish nail is usually satisfactory, depending on the thickness. Panel and contact adhesives may also be

used for this type of interior finish, eliminating the majority of the nails except those at the tongue. On outside walls, use a vapor barrier under the paneling (fig. 81).

Bathroom Wall Covering

When a complete prefabricated shower stall is used in the bathroom instead of a tub, no special wall finish is required. However, if a tub is used, some type of waterproof wall covering is normally required around it to protect the wall. This may consist of several types of finish from a coated hardboard paneling to various ceramic, plastic, and similar tiles.

In the interest of economy, one of the special plastic-surfaced hardboard materials is perhaps a good choice. These are applied in sheet form and fastened with an adhesive ordinarily supplied by the manufacturer of the prefinished board. Plastic or other type moldings are used at the inside corners, at tub edges, at the joints, and as end caps. Several types of calking sealants also provide satisfactory joints.

Other finishes such as ceramic, plastic, and metal tile are installed over a special water-resistant type of gypsum board. Adhesive is spread with a serrated trowel and the 4¼- by 4¼-inch or other size tile pressed in place. A joint cement is used in the joints of ceramic tile after the adhesive has set. The plastic, metal, or ceramic type of wall covering around the tub area would usually cost somewhat more than plastic-surfaced hardboard. However, almost any type of wall finish can be added at the convenience of the homeowner at any time after the cabin is constructed.

Floor Coverings

It is common practice to install wood flooring after the wall finish is applied. This is generally followed by installation of interior trim such as door

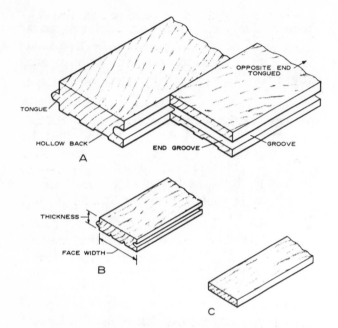

Figure 83—Strip flooring. A, Side and end matched; B, side matched; C, square edged.

Types of Flooring

The term "finish flooring" usually applies to the material used as the final wearing surface. In its simplest form, it may be merely a *sealer* or a paint finish applied to a tongued-and-grooved plywood subfloor. Perhaps one of the most practical floor coverings for low-cost cabins is some type of resilient tile such as asphalt, rubber, vinyl asbestos, etc. These materials may vary a great deal in cost. Because they are applied with an adhesive, the installation costs are usually quite low when compared to other finish flooring. However, when prices are competitive with other materials, wood finish floors in the various patterns might be selected.

Hardwood strip flooring in the best grades is used in many higher cost cabins (fig. 83A). Thinner tongued-and-grooved strip flooring (fig. 83B) and thin square-edged flooring (fig. 83C) are lower in cost than $^{25}/_{32}$-inch strip flooring and might be considered for use initially or at a later date. The use

jambs, casing, base, and other moldings. Wood floors would then be sanded and finished *after* the interior work is completed. Some variation of this is necessary when casing bead and trim are used in dry-wall construction to eliminate the need for standard wood casing around windows and doors. In this instance, the door jambs are installed before the wall finish is applied. Adjustment for the flooring thickness is then made by raising the bottom of the door jambs. Details of the casing bead and trim for dry-wall finishes are included in the next section—"Interior Doors, Frames, and Millwork".

However, for finish floors such as resilient tile and prefinished wood block flooring, it is usually necessary to have most, if not all, the interior work completed before installation. This is especially true of resilient flooring. Manufacturers' recommendations usually state that all tradesmen will have completed their work, even the painters, before the resilient tile is installed. In such cases, a resilient cove base might be a part of the finish, rather than the conventional wood base.

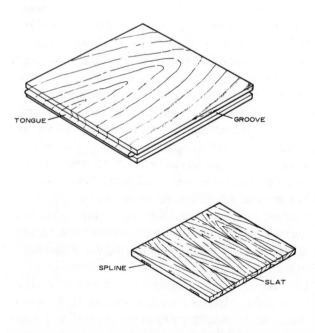

Figure 84—Wood block flooring.

of low-grade softwood strip flooring with a natural or painted finish can also be considered. However, the installation costs of these materials are usually higher than those for resilient coverings. Many types require sanding and finishing after they are nailed in place. Another wood flooring, the parquet or wood block floor (fig. 84) is usually prefinished, is supplied in 6- by 6- or 9- by 9-inch squares, and is installed by nailing or with an adhesive. These materials, while costing more than strip flooring, require no finishing.

Thus, the cost of a finish flooring for a small cabin may vary from a few dollars for a floor sealer or paint on the plywood to an installed cost of $350 or more for finish floors. When a complete floor covering is required, some type of resilient tile is perhaps the best initial choice for a low-cost cabin. Later on, the more desirable wood floors can be easily applied over existing tile floors.

Installation of Flooring

STRIP FLOORING

Before laying strip flooring, be sure that the subfloor is clean and covered with a *building paper* when a board subfloor is used. This will aid in preventing air infiltration and help maintain a comfortable temperature at the floor level when a crawl space is used. The building paper should be chalk-lined at the joists as a guide in nailing the strip flooring. Before laying the flooring, the bundles should be opened and the flooring spread out and exposed to a warm, dry condition for at least 24 hours, and preferably 48 hours. Moisture content of the flooring should be 6 percent for the dry Southwest area, 10 percent for Southern and Coastal areas, and 7 percent for the remainder of the country.

Strip flooring should be laid at right angles to the joists, (fig. 85A). Start at one wall, placing the first board ½ to ⅝ inch away from the wall and face-nail so that the base and shoe will cover the space

and nails (fig. 85B). Next, blind-nail the first strip of flooring and each subsequent piece with eight-penny flooring nails (for $^{25}/_{32}$-inch thickness) at each joist crossing. Nail through the tongue and into the joist below with a nail angle of 45° to 50°. Set each nail to the surface of the tongue. Each piece should be driven up lightly for full contact. Use a hammer and a short piece of scrap flooring to protect the edge. The last flooring strip must be face-nailed atthe wall line, again allowing ½- to ⅝-inch space for expansion of the flooring.

Other thinner types of strip flooring are nailed in the same way, except that sixpenny flooring nails may be sufficient. Square-edge flooring must be face-nailed using two 1½-inch finish nails (brads) on about 12-inch centers.

WOOD BLOCK FLOORING

Wood block flooring with matching tongued-and-grooved edges is often fastened by nailing, but may be installed with an adhesive. Other block floorings made from wood-base materials are also available. Manufacturers of these specialty floors can supply the correct adhesive as well as instructions for laying. Their recommended methods are based on years of experience, and when followed, should provide maintenance-free service.

RESILIENT TILE

Most producers of resilient tile provide detailed instructions regarding installation. This covers the underlayment, adhesives, and other requirements. However, most resilient tiles are applied in much the same way.

The underlayment may be plywood which serves both as a subfloor and an underlayment for the tile. A subfloor of wood boards requires an underlayment of plywood, hardboard, or particleboard. Nails should be driven flush with the surface, cracks and joints filled and sanded smooth, and the surface thoroughly cleaned.

Next, a center baseline should be marked on the

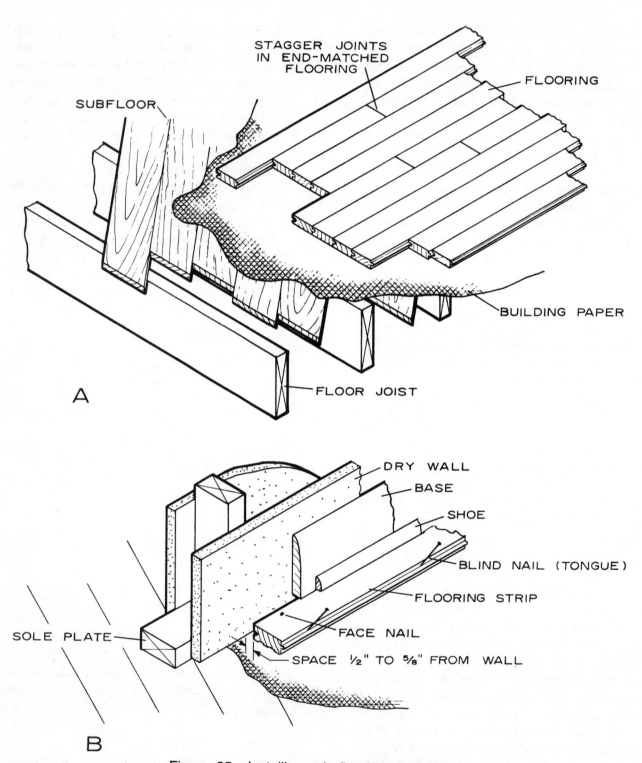

STAGGER JOINTS
IN END-MATCHED
FLOORING

FLOORING

SUBFLOOR

BUILDING PAPER

FLOOR JOIST

A

DRY WALL

BASE

SHOE

BLIND NAIL (TONGUE)

FLOORING STRIP

FACE NAIL

SPACE ½" TO ⅝" FROM WALL

SOLE PLATE

B

Figure 85—Installing strip flooring. A, General
application; B, laying first strip.

From Tent to Cabin

subfloor in each direction of the room (fig. 86A). Centerlines should be exactly 90° (a right angle) with each other. This can be assured by using a 3:4:5-foot measurement along two sides and the diagonal (fig. 86A). In a large room, a 6:8:10-foot measuring combination can be used.

Now, spread the adhesive with a serrated trowel (both as recommended by the manufacturer) over one of the quarter-sections outlined by the center-lines. Waiting (drying) time should conform to the directions for the adhesive.

Starting at one inside corner, lay the first tile exactly in line with the marked centerlines. The second tile can be laid adjacent to the first on one side (fig. 86B). The third tile laid adjacent to the first at the other centerline on the other side of the quarter section. Thus, in checkerboard fashion, the entire section can be covered. The remaining three sections can be covered in the same way. Some tile requires only pressing in place; others should be rolled after installing for better adherence.

The edge tiles around the perimeter of the room must be trimmed to fit to the edge of the wall. A clearance of ⅛ to ¼ inch should be allowed at all sides for expansion. This edge is covered with a cove base of the same resilient material or with a standard wood base. Wood base is usually lower in cost than the resilient cove base, but installation costs are somewhat greater.

Interior Doors, Frames, and Millwork

The cost of interior finish such as cabinets, door frames, doors, and moldings varies a great deal with wood species and styles. For example, pine casing used as trim for door and window frames may cost only half as much as some hardwood trim. However, some types of interior panel doors made of pine may cost twice as much as a mahogany flush door. Choice of materials should be based both on cost and utility. Such details are covered in the building plans and specifications.

The number and types of cabinets used in a cabin can make a substantial difference in the overall cost. Prefinished base cabinets with counter and wall cabinets for kitchens may be much higher than the cost of simple shelving with provisions for installation of the doors at a later date; this may mean a saving of several hundred dollars. When a cost reduction is needed to keep within the limits of available funds, some such substitution may be necessary.

The moisture content of all interior wood finish when installed is important in the overall performance. The recommended moisture content for interior finish varies between 6 and 11 percent, depending on climatic conditions. Recommended moisture content is the same as outlined for wood and fiberboard paneling in the section on "Interior Wall and Ceiling Finish".

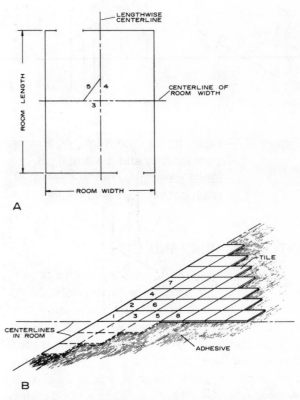

Figure 86—Installing resilient tile. A, Center baseline; B, order of laying tile.

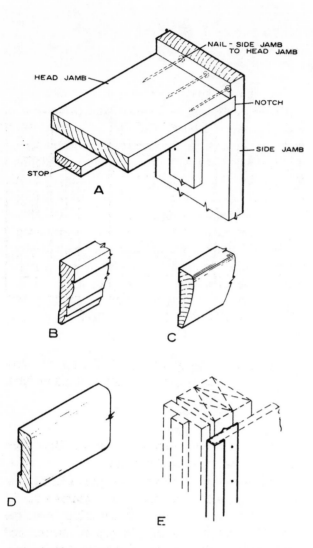

Figure 87—Door frame and trim. A, Frame components and assembly; B, colonial casing; C, ranch casing; D, plain casing; E, metal casing.

INTERIOR DOORS AND TRIM

Door frames.—The rough door openings provided for during framing of the interior walls should accommodate the assembled frames. The allowance was 2½ inches plus the door width and 3 inches plus the door height. When thin resilient tile is used over the subfloor, the allowance is 2¼ inches for door height. Frames consist of a head *jamb* with two side jambs and the stops. When a wood casing is used around the door frame as trim, the width of the jambs is the same as the overall wall thickness.

When a metal casing is used with the dry wall, eliminating the need for the wood casing, the jamb width is the same as the stud depth width. The side and head jambs and the stop are assembled as shown in figure 87A. Jambs may be purchased in sets or can be easily made in a small shop with a table or radial-arm saw.

Casing.—Casing is the trim around the door opening. It is nailed to the edge of the jamb and to the door buck (edge stud). A number of shapes are available, such as colonial (fig. 87B), ranch (fig. 87C), and plain (fig. 87D). Casing widths vary from 2¼ to 3½ inches, depending on the style. Thicknesses vary from ½ to ¾ inch. A casing bead or metal casing used to trim the edges of the gypsum board at the door and window jambs (fig. 87A) eliminates the need for the wood casing.

Doors.—Two general styles of interior doors are the panel and the flush door. The interior flush door is normally the hollow-core type (fig. 88A), which costs much less than the solid core. The five-cross-panel door (fig. 88B) is usually lower in cost than the colonial type (fig. 88C).

Standard widths for interior doors are: (a) Bedroom and other rooms, 2 feet 6 inches; (b) bathroom, 2 feet 4 inches; (c) small closet and linen closet, 2 feet. Interior door heights should be the same as for exterior doors; standard height is 6 feet 8 inches. Doors of these sizes can be obtained from most lumber dealers.

Doors should be hinged so that they open in the direction of natural entry. They should also swing against a blank wall whenever possible, never into a hallway. Door swing directions and sizes are shown on the working drawings.

INSTALLATION OF DOORS

Frames.—When jambs are not preassembled, side jambs are nailed to the head jamb with three eightpenny coated nails (fig. 87A). Cut the side jambs to the correct length before nailing. A temporary brace can then be nailed across the bottom of the side jambs so the width is the same throughout the full height of the door.

The frame is now placed in the opening and fastened to the wall studs with the aid of shingle wedges used between the side jamb and the rough door buck (side stud) (fig. 89A). Plumb and fasten one side first, using four or five sets of wedges along the height, and nail the jamb with pairs of eightpenny finish nails at each wedged area. Square the top corners of the opening and fasten the opposite jamb in the same manner. Use a straightedge along the face of the jambs when lining them up with the wedges.

Casings.—Casings are nailed to the edges of the jamb and to the door buck. First, cut off the shingle wedges flush with the wall. Position the casing with about a 3/16-inch edge distance from the face of the jamb (fig. 89A). Depending on the thickness of the casing, sixpenny or sevenpenny casing or finish nails should be used. When the casing has one thin edge, use a 1½-inch brad or finish nail along this edge. Space the nails in pairs about 16 inches apart.

Casings with molded forms (fig. 87B and C) must have a *mitered joint* where head and side casings join (fig. 89B). Rectangular casing can be butt-joined (fig. 89C). Casing for the interior side of exterior door frames is installed the same way.

Metal casing used instead of wood casing can be nailed in place in two ways. After the jambs have been installed and before the gypsum board is placed, the metal casing can be nailed to the door buck around the opening (fig. 87E). The gypsum board is then inserted into the groove and nailed to the studs in normal fashion. The second method consists of placing the metal casing over the edge of the gypsum board, positioning the sheet properly with respect to the jamb and nailing through both the gypsum board and the casing into the stud behind (fig. 89D). Use the same type nails and nail spacing as described in the section on "Interior Wall and Ceiling Finish" for gypsum board.

Doors and stops.—The door opening is now complete. Without the door in place, it is often referred to as a "cased opening". When cost is a major factor, the use of this opening with a curtain

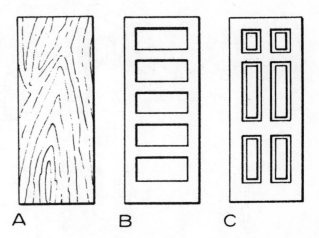

Figure 88—Interior doors. A, Flush; B, five-cross-panel; C, colonial, panel type.

rod and curtain will insure some privacy. Door stops can be fitted and doors hung later.

The door is fitted between the jambs by planing the sides to the correct width. This requires a careful measurement of the width before planing. When the correct width is obtained, the top is squared and trimmed to fit the opening. The bottom of the door is now sawed off with the proper floor clearance. The side, top, and bottom clearances and the location of the hinges are shown in figure 90. Remember that paint or finish takes up some of the space, so allow for this.

The narrow wood strips used as stops for the door are usually 7/16 inch thick and may be 1½ to 2¼ inches wide. They are installed on the jambs with a mitered joint at the junction of the head and side jambs. A 45° bevel cut at the bottom of stops 1 to 1½ inches above the finish floor will eliminate a dirt pocket and make cleaning or refinishing of the floor much easier (fig. 89A).

Before fitting the exterior doors, install a threshold between side jambs to cover the junction of the sill and the flooring (or allow for the threshold). Nail to the floor and sill with finish nails.

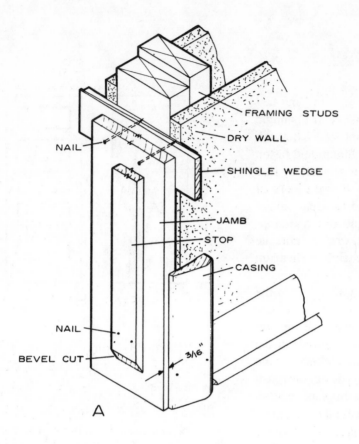

FRAMING STUDS

DRY WALL

SHINGLE WEDGE

JAMB

STOP

CASING

NAIL

NAIL

BEVEL CUT

3/16"

A

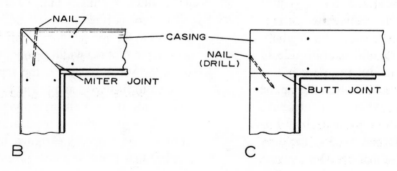

NAIL

CASING

MITER JOINT

B

NAIL
(DRILL)

BUTT JOINT

C

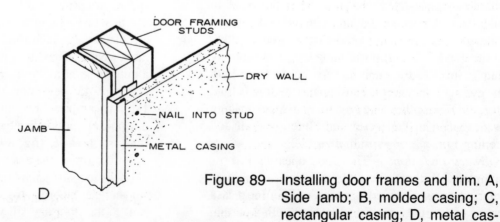

DOOR FRAMING
STUDS

DRY WALL

NAIL INTO STUD

JAMB

METAL CASING

D

Figure 89—Installing door frames and trim. A, Side jamb; B, molded casing; C, rectangular casing; D, metal casing.

From Tent to Cabin

INSTALLATION OF DOOR HARDWARE

Four types of hardware sets available in a number of finishes are commonly used for doors. They are classed as: (a) Entry lock for exterior doors, (b) bathroom set (inside lock control with a safety slot for opening from the outside), (c) bedroom lock set (keyed lock), and (d) passage set (without lock). Two hinges are normally used for 1⅜-inch interior doors. To minimize warping of exterior doors in cold climates, use three hinges. Exterior doors, 1¾ inches thick, require 4- by 4-inch loose-pin hinges and the 1⅜-inch interior doors 3½- by 3½-inch loose-pin hinges.

Hinges.—Hinges are *routed* or *mortised* into the edge of the door with about a 3/16- or 1/4-inch back spacing (Fig. 91A). This may vary slightly, however. Adjustments should be made, if necessary, to provide sufficient edge distance so that screws have good penetration in the wood. Locate the hinges as shown in figure 90 and use one hinge half to mark the outline of the cut. If a router is not available, mark the hinge outline and the depth of the cut and remove the wood with a wood chisel. The depth of the routing should be such that the surface of the hinge is flush with the wood surface. Screws are included with each hinge set and should be used to fasten the hinge halves in place.

The door is now placed in the opening and blocked for the proper clearances. Stops should be tacked in place temporarily so that the door surface is flush with the edge of the jamb. Mark the location of the door hinges on the jambs, remove the door, and with the remaining hinge halves and a small square mark the outline. The depth of the routed area should be the same as that on the door (the thickness of the hinge half). After fastening the hinge halves, place the door in the opening and insert the pins. If marking and routing were done correctly, the door should fit perfectly and swing freely.

Locks.—Door lock and latch sets are supplied with paper templates which provide the exact location of holes for the lock and latch. Follow the

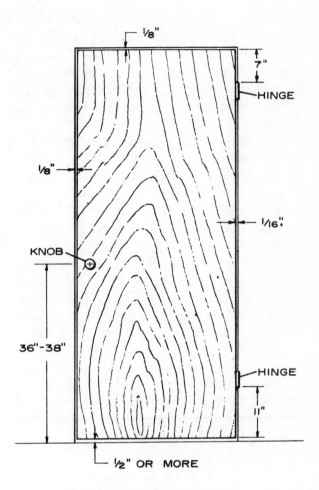

Figure 90 —Door clearances.

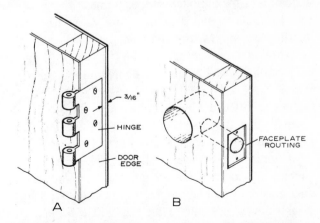

Figure 91—Installing door hardware. A, Hinge; B, lock.

printed directions, locating the door knob 36 to 38 inches above the floor (fig. 90). Most lock sets require only one hole through the face of the door and one at the edge (fig. 91B). Latches are used with or without a face plate, depending on the type of lock set.

Strike plate.—The strike plate is used to hold the door closed by means of the latch. It is routed into the jamb (fig. 92A). Mark the location of the latch on the jamb when the door is in a near-closed position and outline the strike plate to this position. Rout enough to bring the strike plate flush with the face of the jamb.

Stops.—The stops which have been temporarily nailed in place while fitting the door and door hardware can now be permanently nailed. Exterior door frames with thicker jambs have the stop rabbeted in place as a part of the jamb. Finish nails or brads 1½ inches long are satisfactory for nailing. The stop at the lock side should be nailed first, setting it against the door face when the door is latched. Use nails in pairs spaced about 16 inches apart. The clearances and stop locations shown in figure 92B should be generally followed.

WINDOW TRIM

The casing used around the window frames on the interior of the cabin is usually the same pattern as that used for the interior door frames. There are two common methods of installing wood trim at window areas: (a) with a *stool* and *apron* (fig. 93A) and (b) with complete casing trim (fig. 93B). Metal casing is also used around the entire window opening.

In a prefitted double-hung window, the stool is normally the first piece of trim to be installed. It is notched out between the jambs so that the forward edge contacts the lower sash rail (fig. 93A). Of course, in windows that are not preassembled, the sash must be fitted before the trim is installed. The stool is now blind-nailed at the ends with eightpenny finish nails so that the casing at the side will cover the nailheads. With hardwood, predrilling is usually

required to prevent splitting. The stool should also be nailed at midpoint to the sill, and later to the apron when it is installed. Toenailing may be substituted for facenailing to the sill (fig. 93A).

The casing is now applied and nailed as described for the door frames, except that the inner edge is flush with the inner face of the jambs so that the *stop* covers the joint (fig. 93A). The stops are now fitted similarly to the interior door stops and placed against the lower sash so that it can slide freely. A 1½-inch casing nail or brad should be used. Use nails in pairs spaced about 12 inches apart. When full-length weatherstrips are included with the window unit, locate the stops against them to provide a small amount of pressure. Cut the apron to a length equal to the outer width of the casing line (fig. 93A) and nail to the framing sill below with eightpenny finish nails.

When casing is used to finish the bottom of the window frame instead of the stool and apron, a narrow stool or stop is substituted (fig. 93B). Casing along the bottom of the window is then applied in the same way as at the side and head of the window.

When metal casing is used as trim around window openings, it is applied to the sill as well as at the side and head of the frame. Consequently, the jambs and sill of the frame are not as deep as when wood casing is used. The stops are also narrower by the thickness of the dry-wall finish. The metal casing is used flush with the inside edge of the window jamb (fig. 93C). This type of trim is installed at the same time as the dry wall and in the same way described for the interior door frames.

Other types of windows, such as the awning or hopper types or the casement, are trimmed about the same as the double-hung window. Casing of the same types shown in figure 87B, C, D, and E can also be used for these units.

Base Moldings

TYPES

Some type of trim or finish is normally used at

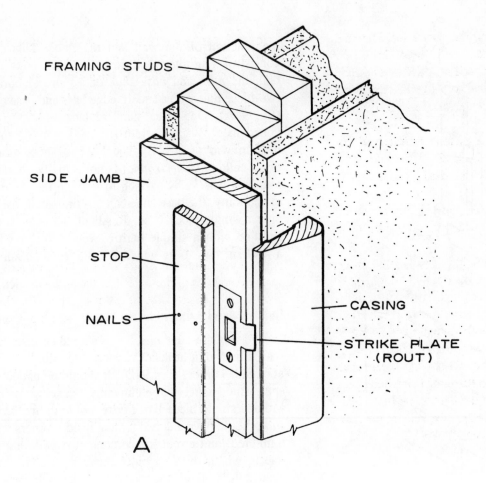

FRAMING STUDS

SIDE JAMB

STOP

NAILS

CASING

STRIKE PLATE
(ROUT)

A

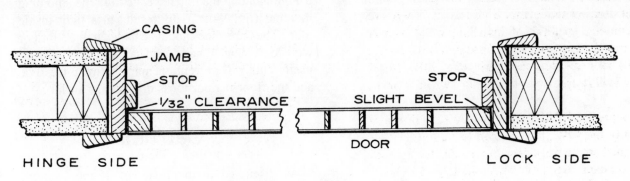

CASING

JAMB

STOP

1/32" CLEARANCE

STOP

SLIGHT BEVEL

DOOR

HINGE SIDE

LOCK SIDE

PLAN VIEW

B

Figure 92—Door installation. A, Strike plate; B,
stop clearances.

From Tent to Cabin

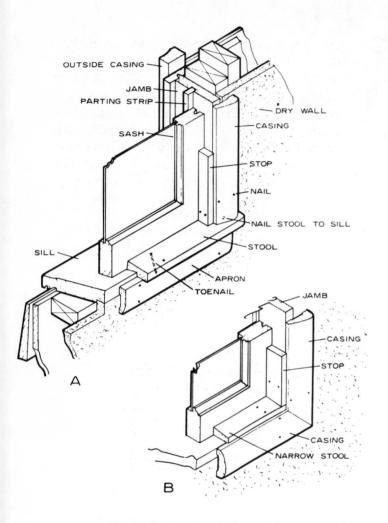

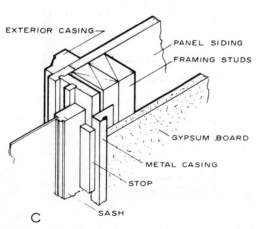

Figure 93—Window trim. A, With stool and
apron; B, wood casing at window;
C, metal casing at window.

the junction of the wall and the floor. This can
consist of a simple wood member which serves as
both the *base* and *base shoe* or a more elaborate
two-piece unit with a square-edge base and base cap
(fig. 94A). One-piece standard base may be obtained in a 2¼-inch width (fig. 94B) or 3¼-inch
medium width (fig 94C). The true base shoe, sometimes called *quarter-round*, is not actually quarter-
round as it is ½ by ¾ inch in size. In the interest
of economy, the base shoe can be eliminated, using
only a single-piece base. Resilient floors may be
finished with a simple narrow wood base or with
a resilient *cove* base which is installed with adhesives.

INSTALLATION

Wide square-edge *baseboard* should be installed
with a butt joint at inside corners and mitered joint
at outside corners (fig. 94D). It should be nailed to
each stud with two eightpenny finishing nails.
Molded single-piece base, *base molding*, and *base
shoe* should have a coped joint at inside corners and
a mitered joint at outside corners. A *coped joint* is
one in which the first piece has a square-cut end
against the wall and the second member at the inside
corner has a coped joint. This is accomplished by
sawing a 45° miter cut and, with a coping saw,
trimming along the mitered edge to fit the adjoining
molding (fig. 94E). This results in a tight inside
joint. The base shoe should be nailed to the subfloor
with long slender nails, and not to the baseboard
itself. This will prevent openings between the shoe
and the floor if floor joists dry out and shrink.

Cabinets

As discussed in the first part of this section,
kitchen and other cabinets can increase the cost of
a cabin substantially. Thus, in many cases, it may
be necessary to use the most simple forms of storage
areas to remain within a limited budget. However,
even when the cabinets might be quite simple, it is

From Tent to Cabin

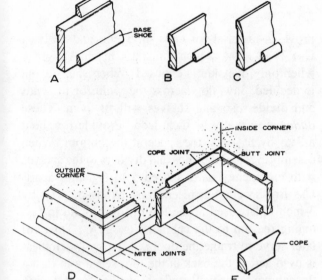

Figure 94—Base moldings. A, Two-piece; B, narrow; C, medium width; C, installation; E, coped joint.

good practice to provide for additions which can be made later such as the installation of the doors and door hardware.

KITCHEN ARRANGEMENTS

A kitchen, no matter how small, should be laid out so that there is a good relationship between the refrigerator, the sink, and the stove. This is desirable in order to save steps and time in the preparation of meals. Kitchen sizes and shapes vary a great deal and usually control the arrangement of the utilities and the cabinets. Figure 95 shows the four common types of kitchen layouts: (a) U-type, (b) L-type, (c) parallel wall, and (d) sidewall type. The L-type and the sidewall type (fig. 95 B or D) are perhaps those most adaptable to a small kitchen. Kitchen layouts are shown on the working drawings for the cabin.

KITCHEN CABINET UNITS

Kitchen cabinets are normally classed as (a) base cabinets and (b) wall cabinets. The base or floor

unit, which contains a counter, may include both drawers and doors and shelves in various combinations. The wall units are normally a series of shelves with hinged or sliding doors located above the base cabinets. The proportions and sizes of these cabinets are shown in figure 96. A standard height for the base unit is 36 inches, with a top width of 25 inches. A low-cost counter top may consist simply of plywood with a resilient surface covering.

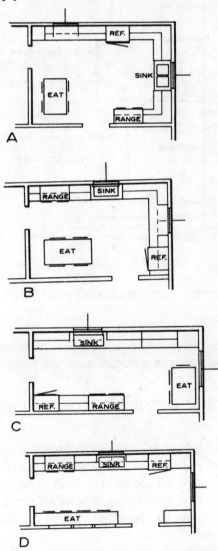

Figure 95—Kitchen arrangements. A, U-type; B, L-type; C, parallel wall; D, sidewall.

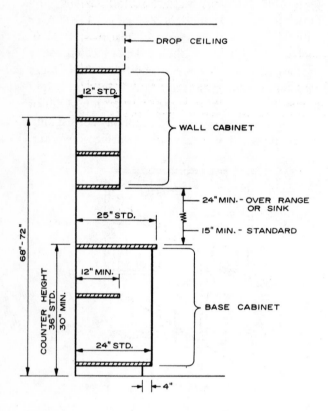

Figure 96 —Kitchen cabinet proportions.

provides material for ends, dividers, and shelves. Use ¾-inch or ¾-inch thickness in an AC grade when only one side is exposed. When shelf layout is decided, saw slots across the width of the ends and dividers so that shelves will fit them. These *dados* are usually ¼-inch deep. Provide for about a 3½- by 3½-inch toe space at the bottom. When assembling, nail the ends and dividers to the shelves with eightpenny nails spaced 5 to 6 inches apart. Use finish nails where ends are exposed. A 1- by 3-inch rail is used at the top in front to aid in fastening the top to the cabinet (fig. 97A). This will later serve to frame the doors. A 1- by 4-inch cleat is used across the back at the top, serving to fasten the cabinet to the wall studs, as well as for fastening the top (fig. 97B). The ends and dividers are notched to receive this cleat (fig. 97C). On finished ends, this notch is cut only halfway through. Fasten the cabinet to the wall by nailing or screwing through the back cleat into each stud with eightpenny nails or 2-inch screws.

The top of plywood or particleboard is nailed in place onto the ends, back cleat, and top rail with eightpenny finish nails. When the top has a plastic finish, use small metal angles around the interior and fasten them to the cabinet and top with small screws. When side stiles and doors are added later, a pleasant, utilitarian cabinet will result (fig. 97D). Until then, however, curtains can be used across the openings.

Any combination of base cabinets can be constructed. The sink cabinet usually consists only of a pair of doors and a bottom shelf. Vent slots are usually cut in the top cross rail. A cutout is necessary in the top to provide for a self-rimming or rimmed sink.

Wall units.—Wall units are about 30 inches high when installed below a drop ceiling. When carried to the ceiling line, they may be 44 or 45 inches in height. The depth is usually about 12 inches. A 4-foot-wide sheet of plywood or particleboard can be ripped in four pieces if this depth is used. As in base unit construction, the wall cabinet can consist of dadoed ends and one or more vertical dividers

The more elaborate tops usually have a plastic laminated surface with a molded edge and backsplash.

CONSTRUCTION OF LOW-COST KITCHEN CABINETS

Low-cost kitchen cabinets can consist of a series of shelves enclosed with vertical dividers and ends. They can be designed so that flush doors can be added later at little cost and with no alterations. Curtains across the top of the opening can be temporarily used.

Base units.—Figure 97 shows the details of a simple base unit. Any combination of opening widths and shelf spacing can be used. Ripping 4-foot-wide sheets of plywood or particleboard in half

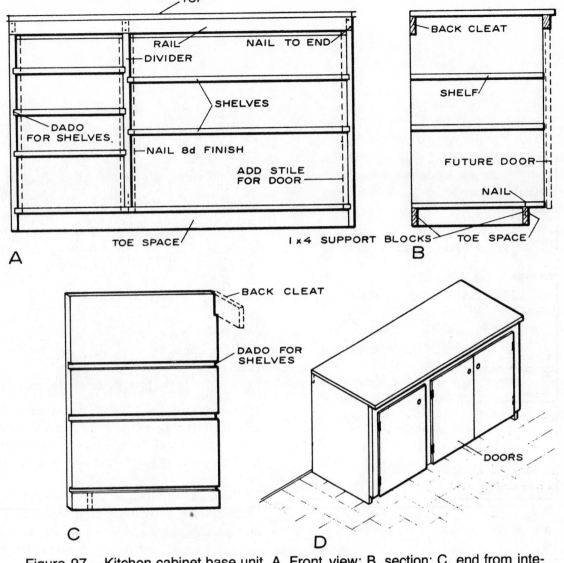

Figure 97—Kitchen cabinet base unit. A, Front view; B, section; C, end from interior; D, overall view.

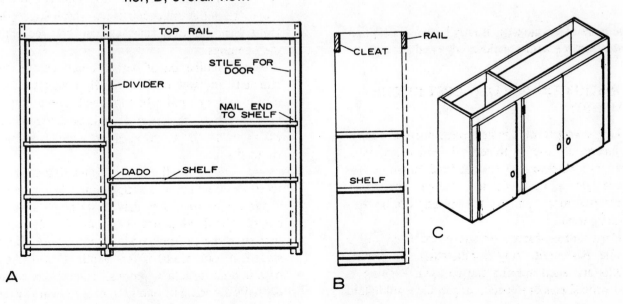

Figure 98—Kitchen cabinet wall unit. A, Front view; B, section; C, overall view.

nailed to the shelves (fig. 98A). Use eightpenny finish nails when the end is exposed. The cleat is used to fasten the cabinet to the wall (fig. 98B). A top rail ties the sides and dividers together and, when the vertical stiles are added, provides framing for doors (fig. 98C).

WARDROBE-CLOSET COMBINATIONS

Closets are often eliminated in a low-cost cabin for economic reasons. A closet requires wall framing, interior and exterior covering, a door frame and door, and trim. However, some type of storage area should be included which will be pleasant in appearance, yet low in cost. Practical storage areas, often called wardrobe-closets, consist of wood or plywood sides, shelves, and some type of door or curtain. Figure 99 shows a simple built-in wardrobe that can be initially curtained. A folding door unit can be added later.

Wardrobe-closets are normally built of ⅝- or ¾-inch plywood or particleboard. Provide dados for the shelf or shelves, as used on the kitchen cabinets. A back cleat at the top provides a member for fastening the unit to the wall. The sides can be trimmed at the floor with a base shoe molding which, with toenailing, keeps the sides in place. Add a simple closet pole. Fasten the unit to the wall at the top cleat and, when in a corner, also to the side wall (fig. 99). Any size or combination of wardrobes of this type can be built in during construction of the cabin or added later. Shelves or partial shelves can be provided in the bottom section for shoe storage.

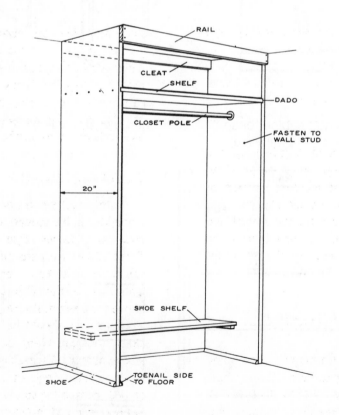

Figure 99—Wardrobe-closet.

13. Steps and Stairs

Outside entry platforms and steps are required for most types of wood-frame cabins. Cabins constructed over crawl space normally require a platform with steps at outside doors. In cabins with masonry foundations, these outside entry stoops may consist of a concrete perimeter wall with poured concrete steps.

Inside stairs leading to second-floor bedrooms in a cabin with a steep roof slope, must be provided for during construction. This includes framing of the floor joists to accommodate the stairway and providing walls and *carriages* for the *treads* and *risers*. Even though the second floor might not be completed immediately, a stairway should be included during construction of such cabins.

Outside Stoops

Outside wood stoops, platforms and open plank stairs should give satisfactory service if these simple rules are followed: (a) All wood in contact with or embedded in soil should be pressure-treated, as outlined in the early section on "Post Foundations"; (b) all untreated wood parts should have a 2-inch minimum clearance above the ground; (c) avoid pockets or areas in the construction where water cannot drain away; (d) if possible, use wood having moderate to good decay resistance; (e) use initial and regular applications of water-repellent preservative to exposed untreated wood surfaces; and (f) use vertical grain members.

WOOD STOOP—LOW HEIGHT

A simple all-wood stoop consists of treated posts embedded in the ground, cross or bearing members, and spaced treads. One such design is shown in figure 100A. Because this type of stoop is low, it can serve as an entry for exterior doors where the floor level of the cabin is no more than 24 inches above the ground. Railings are not usually required. The platform should be large enough so that the storm door can swing outward freely. An average size is about 3½ feet deep by 5 feet wide.

Use treated posts of 5- to 7-inch diameter and embed them in the soil at least 3 feet. Nail and bolt (with galvanized fasteners) a crossmember (usually a nominal 2- by 4-inch member) to each side of the posts (fig. 100 B). The posts should be faced slightly

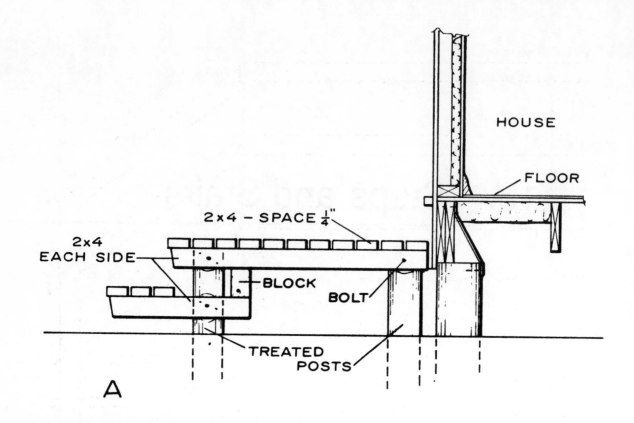

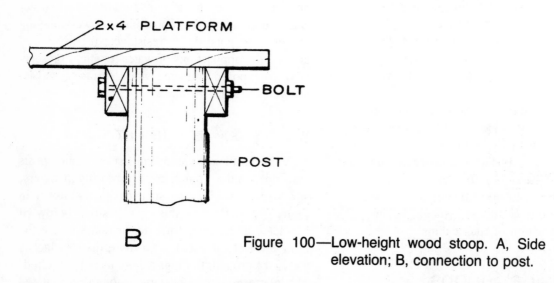

Figure 100—Low-height wood stoop. A, Side elevation; B, connection to post.

at these areas. For a small, 3½- by 5-foot stoop, four posts are usually sufficient. Posts are spaced about 4 feet apart across the front.

Support for the tread of the first step are supplied by pairs of 2- by 4-inch members bolted to the forward posts (fig. 100 A). The inner ends are blocked with short pieces of 2- by 4-inch members to the upper crosspieces (fig. 100 A). Treads consist of 2- by 4- or 2- by 6-inch members, spaced about ¼ inch apart. Use two sixteenpenny galvanized plain or ring-shank nails for each piece at each supporting member.

From Tent to Cabin

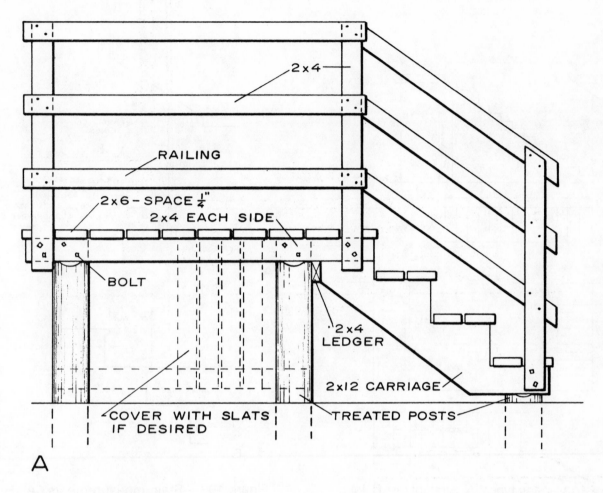

2 x 4

RAILING

2 x 6 – SPACE ¼"
2 x 4 EACH SIDE

BOLT

2 x 4
LEDGER

2 x 12 CARRIAGE

COVER WITH SLATS
IF DESIRED

TREATED POSTS

A

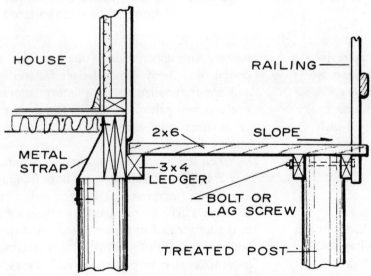

HOUSE

RAILING

2 x 6

SLOPE

METAL
STRAP

3 x 4
LEDGER

BOLT OR
LAG SCREW

TREATED POST

B

Figure 101—Medium-height wood stoop. A,
Side elevation; B, connection to
post.

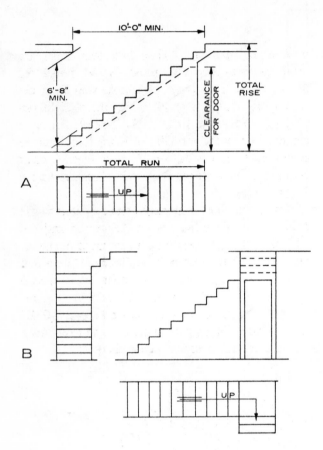

Figure 102—Stair types. A, Straight run; B, long L.

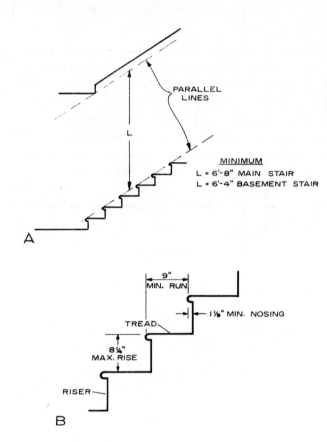

Figure 103—Stair measurements. A, Head room; B, riser-tread sizes.

Some species of wood have natural decay resistance and others are benefited by the application of a water-repellent preservative followed by a good deck paint. If desired, a railing can be added by bolting short upright members to the 2- by 4-inch crossmembers. Horizontal railings can be fastened to the uprights.

WOOD STOOP—MEDIUM HEIGHT

A wood entry platform requiring more than one or two steps is usually designed with a railing and stair stringers. If the platform is about 3½ by 5 feet, two 2- by 12-inch carriages can be used to support the treads (fig. 101A). In most cases, the bottoms of the carriages are supported by treated posts embedded in the ground or by an embedded treated timber. The upper ends of the carriages are supported by a 2- by 4-inch ledger fastened to posts and are face-nailed to the platform framing with twelvepenny galvanized nails. The carriage at the cabin side can be supported in the same way when interior posts are used.

When the platform is narrow, a nominal 3- by 4-inch ledger is fastened to the floor framing of the cabin with fortypenny galvanized spikes or 5-inch lag screws. The 2- by 6-inch floor planks are nailed to the ledger and to the double 2- by 4-inch beam bolted to the post (fig. 101 B). Use two sixteenpenny galvanized plain or ring-shank nails for each tread. When a wide platform is desired, an inside set of posts and doubled 2 by 4 or larger beams should be used.

Railings can be made of 2- by 4-inch uprights

bolted or lagscrewed to the outside beams. These members are best fastened with galvanized bolts or lag screws. Horizontal railing in 1- by 4- or 1- by 6-inch size can then be fastened to the uprights. When an enclosed skirting is desired, 1- by 4-inch slats can be nailed to the outside of the beam and an added lower nailing member (fig. 101A). Treat all exposed untreated wood with a heavy application of water-repellent preservative. When a paint finish is desired, use a good deck paint. See section on "Painting and Finishing" for details.

Inside Stairs

When stairs to a second-floor area are required, the first-floor ceiling joists are framed to accom-modate the stairway. When basement stairs are used, the first-floor joists must also be framed for the stairway. Two types of simple stair *runs* are commonly used in a small cabin, the straight run (fig. 102A) and the long L (fig. 102B). An open length of 10 feet is normally sufficient for adequate headroom with a width of 2½ to 3 feet. A clear width of 2 feet 8 inches is considered minimum for a main stair.

Two of the most important considerations in the design of inside stairways are headroom and the relation of the riser height to the length of the tread. The minimum headroom for stairs should be 6 feet 4 inches for basements or secondary stairs and 6 feet 8 inches for main stairs (fig. 103A). The re-lation of the riser to the run is shown in figure 103B. A good rule of thumb to apply is: The riser times the tread in inches should equal about 75.

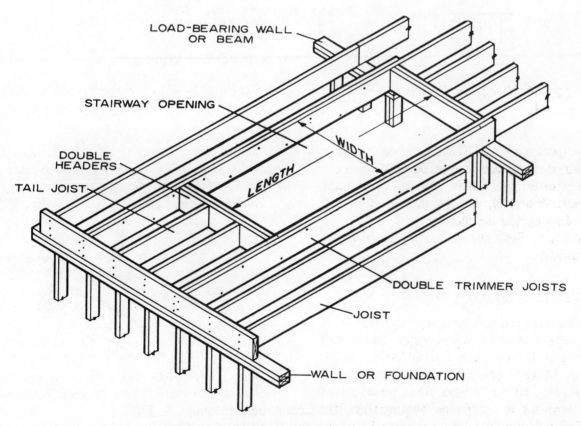

Figure 104—Stairway parallel to joists.

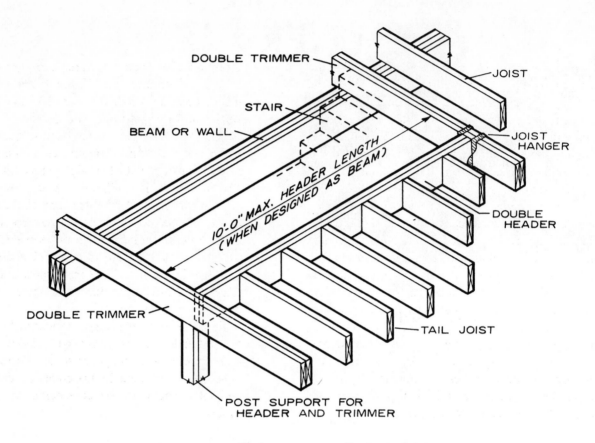

Figure 105—Stairway perpendicular to joists.

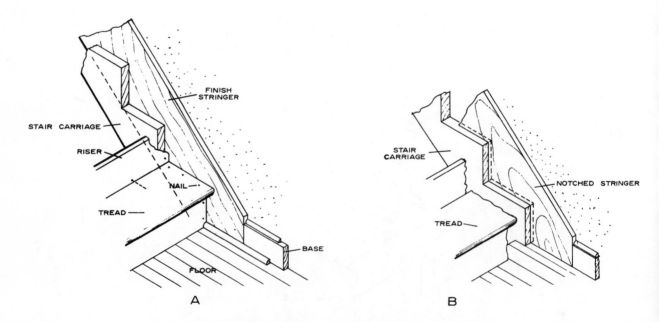

Figure 106—Stair construction details. A, Full
stringer; B, notched stringer.

From Tent to Cabin

When the length of the stairway is parallel to the joists the opening is framed (fig. 104). When the stairway is arranged so that the opening is perpendicular to the length of the joists, the framing should follow the details shown in figure 105. Nailing and framing should comply with table 1 and the descriptions in the section on "Floor Systems".

The stair carriages are normally made from 2-by 12-inch members. They provide support for the stairs and nailing surfaces for the treads and risers. The carriages can be nailed to a finish stringer and the wall studs behind with a sixteenpenny nail at each stud (fig. 106 A). The carriages can also be mounted directly to the wall studs or over the drywall finish and the finish stringer notched to them (fig. 106 B). When no wall is present to fasten the tops of the carriages in place, use a ledger similar to that shown in figure 101 A for an outside stair. The tops of the carriages are notched to fit this ledger. Two carriages are sufficient when treads are at least $1\frac{1}{16}$ inches thick and the stair is less than 2 feet 6 inches wide. Use three carriages when the stair is wider than this. When plank treads $1\frac{5}{8}$ inches thick are used, two carriages are normally sufficient for stair widths up to 3 feet.

After the carriages are mounted to the wall and treads and risers cut to length, nail the bottom riser to each carriage with two eightpenny finish nails. The first tread, if $1\frac{1}{16}$ inches thick, is then nailed to each carriage with two tenpenny finish nails and to the riser below with at least two tenpenny finish nails. Proceed up the stair in this same manner. If $1\frac{5}{8}$-inch-thick treads are used, a twelvepenny finish nail may be required. Use three nails at each carriage, but eliminate nailing to the riser below. All finish nails should be set.

Finish stairs with stringers routed to fit the ends of the treads and risers, and with railing and *balusters* or a handrail, are generally used in main stairs to second-floor rooms in moderate-cost cabins, but probably should not be considered for low-cost cabins.

14. Painting and Finishing

Exterior Wood Finishing

The durability of an exterior finish is materially affected by the wood characteristics. Woods that are high in *density* (heavy), such as dense hardwoods, will be more difficult to finish effectively than lightweight woods.

The amount and distribution of summerwood (darker *grained* portions) on the surface of softwood lumber also influence the success of the finishing procedure. Finishes, particularly paints, will last longer on surfaces with a low proportion of summerwood.

The manner in which lumber is sawn from the log influences its finishing characteristics. Paint-type and film-forming finishes always perform best on *vertical-grain* lumber because the summerwood is better distributed on the surface and because vertical-grain lumber is low in swelling.

All woods shrink or swell as they lose or absorb water. Species which shrink and swell the least are best for painting. Checking, warping of wood, and paint peeling are more likely to be critical on woods which are hard, dense, and high in swelling.

Wood that is free of knots, pitch pockets, and other defects is the preferred base for paints, but these defects have little adverse effect on penetrating-type finishes. Smoothly planed surfaces are best for paint finishes, while rougher or sawn surfaces are preferred for penetrating (non-film-forming) finishes.

TYPES OF EXTERIOR FINISHES

Unfinished wood.—Permitting the wood to weather naturally without protection of any kind is, of course, very simple and economical. Wood fully exposed to all elements of the weather, rain and sun being the most important, will wear away at the approximate rate of only a quarter of an inch in a century. The time required for wood to weather to the final gray color will depend on the severity of exposure. Wood in protected areas will be much slower to gray than wood fully exposed to the sun on the south side of a building. Early in the graying process, the wood may take on a blotchy appearance because of the growth of micro-organisms on the surface. Migration of wood extractives to the surface also will produce an uneven and unsightly discoloration, particularly in areas that are not washed by rain.

Unfinished lumber will warp more than lumber protected by paint. Warping varies with the density, width, and thickness of the board, basic wood structure, and species. Warp increases with density and the width of the board. To reduce warping to a minimum, best results are obtained when the width of boards does not exceed eight times the thickness. Flat-grain boards warp more than vertical-grain lumber. Baldcypress, the cedars, and redwood are species which have only a slight tendency to warp.

Water-repellent-preservative finishes.—A simple treatment of an exterior wood surface with a water-repellent preservative markedly alters the natural weathering process. Most pronounced is the retention of a uniform natural tan color in the early stages of weathering and a retardation of the uneven graying process which is produced by the growth of mildew on the surface. The water-repellency imparted by the treatment greatly reduces the tendency toward warping, excessive shrinking, and swelling which lead to splitting, and retards the leaching of extractives from the wood and water stain at ends of boards.

This type of finish is quite inexpensive, easily applied, and very easily refinished. Water-repellent preservatives can be applied by brushing, rolling, dipping, and spraying. It is important to thoroughly treat all lap and butt joints and ends of boards. Many brands of effective water-repellent preservatives are on the market. A saving could be made by making a solution from the following components:

Penta concentrate (10:1) ....2 quarts
Boiled linseed oil ....1.75 quarts
Paraffin wax ....0.25 to 0.50 pound
Mineral spirits, turpentine, No. 1 or No. 2
   fuel oil .... 4 gallons.

Color pigments can also be added to this type of finish. Mix 2 to 6 fluid ounces of colors to each gallon of water-repellent preservative.

The initial applications may be short-lived (1 year), especially in humid climates and on species that are susceptible to mildew, such as sapwood and certain hardwoods. Under more favorable conditions, such as on rough cedar surfaces which will absorb large quantities of the solution, the finish will last more than 2 years.

When blotchy discolorations of mildew start to appear on the wood, re-treat the surface with water-repellent-preservative solution. If extractives have accumulated on the surface in protected areas, clean these areas by mild scrubbing with a detergent or trisodium-phosphate solution.

The continued use of these water-repellent-preservative solutions will effectively prevent serious decay in wood in above-ground installation. This finishing method is recommended for all wood species and surfaces exposed to the weather.

Only aluminum or stainless steel nails will prevent discoloration on the siding. Galvanized nails will show light stains after several years. Steel nails without rust-resistance treatment should not be used.

Penetrating pigmented stain finishes.—The penetrating stains also are effective and economical finishes for all kinds of lumber and plywood surfaces, especially those that are rough-sawn, weathered, and textured. Knotty wood boards and other lower quality grades of wood which would be difficult to paint also can be finished successfully with penetrating stains.

These stains penetrate into the wood without forming a continuous film on the surface. Because there is no film or coating, there can be no failure by cracking, peeling, and blistering. Stain finishes are easily prepared for refinishing and easily maintained.

The penetrating pigmented stains form a flat and semitransparent finish. They permit only part of the wood-grain pattern to show through. A variety of colors can be achieved with finish. Shades of brown, green, red, and gray are possible. The only color which is not available is white. This color can be provided only through the use of white paint.

Stains are quite inexpensive and easy to apply. To avoid the formation of lap marks, the entire length of a course of siding should be finished without stopping. Only one coat is recommended on smoothly planed surfaces, where it will last 2 to 3 years. After refinishing, however, the second coat will last 6 to 7 years because the weathered surface has absorbed more of the stain than the smoothly planed surface.

Two-coat staining is possible on rough-sawn or weathered surfaces, but both coats should be applied within a few hours of each other. When using a two-coat system, the first coat should never be allowed to dry before the second is applied, because this will seal the surface and prevent the second coat from penetrating. A finish life of up to 10 years can be achieved when two coats are applied to a rough or weathered surface.

Very satisfactory penetrating stains can be prepared by home-mixing the following ingredients:

Boiled linseed oil	3 gallons
Penta concentrate	½ gallon
Paraffin wax	½ pound
Colors-in-oil (tinting colors)	1 quart
Paint thinner	1 gallon

Boiled linseed oil is available in most paint stores and mail-order houses. Penta concentrate is a common name for a solution of pentachlorophenol which is about a 40 percent concentration and is also known as a 10 to 1 concentrate. It is available from several manufacturers by mail order. Paraffin wax, used to seal jelly glasses, can be bought from local grocery stores. Colors-in-oil or tinting colors are available from paint stores and artists' supply stores. Paint thinners which can be used are mineral spirits or *turpentine*. In areas where available, No. 1 or No. 2 fuel oil also can be used. In warm moist areas which enhance fungal growth, the penta content should be doubled.

All ingredients will go into solution quite easily if temperatures are 70°F or above. Dissolving the wax, which is the most difficult step in the process, can be aided by cutting it into fine chips or by melting in a double boiler before adding to other ingredients. Allow the solution to stand overnight and occasionally stir vigorously during use to keep pigments uniformly suspended.

CAUTION: Turpentine, mineral spirits, and other paint thinners are volatile flammable solvents. Their concentrated vapors should not be breathed or exposed to sparks or flames that can ignite them. It is safer to mix ingredients outdoors or in an open garage than in a closed room in a house.

Stained surfaces should be refinished only when the colors fade and bare wood is beginning to show. A light steel-wooling and hosing with water to remove surface dirt and mildew are all that are needed to prepare the surface. Restain after the surfaces have thoroughly dried.

Clear film finishes.—Clear finishes based on *varnish*, which form a coating or film on the surface, should not be used on wood exposed fully to the weather. These finishes are quite expensive and often begin to deteriorate within 1 year. Refinishing is a frequent, difficult, and time-consuming process.

Exterior paints.—Of all the finishes, paints provide the widest selection of color. When properly selected and applied, it will also provide the most protection to wood against weathering. The durability of paint coatings on exterior wood, however, is affected by many variables, and much care is needed in the selection of the wood surface material, type of paint, and method of application to achieve success in painting. The original and maintenance costs are higher for a paint finish than for either the water-repellent-preservative treatment or penetrating-stain finish.

Paint performance is affected by species, density, wood structure, extractives, and defects such as knots and pitch pockets.

Best paint durability will be achieved on the select high grades of vertical-grain western red-cedar, redwood, and low-density pines such as the white pines, sugar pine, and ponderosa pine. Exterior-grade plywood which has been overlaid with medium-density resin-treated paper is another wood-base material on which paint will perform very well.

Follow these three simple steps when painting wood:

(1) Apply water-repellent preservative to all joints by brushing or spraying. Treat all lap and butt joints, ends, and edges of lumber, and window sash and trim. Allow 2 warm days of drying before painting.

(2) Prime the treated wood surface with an oil-base paint free of zinc-oxide pigment. Do *not* use a porous blister-resistant paint as primer on wood surfaces. Apply sufficient primer so the grain of the wood cannot be seen. Open joints should be calked after priming.

(3) Apply two topcoats of high-quality oil, alkyd, or latex paint over the primer. Two topcoats, especially, should be used on the south side, which has the most severe exposure.

Interior Finishes

Interior finishes for wood and dry-wall or plaster surfaces are usually intended to serve one or more of the following purposes:

(1) Make the surface easy to clean.
(2) Enhance the natural beauty of wood.
(3) Achieve a desired color decor.
(4) Impart wear resistance.

The type of finish depends largely upon type of area and the use to which the area will be put. The various interior areas and finish systems employed in each are summarized in table 3. Wood surfaces can be finished either with a clear finish or a paint. Plaster-base materials are painted.

WOOD FLOORS

Hardwood floors of oak, birch, beech, and maple are usually finished by applying two coats of wood seal, also called floor seal, with light sanding between coats. A final coat of paste wax is then applied and buffed. This finish is easily maintained by rewaxing. The final coat can also be a varnish instead of a sealer. The varnish finishes are used when a high gloss is desired.

When floors are to be painted, an *undercoater* is used, and then at least one topcoat of floor and deck enamel is applied.

WOOD PANELING AND TRIM

Wood trim and peneling are most commonly finished with a clear wood sealer or a stain-sealer combination and then topcoated after sanding with at least one additional coat of sealer or varnish. The final coat of sealer or varnish can also be covered with a heavy coat of paste wax to produce a surface which is easily maintained by rewaxing. Good depth in a clear finish can be achieved by finishing first with one coat of a high-gloss varnish followed with a final coat of semigloss varnish.

Wood trim of nonporous species such as pine can also be painted by first applying a coat of primer or undercoater, followed with a coat of latex, flat, or *semigloss oil-base paint*. Semigloss and *gloss paints* are more resistant to soiling and more easily cleaned by washing than the flat oil and latex paints. Trim of porous wood species such as oak and mahogany requires filling before painting.

KITCHEN AND BATHROOM WALLS

Kitchen and bathroom walls, which normally are plaster or dry-wall construction, are finished best with a coat of undercoater and two coats of *semigloss enamel*. This type of finish wears well, is easy to clean, and is quite resistant to moisture.

DRY WALL AND PLASTER

Plaster and dry-wall surfaces, which account for the major protion of the interior area, are finished with two coats of either *flat oil* or latex paint. An initial treatment with size or sealer will improve holdout (reduce penetration of succeeding coats) and thus reduce the quantity of paint required for good coverage.

From Tent to Cabin

15. Foundation Enclosures

A treated wood post foundation is normally constructed with a crawl space having 18- to 24-inch clearance. This access space may be used for placing floor insulation, for installing a vapor barrier soil cover, for examining and treating soil in termite areas, and for other needs. In colder climates, it is often desirable to enclose a crawl space by some low-cost means, even though the floor is insulated. This is commonly done by fastening skirt boards of long-lasting sheet material to the outside beams or floor framing. Enclosed crawl spaces should have a soil cover and a small amount of ventilation to assure satisfactory performance.

When a treated post foundation is not used, a masonry wall of concrete or concrete block construction will provide a satisfactory enclosure. Unlike the skirtboard enclosure, the masonry wall normally acts as a support for the floor framing system. Ventilation and the use of a soil cover are also required for a masonry foundation. The soil cover can consist of a 4-mil polyethylene or similar material placed over the soil under the cabin. Its use reduces ground moisture movement to wood members, which could result in excessive moisture and condensation. Ventilation can consist of standard

foundation vents made for this purpose.

Masonry Cabin Foundations

Although a treated wood post foundation will reduce the cost of a crawl-space cabin substantially, local conditions or personal choice may indicate the use of a full masonry wall. This type of foundation, like the treated post type, will often require only a minimum amount of grading. Concrete block or poured concrete walls and piers with appropriate footings are accepted methods of providing supporting walls for the floor framing. Their use normally eliminates the need for outer beams as the joists are supported by the walls. Only a center flush or drop beam is required. However, the concrete block wall introduces the need for masonry work, which in some areas may be difficult to obtain.

The perimeter layout for the masonry foundation can be made in the same manner as has been outlined for the wood post foundation system (fig. 4). The outside line of the masonry walls will be the same as the outside line of the floor framing. The centerline of the interior load-bearing masonry piers is normally the same as for the posts of the wood foundation. Figure 107 is the plan of typical masonry foundation for a crawl-space cabin. Footings are required for the outside walls as well as for the masonry piers which support the center beam. A soil cover of polyethylene or similar vapor barrier material should be used in all enclosed crawl-space cabins. This prevents ground moisture from moving into the crawl-space area. Uncovered ground can result in high moisture content of floor framing, insulation, and other materials in the crawl space. A poured concrete wall requires some type of formwork while concrete block wall and piers are laid up directly on the footings. The information on concrete and the proper mortar mix for the concrete block is outlined in the chapter on "Foundation Systems".

The spacing of the center piers will depend on the size of the center beams. Longer distances between piers will require larger or deeper beams than moderate spans of 8 to 10 feet. These details are shown on the working drawings for each cabin.

Footings

Footing size is determined by the thickness of the foundation wall. A rule of thumb which is often used for small woodframe cabins under normal soil conditions is: The footing depth should equal the wall thickness and the footing width should be twice the wall thickness. Thus, an 8-inch masonry wall will require a 16- by 8-inch footing (fig. 108). The foundation plan will show the footing size for each cabin. Unusual soil conditions will often require special footing design.

The bottom of the footings should be located below frost line. This may be 4 feet or more in the Northern States. Local regulations or the footing details of neighboring well-constructed structures will indicate this depth. If the soil is stable, no forms are required for the sides of the footing trench. One of the important factors in footing construction is to have the top level all around, especially when concrete block construction is to be used. Drive elevation stakes around the perimeter of the footing

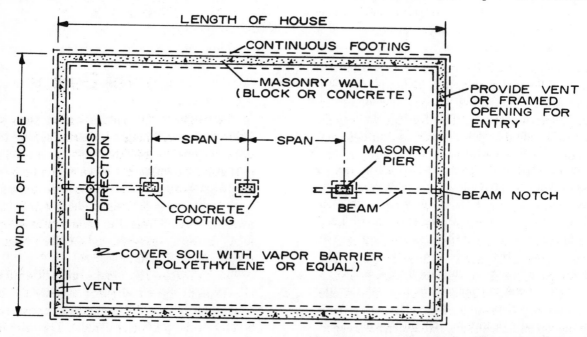

Figure 107—Typical masonry foundation wall (concrete block or poured concrete for crawl-space house).

From Tent to Cabin

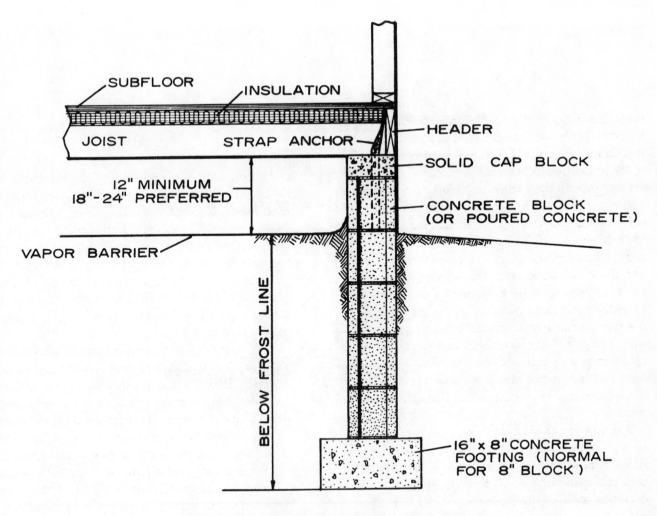

Figure 108—Section through exterior masonry
wall (for crawl-space house).

so that they can be used as guides when pouring the concrete. These elevations can be established by measuring down from the leveling line described in the chapter on "Foundation System". Concrete for footings should be poured over undisturbed soil.

A concrete block wall should normally be finished with a 4-inch solid cap block at the top to provide a good bearing surface for the joists, headers, and stringers (fig. 108). Anchor straps for the perimeter joists or headers are desirable in areas where high winds occur. They often consist of perforated or plain 22-gauge or heavier galvanized metal straps about 2 inches wide. They are used with a bent "L" shaped base which is placed one or more courses below the cap block. They extend above the top of the wall so that they can be fastened to the edge headers, stringers, or joists. Space them about 8 feet apart and fasten by nailing

Center Beams

The height of the center masonry piers with relation to the wall height is determined by the type of center beam used. The flush beam uses ledgers to support the joists, but when a drop beam is used the joists bear directly on the top surface. Each system requires a different depth notch for the masonry end walls. This is to assure that the top of all joists, headers, stringers, and the flush beam, when used, have the same elevation.

Flush beam.—The flush beam allows for more clearance in the crawl space as only the amount equal to the depth of the ledgers extends below the bottom of the joists (fig. 109A). The joists rest on the ledger and are toenailed to the beam. A strap anchor or a bolt should be used to anchor the beam

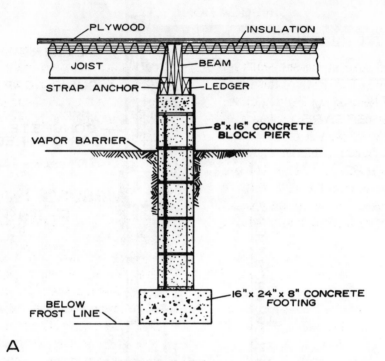

PLYWOOD   INSULATION

JOIST   BEAM

STRAP ANCHOR   LEDGER

VAPOR BARRIER

8"x16" CONCRETE BLOCK PIER

16"x 24"x 8" CONCRETE FOOTING

BELOW FROST LINE

A

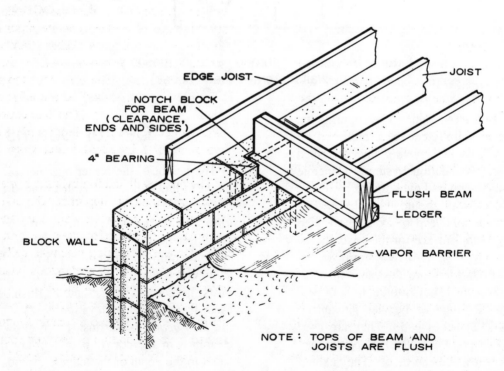

EDGE JOIST   JOIST

NOTCH BLOCK FOR BEAM (CLEARANCE, ENDS AND SIDES)

4" BEARING

FLUSH BEAM

LEDGER

BLOCK WALL

VAPOR BARRIER

NOTE : TOPS OF BEAM AND JOISTS ARE FLUSH

B

Figure 109—Details of concrete block pier for center flush beam. A, cross section; B, detail at exterior end wall.

From Tent to Cabin

in high wind areas.

A notch must be provided in the end walls for beam support (fig. 109). The depth of this notch is equal to the depth of the ledgers. Bearing on the wall should be at least 4 inches. A clearance of about ½ inch should be allowed at the sides and ends of the beam. This will provide an airway to prevent the beam from retaining moisture. The size of the notch or beam opening in the wall (when 2- by 4-inch ledgers are used and the beam consists of two nominal 2-inch-thick members) would be approximately:

Length (along length of wall)	7 inches
Width	4½ inches (4-inch bearing area, plus clearance)
Height (or depth)	3½ inches (or width of ledgers)

The top of the beam should be flush with the top of the joists (fig. 109 B).

In a concrete block wall, the mason provides the beam notch. When a poured concrete wall is used, a small wood box the size of the notch is fastened to the forms before pouring.

Drop beam.—The drop beam is supported by the masonry piers and the end walls of the foundation. Joists rest directly on the beam (fig. 110 A). A lap or butt joint can be used for the joists over the beam. In areas of high winds, it is advisable to use a strap anchor or a long bolt to fasten the beam to the piers. One disadvantage of this type of beam is the difference in the amount of wood at the center piers and at the outer walls which can shrink or swell. It is desirable to equalize the amount of wood at both the center and outside walls whenever possible. The flush beam closely approaches this desirable construction feature. The end foundation walls have a notch to provide bearings areas for the ends of the beams (fig. 110 B). This notch should have the same depth as the beam height. Allow clearance at the sides and end for air circulation. Assembly of the

beams, the joist arrangement, and other general details are discussed in the chapter on "Floor Systems". Specific details on the size, spacing, and location of the beams and joists are included in the floor framing plan of the working drawings for each cabin.

Masonry Foundation for Entry Steps

The construction of wood entry steps has been discussed in the chapter on "Steps and Stairs". This type of wood stoop provides a satisfactory entry platform and steps at a reasonable cost. However, when masonry walls are used in the foundation of the cabin, it may be desirable to also provide a masonry foundation for the entry steps.

Figure 111 A shows the foundation plan for a typical masonry entry platform and step. The walls are normally of 6-inch concrete blocks or poured concrete. Block units 4 inches thick or a 4-inch poured wall have also been used for the supporting front and sidewalls. The size of the top platform for a main entry step should be a minimum of 5 feet wide and 3½ feet deep. The foundation in figure 111 A would result in a 6-foot by 3½-foot top with two steps or 6 by about 5 feet when one step is used.

The outer wall and footings are sometimes eliminated in providing support for the concrete steps. Then only the two wing walls are constructed. In such cases, the concrete steps are reinforced with rods to prevent cracking when the soil settles. Use at least two ½-inch diameter rods located about 1 inch above the bottom of the step.

It is important in constructing a masonry entry stoop to tie the wall into the cabin foundation walls and to have the bottom of the step footings below frost level. A concrete footing should be used for the concrete block wall to establish a level base as well as a bearing for the wall (fig. 111 B). The footing should be at least 6 inches wide even though the wall may be less than this. Footings are normally not required for the 6-inch poured wall as the bearing area of the poured wall is usually sufficient. Ties or anchors to the cabin wall can consist of ½-inch reinforcing rods for the poured wall or standard masonry wall reinforcing for the block wall. These are placed as the cabin wall is erected. In block construction, both the cabin foundation wall and the wall for the entry stoop can be erected at the same time and tied together with interlocking blocks.

The finish concrete slab should be reinforced with a wire mesh when fill is used. Concrete is poured over the block wall forming the steps and platform (fig. 111B). Boards at each side of the step and platform and one at each riser provide the desired formwork for the concrete.

Skirtboard Materials for Wood Post Foundation

Sheet materials such as exterior grade plywood, hardboard, or asbestos board are most suitable for enclosing a wood post foundation. They need little if any framing and can be installed during or after construction of the cabin. When the skirtboard will be in contact with or located near the ground, it is most desirable to use a treated plywood when available. However, a 3-minute dip coat of a penta preservative or a water-repellent preservative along the exposed edges will provide some desirable protection for untreated material. It is also desirable to treat the exposed edges of hardboard with water-repellent preservative. Although asbestos board and metal skirtboards do *not* require preservative treatment, they are not as resistant to impacts as plywood and hardboard. Plywood and hardboard can be easily painted or stained to match the color of the cabin.

Plywood for skirtboards should be an exterior grade to resist weathering. A standard or sheathing grade with exterior glue is the most economical and can be readily stained. Plywood with rough-sawn or grooved surfaces commonly used for panel siding is also satisfactory.

Tempered hardboard probably provides somewhat better performance than regular-density (standard) hardboard. However, with paint or similar protective coatings, the lower cost regular-density hardboard should give satisfactory performance. Asbestos board normally requires pre-drilling to prevent cracking when nailing near the edges.

Skirtboard for House With Edge Beams

Two relatively simple means of fastening the skirtboards to the floor framing can be used. The first method must be employed during construction of the floors and walls. The second can be used either during construction or after the cabin has been completed.

First method.—Figure 112 illustrates the first method of providing a nailing surface for the skirtboard material. The subfloor and the bottom plate of the walls are extended beyond the edge beam a distance equal to the thickness of the skirtboard (fig. 112). The skirtboard is then nailed to the beam and to the foundation posts. Splices should be made at the post when possible. When splices must be made between the posts, use a 2- by 4-inch vertical nailing cleat on the inside. Fourpenny or fivepenny galvanized siding or similar nails can be used for the ¼-inch hardboard or asbestos board. Space them about 8 inches apart in a staggered pattern. Use sixpenny nails for ⅜-inch plywood and sevenpenny or eightpenny nails for ½-inch plywood skirtboards with the same 8-inch spacing. The panel siding is nailed directly over the top portion of the skirtboard. Nailing recommendations for the siding are given in the chapter on "Exterior Wall Coverings".

The detail for the end wall in this type of installation is shown in figure 112B. A 2- by 4-inch cleat should also be used for the skirtboard joints when they occur between the foundation posts.

Some support or a backing may be required for the bottoms of the skirtboard to provide stability and resistance to impacts from the outside especially

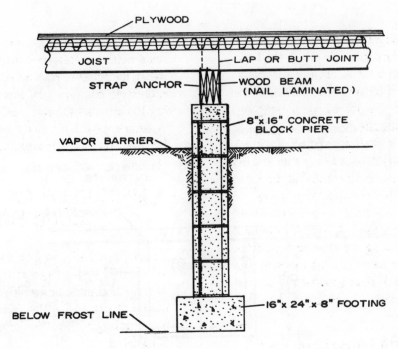

PLYWOOD

JOIST

LAP OR BUTT JOINT

STRAP ANCHOR

WOOD BEAM
(NAIL LAMINATED)

8"x 16" CONCRETE
BLOCK PIER

VAPOR BARRIER

16"x 24"x 8" FOOTING

BELOW FROST LINE

A

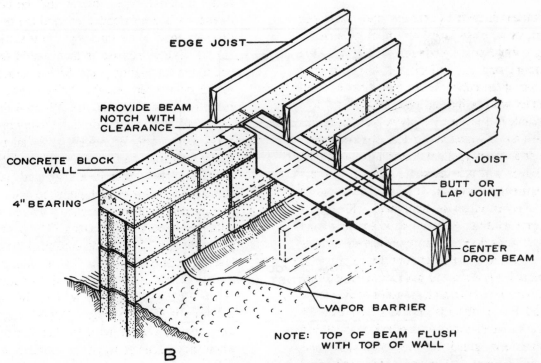

EDGE JOIST

PROVIDE BEAM
NOTCH WITH
CLEARANCE

CONCRETE BLOCK
WALL

4" BEARING

JOIST

BUTT OR
LAP JOINT

CENTER
DROP BEAM

VAPOR BARRIER

NOTE: TOP OF BEAM FLUSH
WITH TOP OF WALL

B

Figure 110—Details of block pier for center
drop beam. A, cross section; B,
detail at exterior end wall.

From Tent to Cabin

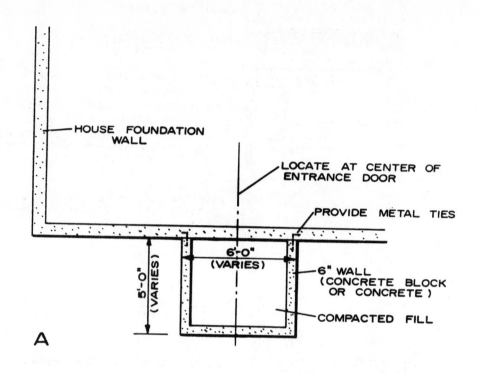

HOUSE FOUNDATION WALL

LOCATE AT CENTER OF ENTRANCE DOOR

PROVIDE METAL TIES

6'-0" (VARIES)

5'-0" (VARIES)

6" WALL (CONCRETE BLOCK OR CONCRETE)

COMPACTED FILL

A

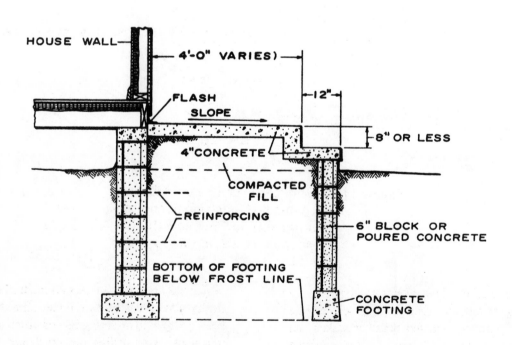

HOUSE WALL

4'-0" VARIES)

12"

FLASH SLOPE

8" OR LESS

4" CONCRETE

COMPACTED FILL

REINFORCING

6" BLOCK OR POURED CONCRETE

BOTTOM OF FOOTING BELOW FROST LINE

CONCRETE FOOTING

B

Figure 111—Details of typical masonry entrance steps. A, plan view; B, section view.

From Tent to Cabin

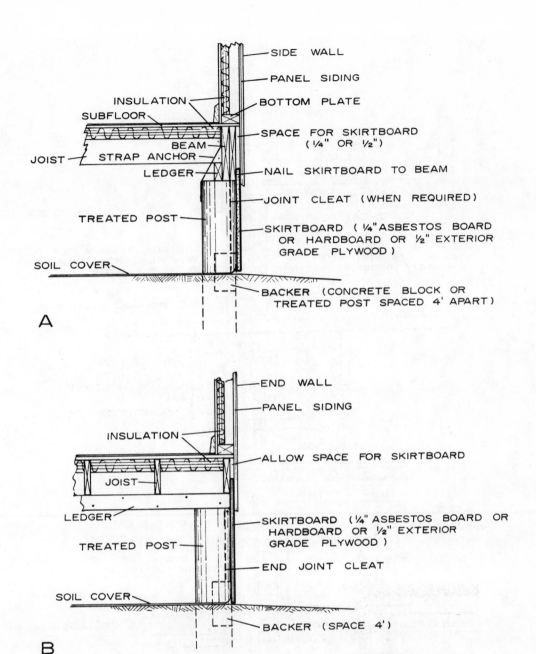

SIDE WALL

PANEL SIDING

INSULATION

SUBFLOOR

BOTTOM PLATE

SPACE FOR SKIRTBOARD
(1/4" OR 1/2")

BEAM

JOIST

STRAP ANCHOR

LEDGER

NAIL SKIRTBOARD TO BEAM

JOINT CLEAT (WHEN REQUIRED)

TREATED POST

SKIRTBOARD (1/4"ASBESTOS BOARD
OR HARDBOARD OR 1/2" EXTERIOR
GRADE PLYWOOD)

SOIL COVER

BACKER (CONCRETE BLOCK OR
TREATED POST SPACED 4' APART)

A

END WALL

PANEL SIDING

INSULATION

ALLOW SPACE FOR SKIRTBOARD

JOIST

LEDGER

SKIRTBOARD (1/4" ASBESTOS BOARD OR
HARDBOARD OR 1/2" EXTERIOR
GRADE PLYWOOD)

TREATED POST

END JOINT CLEAT

SOIL COVER

BACKER (SPACE 4')

B

Figure 112—Skirtboard for house with edge
beams (to be applied during construction). A, Section through
sidewall; B, section through end
wall.

with thinner materials. Treated posts, treated 2- by
4-inch stakes, or embedded concrete blocks can be
used for this purpose. Treated posts or stakes can
be driven behind the skirtboard and the concrete
blocks can be embedded slightly for added resistance (fig. 112A and B). Space these supports about
4 feet apart or closer if required.

Second method.—A second method of installing
the skirtboard can be used either after the cabin has
been completed or during its construction. This system consists of nailing the skirtboard to the inner
face of the ledger (fig. 112). The skirtboard must
be fitted between the posts which are partly exposed. Use the same method of nailing and blocking

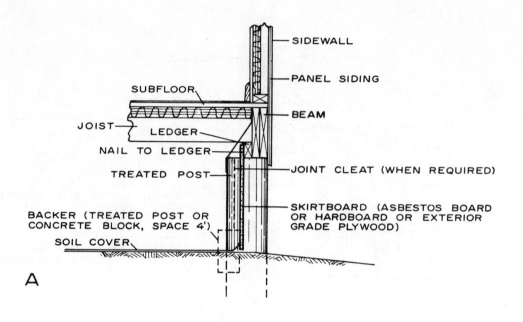

SIDEWALL

PANEL SIDING

SUBFLOOR

BEAM

JOIST

LEDGER

NAIL TO LEDGER

JOINT CLEAT (WHEN REQUIRED)

TREATED POST

SKIRTBOARD (ASBESTOS BOARD OR HARDBOARD OR EXTERIOR GRADE PLYWOOD)

BACKER (TREATED POST OR CONCRETE BLOCK, SPACE 4')

SOIL COVER

A

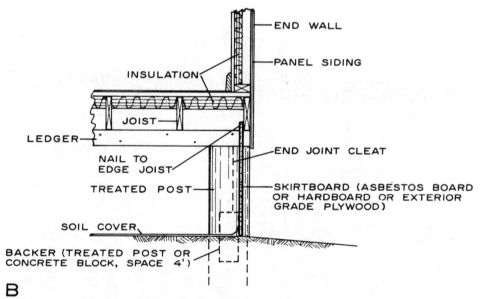

END WALL

PANEL SIDING

INSULATION

JOIST

LEDGER

NAIL TO EDGE JOIST

END JOINT CLEAT

TREATED POST

SKIRTBOARD (ASBESTOS BOARD OR HARDBOARD OR EXTERIOR GRADE PLYWOOD)

SOIL COVER

BACKER (TREATED POST OR CONCRETE BLOCK, SPACE 4')

B

Figure 113—Skirtboard for house with edge beams (can be applied after house is constructed). A, Section through sidewall; B, section through end wall.

at the bottom of the boards as previously described. In addition, toenail the ends of the boards into the posts which they abut. Figure 112A shows the details of installation at a sidewall and figure 112B shows the details at an end wall. Use treated posts or stakes or concrete blocks as backers at the bottom of the skirtboard as previously described.

Skirtboard for Cabin With Interior Beam

In those crawl-space cabins with interior supporting beams and posts and with side overhang, the application of skirtboards is much the same as

172

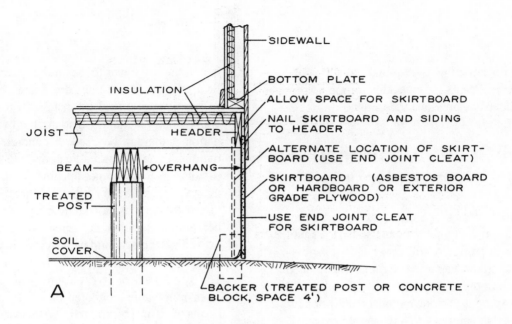

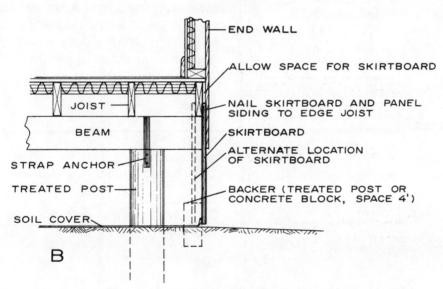

Figure 114—Skirtboard for house with interior
beam (with overhang). A, Section
through sidewall; B, section
through end wall.

when the beams are located under the outside walls.
The skirtboard may be nailed to the outside of the
joist header or to the inner face (fig. 114A). When
it is fastened to the exterior face, the subfloor and
the bottom wall plate are extended beyond the
header a distance equal to the thickness of the skirtboard material. The skirtboard can also be fastened
to the inside face of the header, but then it must be
notched at each joist (fig. 114A). Use the same type
of nails and nailing patterns described for the details
shown in figures.

Details at the end walls of the cabin are much
the same as those at the sidewalls (fig 114 B). When
the skirtboard is nailed to the inner surface of the

edge joist, no notching is required except at the center and edge beams. Use backers for the bottom of the skirtboard as previously described.

Soil Cover, Ventilation, and Access Door

An enclosed crawl space should not only be protected with a soil cover but should also have a small amount of ventilation. A soil cover of 4-mil polyethylene or similar vapor barrier material placed over the earth in the crawl space will minimize soil moisture movement to floor members and floor insulation. Lap the material 4 to 6 inches at the seams, and carry it up the walls or skirtboards a short distance. Use sections of concrete block or small field stones to keep the material in place. When the use of a soil poison is required in termite areas, do not install the soil cover for several days after poisoning or until the soil becomes dry again.

Ventilators should be installed on two opposite walls when practical. Standard 16- by 8-inch foundation vents can be used in concrete block foundations. Usually, in small cabins, two screened ventilators, each with a net opening of 30 to 40 square inches, are sufficient when a soil cover is used. Crawl spaces with skirtboard enclosures should also be ventilated with small screened vents.

Access doors should be provided in crawl spaces. With a masonry foundation, they can consist of a 16- by 24-inch or larger frame with a plywood or other removable or hinged panel. Install the frame as the wall is constructed. With skirtboard enclosures, provide a simple removable section. When practical, the access doors should be located at the rear or side of the foundation and at the lowest elevation when a slope is present.

Glossary of
Terms

Airway. A space between roof insulation and roof boards for movement of air.

Apron. The flat member of the inside trim of a window placed against the wall immediately beneath the stool.

Asphalt. Most native asphalt is a residue from evaporated petroleum. It is insoluble in water but soluble in gasoline and melts when heated. Used widely in building for such items as waterproof roof coverings of many types, exterior wall coverings, and flooring tile.

Attic ventilators. Screened openings provided to ventilate an attic space. They are located in the soffit area as inlet ventilators and in the gable end or along the ridge as outlet ventilators. They can also consist of powerdriven fans used as an exhaust system. See also *Louver.*

Backfill. The replacement of excavated earth into a trench or pier excavation around and against a basement foundation.

Balusters. Usually small vertical members in a railing used between a top rail and the stair treads or a bottom rail.

Base or baseboard. A board placed around a room against the wall next to the floor to finish properly between floor and plaster or drywall.

Base molding. Molding used to trim the upper edge of interior baseboard.

Base shoe. Molding used next to the floor in interior baseboard. Sometimes called a carpet strip.

Batten. Narrow strips of wood used to cover joints or as decorative vertical members over plywood or wide boards.

Beam. A structural member transversely supporting a load.

Bearing partition. A partition that supports any vertical load in addition to its own weight.

Bearing wall. A wall that supports any vertical load in addition to its own weight.

Bed molding. A molding in an angle, as between the overhanging cornice, or eaves, of a building and the sidewalls.

Blind-nailing. Nailing in such a way that the nailheads are not visible on the face of the work. Usually at the tongue of matched boards.

Blind stop. A rectangular molding, usually ¾ by 1⅜ inches or more in width, used in the assembly of a window frame. Serves as a stop for storm and screen or combination windows and to resist air infiltration.

Boiled linseed oil. Linseed oil in which enough lead, manganese, or cobalt salts have been incorporated to make the oil harden more rapidly when spread in thin coatings.

Bolts, anchor. Bolts to secure a wooden sill plate to concrete or masonry floor or wall or pier.

Boston ridge. A method of applying asphalt or wood shingles at the ridge or at the hips of a roof as a finish.

Brace. An inclined piece of framing lumber applied to wall or floor to stiffen the structure. Often used on walls as temporary bracing until framing has been completed.

Buck. Often used in reference to rough frame opening members. Door bucks used in reference to metal door frame.

Built-up roof. A roofing composed of three to five layers of asphalt felt laminated with coal tar, pitch, or asphalt. The top is finished with crushed slag or gravel. Generally used on flat or low-pitched roofs.

Butt joint. The junction where the ends of two timbers or other members meet in a square-cut joint.

Cabinet. A shop- or job-built unit for kitchens or other rooms. Often includes combinations of drawers, doors, and shelves.

Casing. Molding of various widths and thicknesses used to trim door and window openings at the jambs.

Casement frames and sash. Frames of wood or metal enclosing or all of the sash, which may be opened by means of hinges affixed to the vertical edges.

Collar beam. Nominal 1- or 2-inch thick members connecting opposite roof rafters. They serve to stiffen the roof structure.

Combination doors or windows. Combination doors or windows used over regular openings. They provide winter insulation and summer protection. They often have self-storing or removable glass and screen inserts. This eliminates the need for handling a different unit each season.

Concrete, plain. Concrete without reinforcement, or reinforced only for shrinkage or temperature changes.

Condensation. Beads or drops of water, and frequently frost in extremely cold weather, that accumulate on the inside of the exterior covering of a building when warm, moisture-laden air from the interior reaches a point where the temperature no longer permits the air to sustain the moisture it holds. Use of louvers or attic ventilators will reduce moisture condensation in attics. A vapor barrier under the gypsum lath or dry wall on exposed walls will reduce condensation in walls.

Conduit, electrical. A pipe, usually metal, in which wire is installed.

Construction, dry-wall. A type of construction in which the interior wall finish is applied in a dry condition, generally in the form of sheet materials or wood peneling, as contrasted to plaster.

Construction, frame. A type of construction in which the structural parts are of wood or depend upon a wood frame for support. In building codes, if masonry veneer is applied to the exterior walls, the classification of this type of construction is usually unchanged.

Coped joint. Fitting woodwork to an irregular surface. In moldings, cutting the end of one piece to fit the molded face of the other at an interior angle to replace a miter joint.

Corner bead. A strip of formed sheet metal, sometimes combined with a strip of metal lath, placed on corners before plastering to reinforce them. Also, a strip of wood finish three-quarters round or angular placed over a plastered corner for protection.

Corner boards. Used as trim for the external corners of a house or other frame structure against which the ends of the siding are finished.

Corner braces. Diagonal braces at the corners of frame structure to stiffen and strengthen the wall.

Cornice. Overhang of a pitched roof at the eave line, usually consisting of a facia board, a soffit for a closed cornice, and appropriate moldings.

Counterflashing. A flashing usually used on chimneys at the roofline to cover shingle flashing and to prevent moisture entry.

Cove molding. A molding with a concave face used as trim or to finish interior corners.

Crawl space. A shallow space below the living quarters of a basementless house, sometimes enclosed.

d. See *Penny*.

Dado. A rectangular groove across the width of a board or plank. In interior decoration, a special type of wall treatment.

Deck paint. An enamel with a high degree of resistance to mechanical wear, designed for use on such surfaces as porch floors.

Density. The mass of substance in a unit volume. When expressed in the metric system (in g. per cc.), it is numerically equal to the specific gravity of the same substance.

Dimension. See *Lumber, dimension.*

Doorjamb, interior. The surrounding case into and out of which a door closes and opens. It consists of two upright pieces, called side jambs, and a horizontal head jamb.

Dormer. A projection in a sloping roof, the framing of which forms a vertical wall suitable for windows or other openings.

Downspout. A pipe, usually metal, for carrying rainwater from roof gutters.

Dressed and matched (tongued and grooved). Boards or planks machined in such a manner that there is a groove on one edge and a corresponding tongue on the other.

Drier, paint. Usually oil-soluble soaps of such metals as lead, manganese, or cobalt, which, in small proportions, hasten the oxidation and hardening (drying) of the drying oils in paints.

Drip cap. A molding placed on the exterior top side of a door or window frame to cause water to drip beyond the outside of the frame.

Dry-wall. see *Construction, dry wall.*

Ducts. In a house, usually round or rectangular metal pipes for distributing warm air from the heating plant to rooms, or air from a conditioning device, or as cold air returns. Ducts are also made of asbestos and composition materials.

Eaves. The overhang of a roof projecting over the walls.

Face nailing. To nail perpendicular to the initial surface or to the junction of the pieces joined.

Facia or fascia. A flat board, band, or face, used sometimes by itself but usually in combination with moldings, often located at the outer face of the cornice.

Flashing. Sheet metal or other material used in roof and wall construction to protect a building from seepage of water.

Flat paint. An interior paint that contains a high proportion of pigment, and dries to a flat or lusterless finish.

Flue. The space or passage in a chimney through which smoke, gas, or fumes ascend. Each pas-

sage is called a flue, which, together with any others and the surrounding masonry, make up the chimney.

Flue lining. Fire clay or terra-cotta pipe, round or square, usually made in all of the ordinary flue sizes and in 2-foot lengths, used for the inner lining of chimneys with a brick or masonry work around the outside. Flue lining in chimneys runs from about a foot below the flue connection to the top of the chimney.

Fly rafter. End rafters of the gable overhang supported by roof sheathing and lookouts.

Footing. A masonry section, usually concrete in a rectangular form wider than the bottom of the foundation wall or pier it supports.

Foundation. The supporting portion of a structure below the first-floor construction, or below grade, including the footings.

Framing, balloon. A system of framing a building in which all vertical structural elements of the bearing walls and partitions consist of single pieces extending from the top of the foundation sill plate to the roofplate and to which all floor joists are fastened.

Framing, platform. A system of framing a building in which floor joists of each story rest on the top plates of the story below or on the foundation sill for the first story, and the bearing walls and partitions rest on the subfloor of each story.

Frieze. In house construction, a horizontal member connecting the top of the siding with the soffit of the cornice or roof sheathing.

Frostline. The depth of frost penetration in soil. This depth varies in different parts of the country. Footings should be placed below this depth to prevent movement.

Furring. Strips of wood or metal applied to a wall or other surface to even it and usually to serve as a fastening base for finish material.

Gable. The triangular vertical end of a building formed by the eaves and ridge of a sloped roof.

Gloss (paint or enamel). A paint or enamel that contains a relatively low proportion of pigment and dries to a sheen or luster.

Girder. A large or principal beam of wood or steel used to support concentrated loads at isolated points along its length.

Grain. The direction, size, arrangement, appearance, or quality of the fibers in wood.

Grain, edge (vertical). Edge-grain lumber has been sawed parallel to the pith of the log and approximately at right angles to the growth rings; i.e. the rings form an angle of 45° or more with the surface of the piece.

Gusset. A flat wood, plywood, or similar type member used to provide a connection at the intersection of wood members. Most commonly used at joints of wood trusses. They are fastened by nails, screws, bolts, or adhesives.

Gutter or eave trough. A shallow channel or conduit of metal or wood set below and along the eaves of a house to catch and carry off rainwater from the roof.

Header. (a) A beam placed perpendicular to joists and to which joists are nailed in framing for chimney, stairway, or other opening. (b) A wood lintel.

Heartwood. The wood extending from the pith to the sapwood, the cells of which no longer participate in the life processes of the tree.

Hip. The external angle formed by the meeting of two sloping sides of a roof.

Hip roof. A roof that rises by inclined planes from all four sides of a building.

Insulation board, rigid. A structural building board made of wood or cane fiber in ½- and ²⁵⁄₃₂-inch thicknesses. It can be obtained in various size sheets, in various densities, and with several treatments.

Insulation, thermal. Any material high in resistance to heat transmission that, when placed in the walls, ceilings, or floors of a structure, will reduce the rate of heat flow.

Jack rafter. A rafter that spans the distance from the wallplate to a hip, or from a valley to a ridge.

Jamb. The side and head lining of a doorway, window, or other opening.

Joint. The space between the adjacent surfaces of two members or components joined and held together by nails, glue, cement, mortar, or other means.

Joint cement. A powder that is usually mixed with water and used for treatment in gypsum-wallboard finish. Often called "spackle".

Joist. One of a series of parallel beams, usually 2 inches thick, used to support floor and ceiling loads, and supported in turn by larger beams, girders, or bearing walls.

Knot. In lumber, the portion of a branch or limb of a tree that appears on the edge or face of the piece.

Landing. A platform between flights of stairs or at the termination of a flight of stairs.

Lath. A building material of wood, metal, gypsum, or insulating board that is fastened to the frame of a building to act as a plaster base.

Ledger strip. A strip of lumber nailed along the bottom of the side of a girder on which joists rest.

Light. Space in a window sash for a single pane of glass. Also, a pane of glass.

Lintel. A horizontal structural member that supports the load over an opening such as a door or window.

Lookout. A short wood bracket or cantilever to support an overhanging portion of a roof or the like, usually concealed from view.

Louver. An opening with a series of horizontal slats so arranged as to permit ventilation but to exclude rain, sunlight, or vision. See also *Attic ventilators.*

Lumber. Lumber is the product of the sawmill and planing mill not further manufactured other than by sawing, resawing, and passing lengthwise through a standard planing machine, cross cutting to length, and matching.

Lumber, boards. Yard lumber less than 2 inches thick and 2 or more inches wide.

Lumber, dimension. Yard lumber from 2 inches to, but not including, 5 inches thick, and 2 or more inches wide. Includes joists, rafters, studs, plank, and small timbers. The actual size dimension of such lumber after shrinking from green dimension and after machining to size or pattern is called the dress size.

Lumber, matched. Lumber that is dressed and shaped on one edge in a grooved pattern and on the other in a tongued pattern.

Lumber, shiplap. Lumber that is edge-dressed to make a close rabbeted or lapped joint.

Lumber, yard. Lumber of those grades, sizes, and patterns which are generally intended for ordinary construction, such as framework and rough coverage of houses.

Masonry. Stone, brick, concrete, hollow-tile, concrete-block, gypsum-block, or other similar building units or materials or a combination of the same, bonded together with mortar to form a wall, pier, buttress, or similar mass.

Meeting rails. Rails sufficiently thicker than a window to fill the opening between the top and bottom sash made by the parting stop in the frame of double-hung windows. They are usually beveled.

Millwork. Generally all building materials made of finished wood and manufactured in millwork plants and planing mills are included under the term "millwork". It includes such items as inside and outside doors, window and doorframes, blinds, porchwork, mantels, panelwork, stairways, moldings, and interior trim. It normally does not include flooring, ceiling, or siding.

Miter joint. The joint of two pieces at an angle that bisects the joining angle. For example, the miter joint at the side and head casing at a door opening is made at a 45° angle.

Moisture content of wood. Weight of the water contained in the wood, usually expressed as a percentage of the weight of the oven dry wood.

Mortise. A slot cut into a board, plank, or timber, usually edgewise, to receive tenon of another board, plank, or timber to form a joint.

Molding. A wood strip having a curved or projecting surface used for decorative purposes.

Natural finish. A transparent finish which does not seriously alter the original color or grain of the natural wood. Natural finishes are usually provided by sealers, oils, varnishes, water-repellent preservatives, and other similar materials.

Nonloadbearing wall. A wall supporting no load other than its own weight.

Notch. A crosswise rabbet at the end of a board.

O.C., on center. The measurement of spacing for studs, rafters, joists, and the like in a building from center of one member to the center of the next.

Paint. A combination of pigments with suitable thinners or oils to provide decorative and protective coatings.

Panel. In house construction, a thin flat piece of wood, plywood, or similar material, framed by stiles and rails as in a door or fitted into grooves of thicker material with molded edges for decorative wall treatment.

Paper, sheathing or building. A building material, generally paper or felt used in wall and roof construction as a protection against the passage of air and sometimes moisture.

Parting stop or strip. A small wood piece used in the side and head jambs of double-hung windows to separate upper and lower sash.

Partition. A wall that subdivides spaces within any story of a building.

Penny. As applied to nails, it originally indicated the price per hundred. The term now serves as a measure of nail length and is abbreviated by the letter *d*.

Perm. A measure of water vapor movement through a material (grains per square foot per hour per inch of mercury difference in vapor pressure).

Pier. A column of masonry, usually rectangular in horizontal cross section, used to support other structural members.

Pigment. A powdered solid in suitable degree of subdivision for use in paint or enamel.

Pitch. The incline slope of a roof, or the ratio of the total rise to the total width of a house; i.e., an 8-foot rise and a 24-foot width are a ⅓ pitch roof. *Roof slope* is expressed in inches of rise per 12 inches of run.

Plate. Sill plate: a horizontal member anchored to a masonry wall. Sole plate: bottom horizontal member of a frame wall. Top plate: top horizontal member of a frame wall supporting ceiling joists, rafters, or other members.

Plumb. Exactly perpendicular; vertical.

Plywood. A piece of wood made of three or more layers of veneer joined with glue and usually laid with the grain of adjoining plies at right angles. Almost always an odd number of plies are used to provide balanced construction.

Porch. A roofed area extending beyond the main house. May be open or enclosed and with concrete or wood frame floor system.

Preservative. Any substance that, for a reasonable length of time, will prevent the action of wood-destroying fungi, borers of various kinds, and similar destructive life when the wood has been properly coated or impregnated with it.

Primer. The first coat of paint in a paint job that consists of two or more coats; also the paint used for such a first coat.

Putty. A type of cement usually made of whiting and boiled linseed oil, beaten or kneaded to the consistency of dough, and used in sealing glass in sash, filling small holes and crevices in wood, and for similar purposes.

Quarter round. A small molding that has the cross section of a quarter circle.

Rafter. One of a series of structural members of a roof designed to support roof loads. The rafters of a flat roof are sometimes called roof joists.

Rafter, hip. A rafter that forms the intersection of an external roof angle.

Rafter, valley. A rafter that forms the intersection of an internal roof angle. The valley rafter is normally made of doubled 2-inch-thick members.

Rail. Cross members of panel doors or of a sash. Also the upper and lower members of a balustrade or staircase extending from one vertical support, such as a post, to another.

Rake. The inclined edge of a gable roof (the trim member is a rake molding).

Ridge. The horizontal line at the junction of the top edges of two sloping roof surfaces.

Ridge board. The board placed on edge at the ridge of the roof into which the upper ends of the rafters are fastened.

Rise. In stairs, the vertical height of a step or flight of stairs.

Riser. Each of the vertical boards closing the spaces between the treads of stairways.

Roll roofing. Roofing material, composed of fiber and saturated with asphalt, that is supplied in rolls containing 108 square feet in 36-inch widths. It is generally furnished in weights of 45 to 90 pounds per roll.

Roof sheathing. The boards or sheet material fastened to the roof rafters on which the shingle or other roof covering is laid.

Routed. See *Mortised*.

Run. In stairs, the net width of a step or the horizontal distance covered by a flight of stairs.

Sash. A single light frame containing one or more lights of glass.

Saturated felt. A felt which is impregnated with tar or asphalt.

Scab. A short piece of wood or plywood fastened to two abutting timbers to splice them together.

Sealer. A finishing material, either clear or pigmented, that is usually applied directly over uncoated wood for the purpose of sealing the surface.

Semigloss paint or enamel. A paint or enamel made with a slight insufficiency of nonvolatile vehicle so that its coating, when dry, has some luster but is not very glossy.

Shake. A thick handsplit shingle, resawed to form two shakes; usually edge grained.

Sheathing. The structural covering, usually wood boards or plywood, used over studs or rafters of a structure. Structuralbuilding board is normally used only as wall sheathing.

Sheathing paper. See *Paper, Sheathing*.

Shingles. Roof covering of asphalt, asbestos, wood, tile, slate, or other material cut to stock lengths, widths, and thicknesses.

Shingles, siding. Various kinds of shingles, such

as wood shingles or shakes and nonwood shingles, that are used over sheathing for exterior sidewall covering of a structure.

Shiplap. See *Lumber, shiplap*.

Siding. The finish covering of the outside wall of a frame building, whether made of horizontal weatherboards, vertical boards with battens, shingles, or other material.

Siding, bevel (lap siding). Wedge-shaped boards used as horizontal siding in a lapped pattern. This siding varies in butt thickness from ½ to ¾ inch and in widths up to 12 inches. Normally used over some type of sheathing.

Siding, drop. Usually ¾ inch thick and 6 and 8 inches in width with tongued-and-grooved or shiplap edges. Often used as siding without sheathing in secondary buildings.

Siding, panel. Large sheets of plywood or hardboard which serve as both sheathing and siding.

Sill. The lowest member of the frame of a structure, resting on the foundation and supporting the floor joists or the uprights of the wall. The member forming the lower side of an opening, as a door sill, window sill, etc.

Soffit. Usually the underside covering of an overhanging cornice.

Soil cover (ground cover). A light covering of plastic film, roll roofing, or similar material used over the soil in crawl spaces of buildings to minimize moisture permeation of the area.

Soil stack. A general term for the vertical main of a system of soil, waste, or vent piping.

Sole or sole plate. See *Plate*.

Span. The distance between structural supports such as walls, columns, piers, beams, girders, and trusses.

Square. A unit of measure—100 square feet—usually applied to roofing material. Sidewall coverings are sometimes packed to cover 100 square feet and are sold on that basis.

Stain, shingle. A form of oil paint, very thin in consistency, intended for coloring wood with rough surfaces, like shingles, without forming a coating of significant thickness or gloss.

Stair carriage. Supporting member for stair treads. Usually a 2-inch plank notched to receive the treads; sometimes termed a "rough horse".

Stool. A flat molding fitted over the window sill between jambs and contacting the bottom rail of the lower sash.

Storm sash or storm window. An extra window usually placed on the outside of an existing window as additional protection against cold weather.

Story. That part of a building between any floor and the floor or roof next above.

String, stringer. A timber or other support for cross members in floors or ceilings. In stairs, the support on which the stair treads rest; also stringboard.

Stud. One of a series of slender wood or metal vertical structural members placed as supporting elements in walls and partitions. (Plural: studs or studding.)

Subfloor. Boards or plywood laid on joists over which a finish floor is to be laid.

Tail beam. A relatively short beam or joist supported in a wall on one end and by a header at the other.

Termites. Insects that superficially resemble ants in size, general appearance, and habit of living in colonies; hence, frequently called "white ants". Subterranean termites *do not* establish themselves in buildings by being carried in with lumber, but by entering from ground nests after the building has been constructed. If unmolested, they eat out the woodwork, leaving a shell of sound wood to conceal their activities, and damage may proceed so far as to cause collapse of parts of a structure before discovery. There are about 56 species of termites known in the United States; but the two main species, classified from the manner in which they attack wood, subterranean (ground-inhabiting) termites, the most common, and dry-wood termites, found almost exclusively along the extreme southern border and the Gulf of Mexico in the United States.

Termite shield. A shield, usually of noncorrodible metal, placed in or on a foundation wall or other mass of masonry or around pipes to prevent passage of termites.

Threshold. A strip of wood or metal with beveled edges used over the finished floor and the sill of exterior doors.

Toenailing. To drive a nail at a slant with the initial surface in order to permit it to penetrate into a second member.

Tread. The horizontal board in a stairway on which the foot is placed.

Trim. The finish materials in a building, such as moldings, applied around openings (window trims, door trim) or at the floor and ceiling of rooms (baseboard, cornice, picture molding).

Trimmer. A beam or joist to which a header is nailed in framing for a chimney, stairway, or other opening.

Truss. A frame or jointed structure designed to act as a beam of long span, while each member is usually subjected to longitudinal stress only, either tension or compression.

Turpentine. A volatile oil used as a thinner in paints and as a solvent in varnishes. Chemically, it is a mixture of terpenes.

Undercoat. A coating applied prior to the finishing or top coats of a paint job. It may be the first of two or the second of three coats. In some usage of the word, it may become synonymous with priming coat.

Vapor barrier. Material used to retard the movement of water vapor into walls and prevent condensation in them. Usually considered as having a perm value of less than 1.0. Applied separately over the warm side of exposed walls or as a part of batt or blanket insulation.

Varnish. A thickened preparation of drying oil or drying oil and resin suitable for spreading on surfaces to form continuous, transparent coatings, or for mixing with pigments to make enamels.

Vent. A pipe or duct which allows flow of air as an inlet or outlet.

Vermiculite. A mineral closely related to mica, with the faculty of expanding on heating to form lightweight material with insulation quality. Used as bulk insulation and also as aggregate in insulating and acoustical plaster and in insulating concrete floors.

Water-repellent preservative. A liquid designed to penetrate into wood and impart water repellency and a moderate preservative protection. It is used for millwork, such as sash and frames, and is usually applied by dipping.

Weatherstrip. Narrow or jamb-width sections of thin metal or other material to prevent infiltration of air and moisture around windows and doors.

NOTES

NOTES

NOTES

NOTES

NOTES

NOTES

NOTES

NOTES

NOTES

NOTES